THE THIRTYMILE FIRE

THE
THIRTYMILE FIRE

A CHRONICLE OF
BRAVERY AND BETRAYAL

JOHN N. MACLEAN

A JOHN MACRAE/HOLT PAPERBACK

HENRY HOLT AND COMPANY | NEW YORK

Holt Paperbacks
Henry Holt and Company, LLC
Publishers since 1866
175 Fifth Avenue
New York, New York 10010
www.henryholt.com

A Holt Paperback® and 🅗® are registered trademarks
of Henry Holt and Company, LLC.

Library of Congress Cataloging-in-Publication Data

Maclean, John N.
   The Thirtymile fire : a chronicle of bravery and betrayal /
John N. Maclean. —1st ed.
      p. cm.
   ISBN-13: 978-0-8050-8330-9
   ISBN-10: 0-8050-8330-8
   1. Wildfires—Washington (State)—Prevention and control.
2. Wildfire—fighters—Washington (State)   3. Wildfires—North
Cascades (B.C. and Wash.)—Prevention and control.   4. Wildfire fighters—
North Cascades (B.C. and Wash.)   I.   Title.

SD421.32.W2M33 2007
363.37'9—dc22   2006045846

Henry Holt books are available for special promotions
and premiums. For details contact: Director, Special Markets.

Originally published in hardcover in 2007 by
John Macrae Books / Henry Holt and Company

First Holt Paperbacks Edition 2008

Designed by Victoria Hartman

Printed in the United States of America

Boots graphic by Laurel Simos, Bureau of Indian Affairs

D 20

For my father and mother,
Norman Fitzroy and Jessie Burns Maclean,
in grateful memory

NORTHWEST REGULAR NO. 6 CREW LIST

NAME	POSITION	HOME DISTRICT
Ellreese Daniels	Incident commander	Lake Leavenworth
Pete Kampen	Crew boss trainee	Lake Leavenworth

SQUAD ONE

Tom Craven	Squad boss	Naches
Beau Clark	Firefighter	Naches
Jason Emhoff	Firefighter	Naches
Karen FitzPatrick	Firefighter	Naches
Scott Scherzinger	Firefighter	Naches
Rebecca Welch	Firefighter	Naches

SQUAD TWO

Thom Taylor	Squad boss	Lake Leavenworth
Armando Avila	Firefighter	Lake Leavenworth
Nick Dreis	Firefighter	Lake Leavenworth
Elaine Hurd	Firefighter	Lake Leavenworth

Jessica Johnson	Firefighter	Naches
Matthew Rutman	Firefighter	Lake Leavenworth
Devin Weaver	Firefighter	Naches

SQUAD THREE

Brian Schexnayder	Squad boss	Lake Leavenworth
Dewane Anderson	Firefighter	Lake Leavenworth
Emily Hinson	Firefighter	Lake Leavenworth
Jodie Tate	Firefighter	Naches
Marshall Wallace	Firefighter	Naches
Donica Watson	Firefighter	Lake Leavenworth

THE THIRTYMILE FIRE

CHAPTER ONE

You won't find any white collars here.
Don't come looking for easy cash.
We fight the fires in your lost canyons,
Faces stained by sweat and ash.

—from *Storm King Angels* by Chip Kiger

As Kathie FitzPatrick struggled to bring a bickering home buyer and seller to terms, she stole a glance at her watch. It was almost 5:30 PM, and once again her workday had stretched into evening. Kathie had snatched a personal moment a few hours earlier to place a cell phone call to her eighteen-year-old daughter Karen, who had just become a wildland firefighter for the Forest Service, much against her mother's wishes. Karen had left the night before for the first big fire of her career, in the North Cascades Range in central Washington, about two hundred miles north of the FitzPatrick home in the Yakima Valley. The phone had failed to make a connection, a regular occurrence since Karen had graduated from high school the previous month, in early June, and headed for the backcountry and out of cell phone range. Kathie would try again later in the evening, when Karen might be settled in a fire camp.

Kathie put in long hours as a real estate agent, was mother to three grown-up daughters, and in what time remained led a Christian ministry to juvenile delinquents, called the Young Lions Youth Ministry Program. The social fault line for the Yakima Valley, the heart of Washington's bountiful fruit and hops industry, runs between orchard owners and their middle-class allies, and an underclass of low-paid migrant fruit pickers. The resulting high crime rate brought Kathie plenty of prospects to evangelize at the Yakima County juvenile detention facility.

Still, family was the first priority. Her youngest daughter, Karen Lee FitzPatrick, had been a tomboy until her midteens, a lanky, lantern-jawed girl with a handshake like a vise clamp. With the coming of adolescence, though, Karen had blossomed into a real dish, ladylike and elegant. What in the world had possessed the girl to become a fire-fighter? Kathie wondered. Firefighting was dirty, physically demanding, and dangerous, no occupation for a lady.

The callout for Karen and her Naches Ranger District fire crew, based near Yakima, had come just after midnight. They initially were assigned to the Libby South Fire, the first big blaze of the season in the North Cascades. Libby South had grown into a "major rager," likely to destroy a lot of homes and other property if not stopped or turned. That effort would take many hundreds of firefighters, as well as aircraft, bulldozers, and other heavy equipment. Ironically, the fire had been started a day earlier, on Monday, July 9, 2001, by the hot exhaust of a state vehicle on fire patrol. Confined within a narrow canyon, the flames had made a series of wind-driven runs that first afternoon, lofting from the crown of one tree to another in what became a sweeping blanket of fire. Conditions had become so extreme that smoke jumpers, the airborne troops of firefighting and the first to fight the blaze, had pulled back from their lines in late afternoon. Thankfully, no one had been injured.

Weather conditions for the area for the next day, Tuesday, July 10, were a repeat of the first day: temperatures rose into the hundreds in hot spots, and the humidity dropped toward single digits nearly everywhere, on top of three straight years of drought. Gary Bennett, a fire meteorologist assigned to the Libby South Fire, awakened that morning with an ominous feeling that something could go seriously wrong. He had opened his morning briefing at fire camp by warning, "Today will be a carbon copy of yesterday," by which he meant that firefighters should be alert for another wind-driven blowup.

Nobody missed the message. The dramatic fire runs the previous day had galvanized attention across the region. New blazes were sure to break out as well, and with the Libby South Fire grabbing attention and resources, the little fires could cause trouble if not dealt with quickly.

Indeed, a new smoke had been spotted the previous evening, Monday, July 9, not many miles to the north in the narrow Chewuch River canyon near the Canadian border. Named the Thirtymile Fire, the newcomer amounted to no more than a single thread of smoke when first observed. If it ever got going, though, it could burn out the canyon and rampage on into Canada. A local engine crew, dispatched within minutes, had driven into the canyon in the dark and found a handful of glowing spot fires spread over five or six acres along the Chewuch River, which is big enough to hold salmon.

The Thirtymile Fire should have been a mop-up operation, swiftly extinguished after being spotted early. But the fire was an elusive trickster, a grab bag of quirky moves and false signals that masked a lethal potential. Lone trees torched up or "candled" seemingly without an ignition source. Flames in the dense underbrush sent aloft streamers of embers, as though someone was shooting off fireworks left over from the Fourth of July. The glossy, fireproof look of the riverine vegetation was deceiving: the odd ember found a cozy nest in dry duff, incubated, and in time emerged as yet another darting flame or flaring tree.

The firefighters, though, had a major advantage: the Chewuch River ran right through the fire scene, providing an unlimited supply of water. During the night of Tuesday, July 10, FitzPatrick and the rest of her twenty-person crew, named the Northwest Regulars, were rerouted from the bigger Libby South Fire to deal with the smaller Thirtymile Fire. But when the Northwest Regulars reached the fire after dawn on the tenth, they encountered one problem after another simply in getting water out of the river and onto the flames: their two water pumps proved balky, and a helicopter with a water bucket wasn't dispatched to the scene in timely fashion. By midafternoon the Thirtymile Fire had grown beyond anything the Northwest Regulars—or anyone else—could control. With waves of embers crossing firelines, the whole crew sensibly pulled back to a place of safety. There, they ate lunch, napped, took out cameras, and remarked upon the ferocity of the flames only yards away.

Then almost inexplicably, with little or no discussion, the Northwest Regulars rose from their resting places and resumed fighting the fire, even as it grew in ferocity. What happened after that is the story of how a no-account wildfire in a remote corner of the Northwest cut off and trapped a group of firefighters, who were joined by two civilians who came out of nowhere. The fire gave everyone time to prepare, though the time was wasted. And then it rose in fury, took an unexpected twist, and swept to its horrific climax.

THE NORTH CASCADES Range, a world away from the damp coastal forest on the Pacific side of the mountains, is a rugged place to fight fires even during a quiet fire season. The knife-sharp ridges and steep-sided, narrow canyons, formed by a chaotic mixture of geologic events, are best visualized as gigantic ice trays, which filled with glaciers during the last Ice Age. As the glaciers began to melt roughly fifteen thousand years ago, they exposed a mosaic of geologic history that ranged from the docking of "minicontinents" with the North American continent, to volcanic eruptions, to scars from the ineluctable grinding of the ice pack. The North Cascades Range generally runs north-south but has so many unexpected twists, turns, doglegs, and dead ends, thanks to its varied geologic history, that it creates a jigsaw puzzle of baffling solution for earth scientists.

Clouds moving in from the Pacific Coast are blocked by the North Cascades and drop much of their moisture in the form of rain and snow before they clear the mountains' crest. The lack of moisture east of the crest line does not necessarily translate into a high number of fires. On the contrary, under normal circumstances there are few fires in this region because the mountains also block the lightning storms that are the most common cause of ignition for wildland fire. But because the area is dry and the terrain rugged, fires that do start can become intense and difficult to manage in a hurry. The fire staff for the Okanogan-Wenatchee National Forest, where both the Libby South and Thirtymile fires were located, was used mainly for initial attack on fires near roads; if those blazes escaped control, teams of firefighters would be called in to fight them and the local units would return to initial attack duty. If fires broke out in the backcountry, smoke jumpers or firefighters in helicopters could be dispatched, arriving by air in minutes over distances that would take hand crews many hours or even days to cover.

The Libby South Fire never gave the forest's initial attack crews a chance. Flames in the first hours were so blustery that smoke jumpers were immediately dispatched from the North Cascades Smokejumper Base nearby at Winthrop, only twenty miles away. As the jumpers stood in the open door of their airplane at 1,500 feet above the ground, ready to leap out, they were swept by waves of heat. They parachuted in and set to work. Over the next twenty-four hours, as the fire spread to 1,200 acres and threatened fifty homes, more resources were pulled in from across the Northwest. Eventually, over four hundred firefighters arrived. Forty engines rushed to the area to support hand crews and defend homes. A half-dozen airplanes and helicopters, carrying loads of water and fire retardant, buzzed overhead; the steep terrain, though, offered few targets for effective drops.

The firefighters were lucky in one way: flames had burned only a single sidewall of the containing canyon. If flames had jumped to the other side as well, a mass burnout likely would have resulted. Fire on both sides of a canyon creates a wind tunnel, which sucks in oxygen, which in turn accelerates flames. A small blaze can turn into an inferno in seconds. Indeed, on this day the thermometer climbed and moisture wicked from the air, setting the stage for just such an event. But the wind, the missing ingredient, remained calm into the afternoon.

On this Tuesday, the second day of the Libby South Fire, Tom Leuschen, a fire staffer, kept an ear cocked to the radio squawk box to monitor fire chatter around the forest. Leuschen was a fire behavior analyst based at the ranger station in Twisp, a small town located between the Libby South and Thirtymile fires. In early afternoon he was surprised by the sound of excited voices from the smaller Thirtymile Fire; it sounded like the fire was perking up, though everyone had thought it wouldn't last the day. Leuschen figured the crew might have a struggle on its hands, but then the radio chatter quieted down in midafternoon.

He turned his attention back to the draft of a forest fire plan, part of a national effort to forestall the kind of catastrophic wildfire becoming all too familiar in the West. Fires primed by drought and decades of fire suppression were scorching hundreds of thousands of acres at a whack and destroying homes by the hundreds. Every national forest has a similar plan, providing guidance on issues ranging from whether to suppress fire or use it to restore forest health. The national plan called for the deliberate burning of 40 million acres of national forest land, an area nearly the size of Wisconsin, over the first decade of the new century.

The Okanogan-Wenatchee National Forest extends over 4 million acres, and its fire plan took note of just about every one, a formidable task. But this forest had a special problem. As the hyphen implies, the Okanogan-Wenatchee had been two separate forests until merged a few years earlier in an attempt to boost efficiency. Leuschen had survived in his forest post, but the top fire management for the combined forest had been reduced by half, as redundant positions were eliminated. One sure consequence of the merger had been ongoing disruption; Leuschen had been shunted to a temporary cubbyhole in a warehouse while office spaces were being physically consolidated. He wondered if things would ever calm down enough for him to complete his part of the fire plan.

He finished his work, and as he headed for the door, a disturbing call came over the radio from the Thirtymile Fire: "Daniels and crew deployed shelters. Everybody fine." Shaking out even one fire shelter, the aluminized pup tents carried by every firefighter, automatically triggers a formal investigation of a wildfire. If Ellreese Daniels, the incident commander, and his entire crew had used theirs, as the broadcast implied, a brush with catastrophe was certain and far worse was possible—except that the radio message had ended on an upbeat note, "Everybody fine."

Leuschen looked at the office clock and marked the time: 1724 hours, or 5:24 PM, the same time that Kathie FitzPatrick, many miles away, was trying to reach her daughter Karen by cell phone. Leuschen picked up a portable radio, mounted his bicycle, and headed for home, only a few blocks away. He could stay on top of developments from there and return quickly to the office if he was needed. For many minutes after that there was near-radio silence from the Thirtymile Fire, as the furies raged in the Chewuch River canyon.

EARLY JULY IS a common time for wildland fire disasters. The woods have dried out from spring, and firefighters, their skills rusty from the off-season, face the first big blazes of the season. The South Canyon Fire, the most prominent landmark in modern wildfire history, happened on July 6, 1994, another time of drought and high temperatures. In late afternoon a sudden wind struck a sputtering fire in a narrow canyon on Storm King Mountain in west-central Colorado. The fire exploded in a scarlet-orange ball of flame, which raced a fire crew up the canyon and left fourteen of them dead. The loss branded the conscience of the fire world: firefighters on the line that day would remember forever after where they were standing, what they were doing, when they heard the news, just as the Kennedy assassination fixed in the mind of the nation a generation earlier. The South Canyon Fire, or as it became known, the Storm King tragedy was the greatest loss of life for wildland firefighters since another fire on a July 9, the Rattlesnake Fire of 1953 in northern California, which cost the lives of fifteen firefighters.

Perhaps more significant, Storm King helped inspire an era of change in wildland firefighting that continues to this day. The fire raised a host of issues, from firefighter safety and "whose fault is it?" to how to better educate the public to protect homes, structures, and themselves, to whether to fight certain fires at all. Not since the Big Blowup of 1910, which cost more than eighty lives and scorched over 3 million acres in the Northwest, had the culture of wildland firefighting undergone such a fundamental shake-up as a consequence of one fire. The lesson taken from the Big Blowup was to put out every fire as soon as it was discovered, no excuses. But with time, that policy created a legacy of overgrown forests, tightly packed with brush and small-diameter trees because they were protected from fire. In times of drought these forests became tinder-boxes, and fighting them hard became a deadly business.

After a series of multiple-fatality fires around midcentury, a host of new safety measures was put in place that began to reduce the rate of firefighter deaths. Only in the latter part of the twentieth century, however, did the understanding emerge that many fires should be allowed to burn, to enhance forest health as well as keep firefighters out of excessively dangerous situations.

After Storm King, the biggest lesson was this: when fire becomes too extreme, back off. Nothing in a lost canyon is worth a human life. And fires indeed were becoming more destructive, thanks in part to the 1910 Big Blowup but also to drought and the spread of human habitation into forests and prairies. Storm King did not invent these issues. But it brought the fire community together as one to work on them. By the time of the Thirtymile Fire, seven years later almost to the day, it was unthinkable that anything like the Storm King tragedy could happen again. And then it did.

The Thirtymile Fire was started by a neglected campfire along a dirt road in the Chewuch River canyon, a dozen miles short of the Canadian border. The canyon, a V-shaped gorge with knife-sharp ridges, is a classic North Cascades "ice tray" formation: narrow, steep-sided, and with odd twists and turns.* The Chewuch River (pronounced either Chew-Wuch or Chee-wak, as in *cheese whack*, in keeping with an old spelling) and a dirt road share the narrow canyon bottom.

The canyon is a popular camping place. The campfire could have been started during the Fourth of July holiday and smoldered for days before escaping, or it could have been hours old; authorities never established the timing with certainty. The smoke was first spotted Monday evening, July 9, by the pilot of a Canadian lead plane, aptly called *Bird Dog 8*, returning to British Columbia from directing air traffic over the Libby South Fire. The pilot radioed the sighting to the Forest Service central dispatch office in Okanogan. Flames were visible on the "valley bottom next to logging road," the pilot reported at 9:26 PM, according to the dispatch log. The fire covered two hectares, the pilot estimated, or about five acres, "with two spots ahead of it."

The dispatcher gave the fire a number, 103, and a name, the Thirtymile Fire, following the custom of naming fires for a prominent nearby

---

* Though the Chewuch River canyon follows an irregular path, for the sake of clarity and consistency the sides of the canyon will be identified as "north" and "south" in this account, corresponding to left and right as one drives up the canyon.

geographic landmark, in this case Thirtymile Peak, a few miles to the northeast. Many locations in the region are named, as is Thirtymile Peak, for their approximate distance from the town of Winthrop. Sited at the confluence of the Chewuch and Methow rivers, the town was a busy center for trade and mining in the pioneer days a century ago.

The smoke report caused a flurry of activity for already-busy fire managers. Not only was every fire a threat to become big and destructive, considering the drought, but the Chewuch River canyon was prized for its scenic and recreational value. On top of that, the fire was started by negligent humans, and national policy dictates always fighting such fires. There was never a question of letting this fire burn unchecked.

Within three minutes of *Bird Dog 8*'s report, by 9:29 PM, Jack Ellinger, the district duty officer, had diverted one engine and crew from the Libby South Fire to the new smoke. Ellinger poked his head into a meeting room at the Twisp ranger station and reported the unwelcome news to the bleary-eyed district fire management officer, Pete Soderquist, who was engaged in planning for the Libby South Fire. Soderquist had been up since 6:00 AM; he wasn't worn to exhaustion at this point, but he would not see a bed again for many hours. Fire managers at this time considered it a badge of honor to work the same long hours as their fire crews, which meant the occasional twenty-four-hour shift and no days off for weeks at a stretch. By the end of a busy season, managers often had the same haggard look as fireline grunts.

Ellinger had located Engine No. 702, a pickup truck mounted with a water pump, and its three-person crew. He directed Tim Schmekel, the acting engine boss, to throw some bladder bags—backpacks filled with up to five gallons of water and fitted with nozzles—into the back of the rig and head for the fire. "Check it out," Ellinger told Schmekel. "If it's just a campfire that's started some spot fires, see if you can put it out."

Darkness had filled the bottoms of canyons and begun to creep up their walls as Schmekel and his crew motored north. They got a quick start, reporting themselves en route to the Thirtymile Fire at 10:04 PM, barely more than a half hour after the first smoke report. As they entered the Chewuch River canyon, they sniffed the air like actual bird dogs for the scent of smoke. They drove past campgrounds dotted with the tents of a few post–Fourth of July vacationers, but at this late hour no one stirred.

Two of the campers, Bruce and Paula Hagemeyer, had bedded down early at Camp Four, just off the road and about eight miles below the fire. The Hagemeyers had grabbed a few days of vacation to give Paula a break from the stresses of her job as an occupational therapist, taking on the troubles of people with everything from hurt fingers to brain injuries. Earlier in the day, Bruce and Paula had worn themselves to pleasant exhaustion on mountain bikes, pedaling about ten miles up the road to where it dead-ended at another campground, called the Thirty-mile Campground, and then back. They slept uninterruptedly as Engine 702 passed them by, and as a succession of fire rigs followed up the road during the night.

As Schmekel and his engine crew rounded a corner, the roadway ahead suddenly appeared fully lighted, as though someone had switched on flood lamps. "The whole place ahead was glowing," Schmekel said later. While flaring trees illuminated everything near the road, the fire's full dimensions, away from the road, were hidden behind a latticework of tightly spaced trees and brambles. One crew member, Andy Floyd, had fished the Chewuch River, however, and gave the others the lay of the land.

The rocky canyon walls rise steeply, with inclines ranging from 70 percent to sheer perpendicular, to a crest line as ragged as dragon's teeth. The bottom of the canyon is flattish at the place the fire was burning, but about a mile up the canyon there's an enormous rock slump—mounds of rocks that extend for hundreds of yards along the bottom of the canyon and nearly across its width—which later would affect the progress of the fire. The road continues past the slump for about two miles, crosses a bridge over the river, and then dead-ends at the Thirtymile Campground, which is also a trailhead for the Pasayten Wilderness, which extends to the Canadian border. The Wilderness area is said to be a favored route of "drug donkeys" trans-porting illegal substances; a hunter once discovered more than three thousand marijuana plants in the backcountry well nourished by a sophisticated irrigation system. Drug agents on surveillance duty would be among the first to respond after the Thirtymile Fire's catastrophic climax.

In this stretch, from the fire scene to the Thirtymile Campground, the Chewuch River meanders across the narrow canyon bottom, generally deep and slow and broken only here and there by a fast run. The riverbanks are densely covered by willows, thornbushes, black cottonwoods, aspen, and Englemann spruce. Farther back from the water are stands of taller lodgepole and ponderosa pine and Douglas-fir trees. The water level fluctuates widely day to day, Floyd reported, and though the fishing can be good, the abrupt changes in water level make for chancy sport. The river that night appeared full, despite the heat and long-term drought.

Schmekel didn't like anything he had seen or heard. Why was there a fire here in the first place? It takes fuel, oxygen, and a spark to get a fire going. So where had the spark come from? Schmekel made a quick survey of nearby tree trunks but found no scorch marks to indicate a lightning strike. The rare lightning strike was more likely to hit the crests and walls of the canyon than to find its way to the narrow bottom, and anyway there had been no lightning storm in the area for days. On the drive up the canyon, though, Schmekel had seen a fallen tree near the road with telltale saw marks. An escaped campfire could explain everything.

Schmekel's immediate concern, however, was the extent of the fire, which he had to report to the dispatch office. He drove a hundred yards past visible flames, then turned back and parked at the heel, or downriver side, of the fire. He now knew how far up the canyon flames stretched but not how far across. He instructed Floyd to climb the north side of the canyon, opposite the flames, to get an overall view. Schmekel himself started off through dense brush and toward the river. The smell of smoke was everywhere. Within steps, the brush clutched at his clothing and closed around him. With nothing ahead but blackness and hidden flames, he beat a retreat back to the road.

The fire was sending Schmekel a mixed message. The bad news was that trees torched up with drumbeat regularity. The good news was that the flames shot straight up and thus did not set the crowns of other trees aflame. Schmekel could see one spot fire burning low to the ground between the road and the river. Floyd called down from his vantage point that he could see a couple more spot fires, one of which was good-sized, on the far side of the river. Schmekel checked the weather and jotted down the results. The wind was a light 1.5 miles per hour, the temperature a moderate 69 degrees, and the humidity a reassuring 36 percent. All those readings were normal for the time of year. "Fire still on flat," Schmekel penciled in his notebook. But he was worried.

"The fire was burning hard; I was not expecting fire behavior like this," Schmekel said later. When he called in his report, at 11:22 PM by the dispatch log, he also put in a request for a lot of help: a crew of ten or more, two more fire engines, a water pump and hose, and a fire investigator to check for arson. By then Ellinger, the duty officer, had directed another engine, No. 704, to head for the fire. But the Libby South Fire was the big show, and Ellinger asked Schmekel if the Thirty-mile Fire wouldn't hold until morning.

Schmekel said he thought the fire should be dealt with immediately, that night. When the sun rose and the woods had a chance to dry out, the fire was likely to take off up the steep south face of the canyon, which was well timbered in its lower reaches. At this point, Schmekel technically was the incident commander, or IC, meaning he had the power to assemble and command a small army. Being an IC is one of the most responsible jobs in firefighting: an IC can request anything from air tankers to fire engines to hand crews. But Schmekel was no veteran fire boss. He was a twenty-seven-year-old assistant engine foreman who only became an IC because he happened to be filling in for a vacationing engine boss. Schmekel was in over his head, knew it, and to his credit made no effort to cling to power. The dispatcher, Schmekel said, should also send out "someone more qualified to handle this fire."

The dispatcher replied that seasoned help was on the way: the Entiat Hotshots, a highly trained twenty-person crew with a veteran supervisor, had been assigned to the fire. The hotshots had been summoned to the region for the Libby South Fire and had bedded down at the fire camp, near Winthrop, twenty miles to the south. They already had been awakened and should be arriving shortly. The Entiat superintendent, Marshall Brown, would take over as IC when he arrived, a solution Schmekel greeted with relief.

At this point, as midnight approached, the fire had been scouted but not engaged. Schmekel's engine crew had five-gallon bladder bags but no portable water pumps, one of which can spew up to 7,200 gallons of water an hour, enough to wash a small fire off a mountainside. They did have a pump attached to the water tank on the truck. But no one was eager to march off into darkness, nozzle in hand, with burning trees ready to fall on them from every side. And so they waited.

The second engine, No. 704, showed up at 11:44 PM, ahead of the hotshots. The new engine crew had been working at the Libby South Fire since early afternoon and looked it. "They were moving slowly, just shuffling around," Schmekel said later. "Their eyes had a droopy, 'Why are we here?' look." Schmekel asked the engine boss, Dave Laughman, if he wanted to take over as IC, considering that he was a regular engine boss and Schmekel was a fill-in. Laughman had another water pump and plenty of hose on his truck. The two engine crews, it seemed, had enough manpower and equipment to mount an attack.

Laughman took a long look at the fire and concluded, as Schmekel had before him, that it was worrisome. Laughman had been told the fire was a mere two to five acres, but it appeared to him more like twenty to twenty-five acres "with multiple snags and numerous candles," as he would say later. On top of that, his two crewmen were rookies, not veterans.

Laughman turned down the IC assignment. "I refused because I knew it was beyond what I could handle," Laughman said later. "It was dark, and I did not know the country very well." Laughman and Schmekel decided to keep their crews on the road, out of harm's way, and wait for the hotshots.

The Entiat Hotshots are local heroes and have been for decades. They're headquartered at a work center near the town of Entiat, which occupies a scenic perch on tawny hills above the Columbia River about eighty-five miles south of the site of the Thirtymile Fire. The region is renowned as part of Washington's "apple bowl," and local youth vie to join the Entiat Hotshots, a job that provides instant status along with a better paycheck than apple picking. The Entiat Hotshots have been around for thirty years and were known until the mid-1980s as the Bushmen, famous—or infamous—for being as vulgar and coarse as they were tough and hardworking, a reputation reported without a blush on their Web site today. They were ordered to drop the "sexist" name Bushmen as women and minorities made entry, by force of law and cultural change, into the fire world. Today, the Entiat Hotshots are "hard working, clear thinking crew members led by dedicated, experienced supervisors," according to their Web site. They now post physical fitness records instead of "vulgar" pinups; the crew record for sit-ups is 104 in a minute, and for push-ups an even more remarkable 110 in a minute, both exercises reflecting the demands of wildland fire for upper-body strength.

Entiat superintendent Brown has a law degree, three decades of experience, and a reputation as a heavyweight with a quiet, reserved manner. "He knows as much about fire as you can learn in a career," said a fellow hotshot superintendent. "But he doesn't talk much."

The Entiat Hotshots had been released that Monday morning from a fire near Spokane, about 175 miles to the east, after a long night on the fireline. They drove out of the low hills near Spokane and onto the barren moonscape of eastern Washington, the outwash of a series of gigantic floods in glacial times emanating from western Montana and the panhandle of Idaho. They crossed the scablands and started into the mountains, arriving in Entiat by late afternoon. Within minutes, a telephone call summoned them to the Libby South Fire. They were told to report at the fire camp at the Liberty Bell High School near Winthrop and be prepared to go on the fireline at first light Tuesday morning. The drive to fire camp would take under two hours, so at least they would get a night's rest. They drove north from Entiat, followed the Columbia River for half the distance, and then headed into the Okanogan-Wenatchee National Forest. They checked in at fire camp, put up tents, and bedded down. They had been in their tents less than an hour, however, when two local firefighters acting as escorts, Shaun Rambo and Eric Nichols, awakened them with the news that they were to head for the Thirtymile Fire.

Dazed and sleepy, the hotshots stumbled aboard their vehicles, two "crew buggies" with eight seats each and a chase truck for gear. The escorts, Rambo and Nichols, had their own truck, which carried yet another water pump and a thousand feet of hose. The vehicles set off in a caravan and arrived at the scene of the fire about 1:00 AM—it was now Tuesday, July 10. On the road ahead, illuminated by flames, were the two fire engines, Nos. 702 and 704, and their loitering crews. Someone had squirted water on a burning stump, scattering embers. One crew member snoozed in the cab of a truck.

Brown was less than impressed with the sight. "Not much work had been accomplished," he remarked afterward, with characteristic understatement.

Schmekel briefed Brown, who now assumed the role of incident commander, and showed him the spot fires. In his opinion, Schmekel said, the situation required immediate attention. Brown talked separately with his hotshot crew and then returned and told Schmekel that the hotshots would take it from here. "You guys are initial attack," Brown said, "so if you want to, go home, get your rest, and get back on initial attack tomorrow morning."

Schmekel felt the sting of humiliation. Given proper supervision, the engine crews—eight firefighters, counting the escorts, with two water pumps—could be an effective force. Others, too, felt left out. "Boy, don't we feel like a bunch of jackasses," one local firefighter commented. Days later, one of the escorts, Nichols, would lament: "The ground was flat, the fire was by the road, and there was a river right next to it. It was a firefighter's dream. But the hotshot superintendent said he didn't need us and sent us away. I just have to wonder, if we had gotten that water show going . . ." But it was the middle of the night, everybody was tired, and most of the locals were happy to pack up and leave. The engine crews boarded their vehicles and departed.

Schmekel was on his way home to Winthrop when he heard Brown on the radio make an equipment request that included two water pumps. Schmekel couldn't believe it. "Why didn't he take our hose and pump?" Schmekel remarked to his seatmate, Floyd. "That was kind of messed up, wasn't it?"

Every hotshot crew worthy of the name prides itself on fighting fire by hand. Hotshots never rely on the chance presence of a river or lake to help them put out a fire, and even when a water source is available they often prefer to dig fireline, because nobody digs fireline like a hotshot crew. Old hands can tell at a glance who worked a fire, whether it was hotshots, smoke jumpers, or local hand crews, known as Type II crews. Smoke jumpers scratch out just enough of a line to hold the flanks of a fire while they pinch it off at the head. National Park Service crews are noted for cutting minimal firelines, sometimes only a few inches wide and often tied to existing trails, to reduce environmental impact. Type II crews cut lines that vary from slim and trim to wide and slovenly. Hotshots, however, make the effort to cut lines in orderly fashion, about eighteen inches wide and down to mineral soil. They clear vegetation from the sides of that line by prescription, from a few extra inches to many extra feet. They do their work quickly and without fuss, and when completed their lines run as neat as the contour lines on a map.

Brown's decision to send away Schmekel and the water pumps seems dismissive in hindsight. But considering their reluctance to engage the fire, the engine crews might have been more of a burden than a help. Brown soon realized, however, that the job was too big for the hotshots alone. He put in the order for more resources overheard by Schmekel at 2:15 AM, soon after Schmekel and the others had departed, and he may have tried earlier; the rough country blocked radio signals, and it was only by using a powerful radio set in one of the crew vans that the hotshots were able to contact Okanogan dispatch. "It was the middle of the night and quite confusing because we weren't sure what we had," the hotshot foreman, Kyle Cannon, said later. Brown asked the dispatch office for the water pumps, a fresh hand crew, and a helicopter to make water drops, all for morning.

The hotshots, meanwhile, no sooner had cut lines around a couple of spot fires near the road than their scouts across the river found half a dozen more. The hotshots crossed the river in waist-deep water— they eventually found a crossing log, but it was tricky to use—and set to work on the new spot fires. By 5:00 AM they were ready to call it quits, and they reassembled at the road. Everyone's hair was stiff with grit and smoke. The men had prickly beards. Socks were squishy wet from the river. The hotshots were hungry, weary, frustrated, and badly in need of a break.

They held a conversation with the dispatch office at 5:26 AM and reported that the fire amounted to five or six acres of active flames scattered over twenty to twenty-five acres of ground, which helps account for the conflicting early reports about the fire's size, which ranged from five to twenty-five acres. They had found seven spot fires altogether and contained five of them. The remaining two, each about an acre in size, burned unchecked. A few minutes after this exchange the dispatcher ordered the helicopter and its water bucket, just the ticket to handle a couple of spot fires scattered in heavy brush.

The hotshots dug out high-energy rations—hungry as they were, even a combination like beef jerky and dried papaya could sound tasty. The food brought on a lethargy none could resist. Dawn was on the rise, and help was on the way. They could catch a wink of sleep and still get up for a last swipe at the fire before they handed over the job to their relief. Brown and Cannon made themselves comfortable on the van's seats, the others found nesting spots, and the hotshots fell into restless slumber.

CHAPTER TWO

> *Battling Western wildfire enlists up to 50,000 people every*
> *summer. The top of the organizational pyramid is occupied*
> *by full-time professionals. But its broad base is anchored by*
> *thousands of seasonals—small-town kids, college students,*
> *and perennial firefighters.*
>
> —Mike Thoele, author and journalist,
> from a 1994 media interview

Word went out that Monday afternoon to firefighters across central Washington to stay near a telephone. Expect a callout within hours, they were told; the Libby South Fire, a "growler," was drawing resources from far and wide. The news sent a tremor of excitement through the fire community, from rookie to experienced hand. For the rookies, this would be the first experience with big-time flames; for veterans, it would be an opportunity to show their stuff in their own backyard. For everyone, it offered the possibility of a two-week assignment with overtime. The day shift ended without a summons, but the moment was near.

Karen FitzPatrick had spent the evening with her father, John, practicing driving a stick shift, in the family's sport utility vehicle. They had stopped on the way home to visit their minister, Tom Hagerman, who had turned from a life of drugs and violence to become a preacher. Hagerman had a tiny flock of about a dozen souls, to whom he preached a fundamentalist version of Christianity that allowed no compromise. He was on the outs with established clergy in the Yakima Valley, whom he "despised," as he often remarked, for preaching a "soft Christianity."

On this evening, a radiant light shone from Karen's eyes as she, her father, and Hagerman read scripture together. "I don't know where

I'm getting all this energy!" Karen said. She glowed with an inner fire, Hagerman would remember, "like a lightbulb without a shade." Hagerman prized Karen, whose name means "pure," for her ardent faith and obedient nature. "I never met anyone so *submissive* to instruction and correction," he said. She once had shown up at a prayer meeting wearing a skirt with a slit up the side exposing a comely thigh, and Hagerman had reproached her. "You will cause us to lust!" She went home, changed clothes, and returned in modest dress.

Karen was no plastic angel. Though only a teenager, she already had experienced some of life's strongest passions—from the sexual to the divine—and had made major, life-changing decisions as a result. For her, the turn to firefighting was an attempt to resolve the ageless conflict between the desires of the spirit and those of the flesh. "It takes a certain kind of person to be a firefighter," she had said a month earlier, in a high school speech just before graduation, "and I think I am one of them." The path to that conclusion had not been an easy one.

Before she entered adolescence, Karen had been muscular enough to be mistaken for a boy. She had "six-pack abs" and a bicep muscle that when flexed ran up and down her arm like a live animal, an effect males can spend years in the weight room to achieve. She loved camping. She excelled at gymnastics, soccer, swimming, and any other sport she took up, and once won a medal for weight lifting. Coaches thought she had Olympic potential, but neither she nor her family wanted their lives taken over by sports training, even for the Olympics.

"She was born strong," said her older sister Jaina, a blonde beauty whose soft, feminine looks made a sharp contrast with those of Karen, who was sometimes wrongly taken for Jaina's little brother. The two were best friends; their mother, Kathie, described them as a "Mutt and Jeff" team. A family photo taken in their early teens at a swimming pool shows Jaina floating with supreme self-confidence in an inflatable plastic ring, her face turned upward to embrace the sun, a cool drink ready at hand. Karen sits hunched over in the pool's spill trough, her dark hair fallen over her face, as though she is hiding from the world.

Then Karen entered adolescence, and the lanky tomboy began to fill out. She took up cooking and dressmaking, began to prepare elegant Sunday brunches for girlfriends, developed her natural talent for singing, and became a drum majorette. As Karen became more lady-like, tensions inevitably arose with Jaina, and the two began to drift apart.

Karen had bold liquid eyes, full lips, and glossy dark hair, which was sometimes brownish and sometimes reddish as teen fashion and a dye bottle dictated. Her long jaw, which had given her a mannish look when she was younger, now imparted an exotic touch to her face, saving it from mere prettiness. She began to spend hours in front of a mirror with powders, pencils, lipsticks, and creams arrayed before her like a surgeon's instruments, experimenting first with one look and then another.

She tried out for the lead role of Eliza Doolittle in *My Fair Lady*, the Lerner and Lowe musical about a little flower peddler who is transformed into a woman of charm and sophistication under the guidance of a speech instructor, Henry Higgins, who then falls in love with her. But she lost the part to a friend and fellow drum majorette, Cheryl Purcell. "Congratulations," she generously wrote Cheryl. "You really fit that part!" So did Karen.

She took up photography and learned darkroom techniques that she applied to self-portraits, highlighting her facial features and making her hair thicker and more abundant. The new Karen no longer hid her face and hunched her shoulders. Photos from this time show her pointing a toe and gazing outward. The effect is stunning. The tomboy had become a beauty, ready for the pages of a European high-fashion magazine. But instead, Karen turned to firefighting.

Kathie made a desperate bid to talk her daughter out of the decision, but Karen offered in her defense a piece of career advice from the apostle Jude: "Strive to save others, snatching them out of everlasting fire and destruction." As a Christian minister, Kathie couldn't argue with scripture.

Karen possessed a determined spirit to match her physical strength and had already used those qualities to prove herself as a firefighter, on a Fourth of July back when she was fifteen years old. After watching a fireworks display on television with her family that evening, Karen had headed to bed early, taking advantage of the holiday to catch up on sleep. The family could hear rockets and other fireworks popping outside the house. A pickup truck full of rowdy teenagers raced up and down the street tossing firecrackers. John went to lock up the family cars but a moment later came rushing back into the house.

"Don't anybody go to bed," he warned. "There's a big fire that just got started in the field out there. It must have been those kids with fireworks."

Flames twenty feet high and higher headed for the FitzPatrick house. Within minutes, a big fire engine pulled up, but it was a "pavement queen" with no off-road capability, and its hoses could not reach the flames. Kathie made a frantic call to 911, but the operator said every engine had been dispatched and the fire stations were empty. At this moment Karen appeared in the living room wearing shorty pajamas and combing her hair with her fingers.

"What's all the ruckus?" she asked sleepily, and was told to look out the window.

The fire edged closer.

"You better move your car," John told Kathie, who grabbed her keys and bolted for the door. As Kathie started to drive away, she looked back and saw Karen, still in her PJs, vaulting a five-foot fence next to the house, trailing a couple of garden hoses.

The fight was touch and go, but Karen stood her ground. "The flames came down pretty fast, but I went up against the fire with the two hoses," Karen recounted later. She directed one stream of water onto the flames and the other against the side of the house. After a half hour, she had squelched the last of the flames.

Kathie, who had watched the drama from a neighbor's house, drove back home and listened to the fire story with a mixture of pride and alarm. Where did her daughter find the guts to behave like that? Kathie wondered.

"Karen put the fire department to shame!" John chortled with pride. Forever after, the event was known in the FitzPatrick family as the Shorty Pajama Fire.

As part of Karen's maturing process, she also had an awakening of latent Christian faith. Kathie and John were Pentecostal Christians who made faith the center of family life, but Karen had not taken a serious interest in religion when she was younger. Jaina says *she* was the Bible-thumper, telling her sister she was on her way to hell unless she mended her careless ways. Karen's turn to religion sparked a fresh conflict, though, with another new interest: boys.

Karen had thirsted for the attention she now attracted in abundance from Yakima's adolescent male population. She felt the rush of desire in all its masks. There was a "crazy missing part in my heart," she once wrote in a school essay. "Inside, I felt so alone that I thought even God didn't really feel my pain." Oftentimes she wasn't sure what she felt, a passion for purity and godliness or a baser desire, except whatever it was raged and burned within her, seeking an outlet.

On occasion Karen would take a Bible to the Yakima Mall, buttonhole strangers, and tell them about her growing faith. She wrote book reports for school about Bible stories. She kept a Bible ready at hand while working part-time at Valerie's Espresso, a drive-in coffee shop in downtown Yakima, and sometimes recited scripture to startled customers. When an obviously troubled young man rode up to the drive-in window on his bicycle one day, looking disheveled and downcast, she introduced herself: "My name is Karen FitzPatrick, and I'm a Christian. I'm a virgin, and I'm going to remain one until my wedding night."

Not sure how to respond, the young man said, "My name is Robert Trevino, and I'd like a double mocha." The two became fast friends, and as Trevino struggled to turn around his life they made plans to be students together at community college. "She helped me get right; she empowered me," Trevino said later, after he had become a student at "Karen's school," Yakima Valley Community College.

Then one day a young man named Mark pulled up at Karen's window with something more than a double mocha in mind. After a little conversation, Mark asked Karen for a date.

"I should have said no," Karen later recounted. "But here I was with little dating experience and confidence." Mark was only seventeen years old but already smoked and drank. He traveled as a sales representative but returned to Yakima on weekends, when he and Karen dated. She found herself slipping into a relationship filled with dangers. But his "bad boy" type and seeming worldliness "made me like him even more," Karen admitted.

Mark stepped up the pace. As spring came around, he asked her to go away with him to "join the crew and spend the summer." The idea scared Karen. She was sexually inexperienced but fully comprehended what Mark was talking about. Would the fun be worth the loss of trust and respect from friends and family? Mark seemed to lack understanding of her world or appreciation for the values she held most dear. He was godless, and so they couldn't share her blossoming faith. But perversely, this only made Karen want him more.

Mark pressed his advantage. His eighteenth birthday was coming up, he told Karen. Why not come and celebrate with him? This would be no quickie affair, he promised. He would settle down in Yakima, just to be near her, if only she would spend this coming-of-age birthday with him.

Karen managed to blurt out, "No, I can't, Mark. I can't do this anymore," but inside she felt weak and troubled. If he asked again she had no idea how she would respond. "Our goodbye was a little much and longer than I expected," she recounted in her diary. "I knew he wasn't what I needed. I felt wrong inside for liking him the way I did. He brought out everything in me that I hated." Mark went off on a trip to Seattle but promised to call again.

That evening, Karen found herself alone in her bedroom, which looked out on a jumble of flowers and shrubbery the family called "Karen's forest"; the view gave the room the feel of a vivarium, teeming with new life. The walls of the room were covered with inspirational notes, posters, and photos: a humanistic drawing of Jesus faced a poster of Rosy the Riveter, who flexed her bicep and made her famed declaration, "We Can Do It." The ceiling sparkled with a pasted-on heaven of glittering stars. On the wall next to the bed was a weight-lifting medal inscribed "1st Place, West Valley High School Lift-a-Thon"—for bench-pressing 115 pounds.

Deeply troubled, Karen knelt on a throw rug by the bed. "Jesus, come into my heart and be my Savior," she prayed, as she later recounted. "I can't live a good life without you." She had tried this approach before, after hearing fellow Christians describe their experience of being born again. Once during a prayer meeting, Karen had listened with rapt attention as another participant, Don Chen, told how God had come to him moments before, in that very room. Chen had felt "God's touch," he declared, as though the Supreme Being had made

Himself manifest to him alone. Karen came up to Chen afterward, happy for him but more than a little jealous.

"Wow, Don, you got touched!" Karen said. "I want to get touched too. Please, Don, pray for me to be touched!"

Chen, a Chinese immigrant who had built a successful restaurant business, counseled patience. If Karen prayed with all her heart and soul, Chen said, God would come to her in His own time. Karen prayed hard for the next several weeks, but nothing dramatic happened.

As she knelt by her bed on this evening, she sensed a brightening light as though a sun was rising on a far, inner horizon, an experience shared by many over the ages. The light had a life of its own, beyond anything she could control. At first it was a soft glow. But it quickened, turned an unearthly white, and in a rolling, unstoppable wave filled the dark and undiscovered spaces of her being. The wave of light broke over her consciousness with a fiery touch that inflamed her spirit and made every cell of her physical being come alive with energy. Karen broke into deep sobs of surrender, and her mother, hearing her from upstairs, guessed what was under way. The ecstatic moment faded into afterglow, a sense of peace and belonging unlike anything Karen had ever experienced before. "I finally felt the end of myself," she wrote in her diary. "I knew from that moment on, He received me just as I was. I was forgiven."

Karen never saw Mark again.

On the evening of the callout for the Libby South Fire, Karen was too excited to sleep. After returning home with her father, she darted around the house, her mind a whirl. The "boy thing" was behind her, she assured John. Then she said something he would remember afterward: "I know I've been busy, but whatever time I have I'll help you do things around here. I want to do that."

Karen pulled her gear together and flung herself on her bed. If she had any doubts about becoming a firefighter, she had only to look over at her boots for reassurance. Her mother, Kathie, had nearly fainted when Karen bought the boots—Karen paid half, but the $350-plus price tag was an eye-popper for Kathie, who paid the other half. When they got home from the store, Karen took the boots to this same bedroom to try them on. A minute later she cried out: "Come down and look, Mom! On the inside, it's the date the boots were made." Stamped inside the boots were the numbers 6-20-00. "That's the same date I was born again!" Karen said happily.

Karen was stretched out sleepless on her bed when the telephone rang with the summons to the fire. She eagerly reached for the phone.

CHAPTER THREE

In the spring of '99 I gave notice...that a limited number of college students who had definitely made up their minds to take up Forestry as a profession could get $25 a month and their expenses in the field...But only on condition that they could convince us they had the earnestness, the physical hardiness, and the love of the woods to fit them for the job.

—Gifford Pinchot, first chief of the U.S. Forest Service,
from *Breaking New Ground*, 1947

The Naches Ranger District is headquartered in trim, low buildings on the main highway in Naches, a dozen miles northwest of Yakima. Between the two towns lies the tenderloin of the fertile Yakima Valley, the heart of Washington's fruit industry. The towns are joined by U.S. Highway 12, which parallels the Naches River, a key artery in the valley's liquid lifeline. Streams that rise in the Cascade Range feed an irrigation system that makes the Yakima Valley, acre for acre, among the most productive fruit orchards on earth; it actually leads California's much larger Great Central Valley in hops production.

The night of the callout was balmy, the air filled with the sweet smell of a ripening harvest. Headlights along U.S. 12 illuminated a succession of huge, hand-lettered road signs that proclaimed the valley's riches: "My Big Fat Sweet Peaches," "Sweet Walla Walla Onions," "King Kong Peaches." The valley's every product proclaimed its sweetness, from sweet cherries to "sweet bottled water." Close by the road signs stood clapboard sheds with covered stands, humble by comparison with the come-on signs, where just-picked fruits and vegetables would be set out for sale in the morning.

The assembling fire crew was a study in diversity, a mix of ages, genders, races, and backgrounds. Four of them, though, were linked by an unseen bond, a separate determination by each to resolve deep-seated personal issues by joining the fire world. Of this group, two were teenagers: Karen FitzPatrick and Jessica Johnson, who was two weeks shy of her twentieth birthday. The other two were Devin Weaver, a twenty-one-year-old headed for college, and Tom Craven, a thirty-year-old squad leader and fire veteran.

For these four, the lure of fire went beyond action adventure and a paycheck. They had counted the dangers and knew the risks, or thought they did. They embraced the discipline, the drudgery, and the dirt. They expected in return an outdoor life of service to others, with defined rules and rewards. They shared a faith, in varying degrees of intensity, that their chosen path would lead to better things ahead—not to riches in the usual sense but to satisfying careers, good families, and the abiding comradeship that comes from facing danger together. In the next hours these four would form a physical bond and confront, in a supreme test, the very flames that had called them out.

Weaver, waiting for the phone to ring at home, was rubbing waxy goo into a new pair of fire boots when his father, Ken, came in from a Yakima baseball league meeting. Devin fanned a hair dryer over the boots to melt the wax, so it would absorb into the leather. How Devin loved those boots, Ken thought. Devin always had to have the best toys—the fanciest fishing rod, hunting bow, or pickup truck—and though Devin was a rookie firefighter, he had bought a pair of White's, the legendary fire boots. Legends come at a price, in this case over $350. But Devin never counted the cost, Ken thought, and why should he?

Devin was the brightest star in the Weaver family constellation, the only son to Ken and his wife, Barbara, and best friend to his sisters Jeanette and Andrea Michelle. Devin was such good friends with Andrea Michelle, who had a learning disability, and Jeanette, the pretty sister, that neither girl took much interest in dating. And Devin felt the same way about them: he liked other girls as friends but had no runaway romantic interests. He was the fulfillment of his parents' family ambitions. As long as Devin filled those roles, all was well in the Weaver household. Ken dug out his own heavy boots, settled himself next to Devin on a sofa, and dipped his fingers into the can of wax.

It was about 10:00 PM when Ken left for bed. He had a long work-day behind him and another one ahead at Weaver Flowers, his dry flower business. Manufacturing ornamental flower arrangements might seem a curious occupation for a man like Ken, a weight lifter, hunter, and all-around macho guy. But he had built the company from scratch into a successful family enterprise, and that mattered more to him than anything: Barbara and the children had all worked for Weaver Flowers at one time or another.

Devin was too keyed up to sleep, so when the phone buzzed around midnight he answered before the ring wakened his father. A voice ordered him to report immediately to his duty post, the Naches ranger station. "Pack a double lunch," the voice said. "We don't know when we can feed you."

The buzz of the phone stirred Barbara, and she slipped out of bed, leaving Ken to sleep. She found Devin in the kitchen, excited and happy, but anxious that his crew might take off without him. Could she micro-wave a favorite dish, he asked, macaroni and cheese with jalapeño peppers? He would need the extra carbohydrates for energy on the fireline.

"Yeah, we can do that," Barbara said with a smile, glad to be of use. The brightly lighted kitchen was a cozy haven against the dark world outside. The sight of Devin, strong, tall, and aglow with enthusiasm, brought a rush of old feelings to Barbara, like the good times before that awful day not long ago when the bond that united the Weavers had snapped and the stars of the family constellation had tumbled in their courses. Until that moment, Devin had been the wonder child; after that moment, well, Barbara didn't let her mind go there.

Devin had been a star baseball player, his pitching arm the pride of the Weaver family. There was simply nothing like it in the Yakima Val-ley. Adoring fans chanted "Weaver! Weaver! Weaver!" when he walked to the mound, ready to mow down opponents. His father coached and cheered from the dugout. (Ken never screamed at his son, he said, but others remembered him yelling impassioned advice and criticism.) Barbara and the girls shouted their approval from the stands.

Devin's success at baseball helped the Weavers make up for a dark past. Ken grew up in a huge family, along with seven brothers and two sisters. His father was consumed by an angry desire to get rich and his failure to do so made him a bitter man. According to Ken, his father often doled out discipline with a razor strop. When Ken grew up and had children of his own, he became a superparent by way of compensation, as did others of his siblings. Ken poured the love and comradeship denied him into Devin, his "soul mate and best boy friend." He drove the relationship closer and closer until he and Devin became more brothers than father and son. "If I lost you, I'd flat die," Ken once told Devin, after they had seen a Mel Gibson movie, *The Patriot*, about a Revolutionary War hero who loses two sons. "When I die, I want you to give my eulogy," Ken said.

"Aw, Dad," Devin replied bashfully, "what am I going to say?"

Devin carried off his weighty family role with a shy, engaging smile and a quiet, self-effacing manner. "He could bring a smile to anyone's face without saying a word," one admirer remarked. During the busy holiday season at Weaver Flowers, Devin worked long hours, often seven days a week. He took on nasty jobs like running the dye machine, which required wearing heavy protective clothing. Even when he came home tired, he could summon the energy on occasion to wrestle with Andrea, whom he affectionately called "Little Piggy"—she was seriously overweight. Devin and Andrea would stay up "babbling" together into the wee hours, as Andrea remembered. Devin was, she said, "my brother, my best friend, the guy I could sit and talk mindless conversation with, play darts, beat the crap out of each other." Devin's faithful attentions helped Andrea gain the self-confidence to graduate from high school and go on to community college.

Ken's passions and pastimes became Devin's keenest interests. They hunted, bowled, golfed, and worked out together. "He wanted every bit of skill I had," Ken said. "Never in my life had anyone wanted to be me, and a little better. My daughters don't want it. He couldn't get enough, and I poured my heart and soul into that." Devin had a head for numbers and would work out velocity, tangent, and energy formulas for whatever sport they pursued. "Devin was always conflicted between his IQ and his love of dirt," Ken said.

Once on a hunting trip, Devin worked out vectors for the interception point of shot and a flying turkey, using a variety of values for the objects in motion. "Are we hunting turkey or conducting a physics class?" Ken asked in exasperation. "The world is a physics class," Devin responded, to his father's delight.

Family pride, though, came from Devin's very public success as a pitcher. The Yakima All-Star team took on every comer, except the dominant team in the region, West Sound, who turned up their noses at the All-Stars' challenge until finally shamed into a meeting. The All-Stars started another pitcher, Tony Alexander, for the first three innings; Devin was to pitch the final innings, his customary assignment. Alexander left Devin the barest of leads, three runs to two. As Devin started for the mound, Ken noticed a nervous look on his son's face. Ken trotted to the mound.

"Nobody could bring out in him what I could," Ken recounted with pride. "Nobody else could do it." Ken massaged Devin's pitching arm.

"Why are we here?" Ken asked, smiling confidently.

Devin was silent.

"We're here because they're the best we could find to play," Ken said.

"Now, how good are we?"

Again Devin was silent. Ken patted his arm and left him to his fate.

The first batter to face Devin slapped a slow roller into the infield and beat the throw to first base by a step: runner on first, nobody out. The anxious look on Devin's face vanished and was replaced by a smile. Ken recognized the smile as a nervous tic, not necessarily a sign of happiness, which sometimes got Devin in trouble—like the time he hit a batter with a pitch and the smile broke out. But it had another meaning, too. Devin had never yet lost a game with the smile on his face.

The next batter rapped a sharp grounder into the glove of Alexander, who had moved from the mound to shortstop. Alexander flipped the ball to the second baseman, who fired the ball to first to complete a double play. After that, Devin never faltered. The All-Stars went on to beat West Sound by a wide margin, a high point in Yakima baseball history to this day.

A year or so later Devin damaged the rotator cuff in his pitching arm, and the injury was misdiagnosed as a sore shoulder caused by overuse. Devin worked his arm hard in the off-season, which further inflamed the shoulder. His arm slowly lost effectiveness. By the time Devin reached his senior year, which should have been his strongest season, he couldn't buy three outs.

"He couldn't believe he could not do it," Ken said. Four years earlier, Devin had pitched fourteen innings a week, half the weekly schedule. Now he was pulled out of games, making the long walk from the mound to the dugout in humiliation. The smile was gone; no longer was Devin the hero of Yakima Valley. The pride went out of his life, and so too out of the Weaver family.

Devin began spending a lot of time in the woods with three baseball buddies, who called themselves the "Four Horsemen" and adopted nicknames: Corey "Kingfish" Kingman, who was Devin's catcher, known for his appetite for hot dogs and hamburgers "by the pound"; Brent "The Quiet One" Colby; Doug "Wolfman" Mitzel; and "Mustardman" Weaver, for his fondness for mustard. "Four Horsemen for life, we rode side by side, through adventure and growth, together in stride," the Kingfish rhymed.

One winter weekend Devin and company took a supply of Jack Daniels whiskey, provided by Devin, the only one with a job and ready cash, to a cabin on a lake. They finished the whiskey outdoors looking at the stars, and Devin, in worse shape than the others, passed out on bare ground. The night grew bitterly cold. Luckily for Devin, his friends sobered up enough to drag him into the cabin and save him from hypothermia. After that, Devin sank deeper into depression, and his drinking bouts became more frequent.

Ken and Barbara could see the outward changes in Devin's behavior: he was listless and sullen, the opposite of his usual cheery and optimistic self. The cement that bound the family together was visibly crumbling. One day as Ken and Devin stood together outside the house, a friend of Devin's came by. Devin edged away from his father and held a furtive, whispered conversation with the friend.

Oh, that's interesting, Ken thought. The proper functioning of the Weaver family constellation depended upon frank and open discussion among its members. Ken, who was not a man to avoid confrontation, took Devin into the house and sat him down.

"Now, what's this all about?" Ken said with a tight smile.

Devin had no heart for defiance. "I'm going drinking later," Devin confessed. "I drink a lot."

"What's a lot?" Ken asked.

"Maybe fifteen beers."

"What, a week, a month, what are we talking about?"

"No, Dad, fifteen beers a night."

"You can't do that! If you drink that much, you pass out and throw up and you can strangle on your vomit and die."

"No, Dad, I won't strangle; when I fall down, I try to land on my stomach."

The conversation was shattering for both Ken and Devin, but they agreed to keep talking. Meantime, Devin was grounded. Devin was no rebel; he wanted nothing more than to fulfill the family role laid out for him. But something deeply troubling had happened, far beyond the injury to Devin's pitching arm, and everyone in the family had been damaged by it. Night after night, Ken and Devin talked together, trying to sort out what had gone wrong. Finally, Ken told Devin that he realized he had put too heavy a burden on him. Righting the wrongs of Ken's childhood had become mixed up with Devin's success as a pitcher. Devin's pitching arm had been an outward and visible sign of the loving pride the members of the Weaver family took in themselves, and of the support they could offer a son, the support Ken had been denied by his father. And magically it had healed the wounds of the past. When Devin's pitching arm failed, the Weaver family structure failed, too. "I put half of this on you," said Ken.

Devin's recovery was helped by the Four Horsemen, who talked openly about their drunken escapades as a passing stage; they were ready to move on to healthier pastimes. But Devin had nothing to replace the role baseball had played for him and his family. Then one day as Devin walked down the hall at Yakima's Eisenhower High School he was met by the wrestling coach, Ray Harris.

"Guess what, Weaver," Harris boomed. "What are you doing with yourself?"

"I don't know," the fallen athlete responded, sheepishly.

"You're wrestling!" Harris announced. Harris had an opening on the wrestling squad for a big fellow, and Devin, at six feet tall and just over 170 pounds, fit the need. Devin showed up at practice that afternoon. He had never wrestled before and had to suffer the pains of apprenticeship on the junior varsity squad. But he was grateful to find a physical outlet with even the hope of glory. Two weeks later he had his first match and lost badly. He plugged away nonetheless, learned holds and strategy, and began to win an occasional match. He was no star—except to the Weavers. The family was well represented at every match; sometimes Weavers were the only ones in the stands. "Mom, nobody goes to JV wrestling matches," Jeanette once told Barbara, "and *nobody* screams like that."

"I do," Barbara replied with a secret smile.

The Weavers became JV wrestling's biggest boosters. "I get these parents who want their kids to be undefeated state champs," Harris said. "It doesn't happen. Ken and Barb were happy to have Devin out there. If Devin lost, Ken would say, 'That's pretty good for a kid who never wrestled before.' They enjoyed it for the camaraderie, for the joy of it." And for a great deal more.

The big match of the year was the President's Invitational in Tacoma, when schools like Eisenhower, named for U.S. presidents, faced each other. Devin lost one match but won three others, a good enough record to place him in the JV consolation bracket. As he faced his last opponent of the day, with a third-place medal in the balance, his teammates gathered around the mat and started the old familiar chant, "Weaver! Weaver! Weaver!" Devin won by the narrowest of margins and took home the bronze.

Devin went on to Yakima Valley Community College, where he studied physics, and made plans to attend the University of Washington in Seattle, majoring in electrical engineering. The thought of leaving home, though, made him sick to his stomach, and he spent sleepless nights throwing up.

One day while Devin and Ken were shopping together, they ran into Jason Emhoff, an old classmate and fellow athlete of Devin's from Eisenhower High School. Emhoff, short, burly, and outdoorsy, was working for the Forest Service, assigned to the nearby Naches Ranger District. "We spend all day in the woods, and they pay us for it!" Emhoff enthused. His crew did a lot of chore work, he acknowledged. "But sometimes we fight fire."

It sounded like the solution to Devin's summer. A job close to Yakima would allow him to live at home until the last possible minute, before leaving for college. A Forest Service paycheck would help with tuition. And the work had the allure of outdoor adventure, within limits. Perhaps best of all, the job paid a handsome dividend in public pride. Being young and with the Forest Service in small-town America means walking tall—more so if you fight fire.

Devin applied, was accepted, and came home after a week of fire training with a beaming smile. "Hey, Dad, I'm a Fed!" he told Ken. There was no need to worry about safety, Devin said. The basic safety rules were in red ink because they "are written in blood." Devin got the assignment he wanted, the Naches Ranger District fire crew, and within weeks, in early July, the promise of his first big fire.

Barbara threw everything she could find into a lunch box and handed it to Devin as he bolted for the kitchen door.

"Wait," she said, "I gotta have a hug." She had to pull his head down to plant a kiss, he was so tall. "Be careful and have fun," she said. Devin started up his GMC Sonoma pickup, a black beauty Ken had bought for the family hero, and headed out.

IT TOOK MORE than an hour for Weaver and all the others to assemble at Naches. Among the earliest arrivals was Jessica Johnson, who came from the Forest Service fire barracks at a work station several miles from Naches. She showed up with her blonde hair sticking out from under her hard hat, in trademark disarray. Jessica was a pretty girl, athletic and robust, a stunner in makeup and a prom dress. But she felt more at home with her face smudged by ash and wearing work clothes. She had moved into the fire barracks barely more than twenty-four hours earlier, on Sunday night, after making one of the biggest decisions of her life. Over the weekend she had walked out on her longtime boyfriend, Nathan Craig, a fellow firefighter.

Jessica and Nate had made a pair, similar enough to be bookends. They both had firefighter builds—not too big and not too small, strong and fit. They had wild, blondish hair and round, attractive faces. And they loved the same things: hard physical work, trips to the Wind River for salmon fishing (Nate had a reputation as a fisherman, but Jessica often caught more and bigger fish), and partying. Way too much partying.

In the last few months, Johnson had realized she could not go on being a "wild child" with Nate and fight fire at the same time. This was her second season as a wildland firefighter, and the job demanded every bit of strength, fitness, and mental alertness she could muster. The late nights and beer guzzling with Nate left her bleary and unfit for duty the next day.

Jessica and Nate had lived together for two years, from the time she was seventeen, despite severe parental disapproval. Jessica had been a longtime challenge for family and teachers. She was "squirrelly, loud, gutsy," according to Holly Dunham-Wheeler, her swimming coach at West Valley High School. "She was wild and outgoing, and if she disagreed with you, you knew it. But then she started firefighting, and she really grew up. She found herself. She found confidence, and it made her feel good."

Jessica had seemed destined for the fire world from infancy. She had been a pretty baby with platinum-colored hair, a beaming countenance, and an untamable spirit. While out driving one day with her parents, Jody and Rick, she had shrieked with delight as a fire truck swept past, lights flashing and siren wailing. "Fire fuck! Fire fuck!" she cried out, and the story entered family lore.

"She would jump in a swimming pool when she was a year old and come up laughing," Jody said. "I'm thinking, I have this child here that is way beyond me."

Jody and Rick divorced when Jessica was nine years old, and difficult times followed. Jody, an intensive care nurse, was granted custody of Jessica but found raising a child alone to be a heavy burden. Thrown on each other's company, Jody and Jessica formed a close bond, but that made it difficult for Jody to play the disciplinarian. "We were really close, but then as she got older she got into teenage-hood," Jody said.

"She was kind of wild—okay, she was a wild kid. And so I had a lot of problems."

Jody remarried, to Greg E. Gray in 1994, and had another daughter, Ashley, who worshiped Jessica, her senior by fifteen years. Whenever Jessica climbed into her vintage Nissan pickup truck to leave for a fire, Ashley would stand at the curb, wave, and cry out, "I love you, Jess! I miss you! Come home soon."

Jessica tried to maintain a relationship with her birth father, Rick, a man of few words, hard ways, and deeply felt emotions. And she succeeded. It was Rick, a bricklayer by trade, who taught her how to put her back into a job. She worked one summer for him as a hod carrier—carrying bricks up scaffolding on construction jobs, which is a physically taxing job for a strong man.

"She was very strong, very stout," Rick said. "There are few, if any, female hod carriers. She didn't back down; she hung in there and worked all summer. She thought it would help her get a firefighting job the next summer." It did.

That summer cemented a bond between father and daughter. As Rick put it, Jessica was "my angel, my joy and my sorrow, my little girl, my grown woman, my helper, my confidante, my ambassador of cheer, my admirer, my hero."

Jessica came home to Jody so exhausted at the end of a day with the bricks that she went from the dinner table straight to bed. The summer was trouble-free, Jody remembered, their easiest time together since Jessica turned teenager. "That was hard work out there in the heat," Jody said. "She had no time for trouble. I was like, 'Jess, do you want to quit?' And she was like, 'No, Mom. I'm going to do this . . . but I'm not doing it again!'"

School days remained a difficult time; Jessica saw to that. "If I didn't have troubles, I would create some," she once said to explain her learning style.

Jessica tried various sports—swimming, volleyball, rugby—but never found a physical outlet that fit her needs and talents exactly until she discovered firefighting. Even so, she pursued each new activity with commitment. And no matter what else was going on in her life, she ran three to five times a week and ate a proper diet. "She always had her daily square meals with five fruits and vegetables," remembered a friend, Anne Miller.

Despite her outgoing nature, Jessica kept a part of her self secret, as though she had a sore spot to protect. On one occasion, during her sophomore year in high school, her mother picked her up at a party and noticed for the first time that Jessica seemed "a little boozy." The next year Jessica was old enough for a driver's license. Jody repeatedly cautioned her daughter against drinking and driving, but without effect.

One night, Jessica came home late, parked her pickup, and staggered into the house so drunk that she walked into a wall and fell down. The noise awakened Jody. She decided the time had come to call the sheriff, who cooperated by giving Jessica the dressing down of her life. "You just be glad I didn't find you sitting in the front seat of your truck, young lady," the sheriff said gruffly. If he had, the sheriff said, it would have meant a drunken-driving charge and the possibility of jail time. Instead, he charged her with drinking as a minor, a lesser but still serious offense.

"She was infuriated," Jody said.

Jessica was sentenced to six months' probation and three hundred hours of community service, which included meetings with families of people killed by drunk drivers. After that experience, Jessica stubbornly continued her romance with Coors Light beer but left the Nissan pickup at home.

Worse trouble lay ahead. Jessica and Nathan had begun dating, and one night Jessica did not come home at all. Jody went to Nathan's apartment and confronted the couple. "Jess, you come with me," Jody said. "You're going to wind up as trailer trash if you keep on. And you," she lashed out at Nathan, "you keep your hands off my daughter!"

Shortly thereafter, Jessica moved in with Nate and told her mother there was nothing she could do about it. By that time, Jessica was a cadet with West Valley Fire District, which covers the sprawling suburban area west of Yakima. The program, available through West Valley High School, offered "job shadowing" of firefighters to students sixteen years old and older.

Jessica had applied on a lark. One day she and two friends, Anne Miller and Lisa Heinzen, were sweating over an upcoming English test, until they heard an unexpected message of salvation come over the school's public address system. A metallic voice announced that anyone interested in the fire cadet program should go immediately to the school commons to sign up.

"I looked at Jess, and she looked at me, and we knew we were in the clear," Anne recalled. The three girls trooped off to the commons room, leaving English exams for the misty future. All cadets, however, had to pass a drug test.

The three girls passed with flying colors and were accepted into the cadet program. They had to show up every Wednesday night at a firehouse for training and work details such as waxing fire apparatus and cleaning hose.

"When she first came in, she was quiet as a church mouse," said Dave Leitch, then deputy fire chief and later chief. "She was never in a big hurry to go home. She never had a bad attitude."

On one of those evenings, Jessica met Nate, a fellow cadet who was older than Jessica by several years. Like her, Nate had a wild side. But unlike her, he passionately wanted to become a professional firefighter, though wiser heads at the firehouse judged him far from ready for so much responsibility.

Nate and Jessica recognized their kindred spirits. "She got down and did the dirty work and enjoyed it," Nate said. "She was fun to be around." Nate introduced Jessica's friends, Lisa and Anne, to two of his friends, and the six of them became regulars on the West Valley party circuit.

"The moms didn't take it as well as we did," Lisa remarked dryly. The cadet program quickly turned into more than a lark, especially after the girls were allowed to take the wheel of a fire engine. A high point came when Jessica drove a West Valley engine up to the front of her house and hit the emergency lights and siren, with little Ashley watching in adoration.

When Jessica began cutting classes and missing swim practice to hang out at the firehouse, her coach, Dunham-Wheeler, sat her down for a talk. "Her true passion was firefighting," Dunham-Wheeler said. "Because she wasn't someone I wanted to lose from the swim team, I gave her the freedom to pursue firefighting. She made it all the way to districts with us that year."

A photo from those days shows Jessica, Lisa, and Anne posing together in bunker pants, red suspenders, and sleeveless T-shirts. Their arms and shoulders are tanned and buff. Their hair gleams in sunlight. Each has a toothy, mischievous grin—girls-next-door gone to the fire-house. They earned the nickname "Al's Angels" because of their knock-out looks and because a Yakima volunteer firefighter, Al Schoonhoven, took them under his protective wing; looking at the photo, though, one wonders who needed protection most, Al's Angels or any normal male caught in their orbit.

The summer Jessica turned eighteen, the minimum age to fight wildland fire, she got a job with the Washington Department of Natural Resources. "Mom, it's the most awesome job in the world; you hike around and get paid for it," she said, echoing many others. Jessica celebrated her nineteenth birthday on July 25 while battling a wildfire north of Lake Chelan in the foothills of the Cascade Mountains. At the end of the summer she came home bursting with stories. "She thought she was bulletproof," said her father, Rick.

Signs began to appear of a turnaround in her life. Jessica had never been the studious type, but she wanted to do something to help people live healthier lives. She and Jody discussed career alternatives, and Jessica considered becoming a nurse like Jody. She found the sight of blood "too yucky," though, and decided instead to major in food science and nutrition at Central Washington University. She was determined to do whatever it took to become a certified dietitian. For the first time, her report card had Bs and As.

As the new fire season approached, Jessica landed a job with the Forest Service on the Naches Ranger District fire crew. When Jody tried to caution her about the dangers, Jessica had a ready answer. Jessica was in the middle of reading *Fire on the Mountain*, a book about the 1994 South Canyon Fire and its heavy loss of life. The account includes a description of how firefighters—some who survived and some who did not—deployed fire shelters to protect themselves. "We'll never have to deploy shelters like that," Jessica assured Jody. "I'll never be in harm's way. Our supervisors are well trained; they would never do that to us.

"Safety first, Mom. That's what they tell us every day. Safety first!"

She also told Jody she had decided to end her firefighting days: she would answer the fire bell this season, but it would be her last. The news surprised Jody, and Jessica offered no explanation for it. Jody took it as another step by Jessica to bring control to a life that was running heavy crosscurrents.

The Saturday before the callout, Jessica and Nate went to a party together. The next morning Jessica showed up at her friend Lisa's house in an uncharacteristically subdued mood. Jessica was always the optimistic one, Lisa remembered, always confident that everything would work out well. When her Nissan pickup ran out of gas, as happened regularly, Lisa would say, "Damn, Jess, what are we going to do?" and Jessica would laugh and figure out a solution. But as they hung out around the pool on this Sunday, Jessica had a new seriousness about her.

Jessica finally confided to Lisa that she had broken up with Nate the night before. She still cared for Nate—in fact, had kissed him goodbye—but the relationship had become a burden. But she felt she was too young. She wanted to move on and try new things in life, not settle down and nest. And she couldn't party with Nate night after night and do the work expected of her as a firefighter. She had packed up her things, she said, and was on her way to the Forest Service barracks.

Jessica and Lisa were not the kind of girls who hugged, shrieked, and blew air kisses—ever. But as Jessica left, she kissed Lisa on the cheek.

"I love you," she said.

"I love you too," a startled Lisa responded.

Jessica telephoned her mother later with the news. She was going to "take a break" from Nate, she told Jody. Maybe they would get back together, maybe not. Meantime, she was on her own at the barracks. "Mom, I can't live like that any longer," she said.

"I'm so proud of you, Jessie," Jody said, her voice flushed with relief. "You did it!"

When the callout came for the Libby South Fire barely twenty-four hours later, Jessica put on her hard hat and went out the barracks door. She had cut her hair short for fire; a new friend, Karen FitzPatrick, had cut hers short, too.

Karen was an odd duck who sometimes appeared on the fireline looking as though she was out on a date. "There's this girl on the crew, and she shows up in lipstick and makeup, and the guys are razzing her," Jessica had told Jody. Earlier in the season the crew supervisor, Julius Sims, had noticed Karen standing and not working on the fireline. Karen had surprised him the first time they met with her strong handshake; she was a slim girl, but with strength like that she would do well as a firefighter, he had thought. So he observed unbelieving as Karen non-chalantly took out a makeup bag and began to apply fresh lipstick. "Karen," Sims said, as kindly as possible, "we don't do that here."

Karen, though, had proved herself physically stronger than most of the crew members, and that had drawn Jessica. One day during man-datory PT the crew decided to push the limits of physical endurance in a game they gave the melodramatic name "Cards of Death." A deck of playing cards was placed on the ground, and cards were turned face up, one after another. Depending on the value of the card, the whole crew did that number of sit-ups or push-ups (aces counted fifteen, face cards ten, and the other cards their numbers). This morning, the exercise was push-ups. Normally the game stopped at a predetermined point, but this time the crew pressed on. Person after person dropped out until only Karen and one or two others remained. The game finally ended after the survivors completed more than two hundred push-ups each. After that Karen was known on the crew as "Mighty Mouse," which she embraced as a replacement for the family nickname "BK" for Baby Karen.

Jessica and Karen found more common ground than just a love of exercise. As Jessica struggled to get her life in order, she began talking with Karen about matters of the spirit and found that Karen's take-no-prisoners Christian message hit a vein. "We're talking, and she's interested," Karen told Pastor Hagerman. The talks helped things fall into place for Jessica, and for her that place was the fireline.

CHAPTER FOUR

The mountains are calling and I must go.

—from a letter by John Muir, 1873

The news spread quickly among firefighters arriving at the Naches station that only half their twenty-person crew was going to the Libby South Fire. They would pick up the other half along the way, at the Leavenworth Ranger District station. Crews from different districts were often mixed together at a moment's notice; in this case, the Naches crew already had fought one fire this season, a small one, and work was being spread around to give others a chance. Julius Sims, the popular Naches fire crew boss, was one of those left behind. Telephone calls had failed to reach him, a missed connection that would later haunt his days. Instead, the Naches crew would be led by two supervisors they would not meet until they reached the Leavenworth ranger station.

They had a long drive to the fire, about two hundred miles. But there would be little traffic at this hour, about 1:00 AM. With a short crew there should be room to stretch out and doze in the crew rigs, if the excitement level ever died down. As they loaded up, FitzPatrick, Johnson, and Weaver made trim silhouettes against the bright halos cast by the lights in the parking area. Two other figures stood out in large, round outline: Jason Emhoff, who had inspired Weaver to join the Forest Service; and Rebecca Welch, a rookie who would shame veterans in the hours ahead with a selfless act of courage. Emhoff and Welch were each over two hundred pounds, but neither was tubby: Emhoff kept strong with outdoor work; Welch was an accomplished athlete who attended the University of Sioux Falls on a soccer and basketball scholarship.

Curiously, Welch had been inspired to apply for a fire job because her father, Alan, had a dream in which he saw her battling flames. Most people would have regarded that as a caution signal; Welch, to the contrary, sent out more than a dozen applications to fire agencies. "I told them basically, 'Pick me because I am physically fit,'" she said. She was a dream-come-true for federal fire managers, who are rated on how well they recruit minorities, women included.

Responses flooded in. "I had to turn off my phone," Welch said. A native of California, she chose Washington because she had never been to the state before and liked the idea of a cool climate for hot work. She wound up in the basic wildland firefighter course at West Valley High School, where Emhoff was one of her instructors.

The others on the half-crew were Beau Clark, Scott Scherzinger, Jodie Tate, and Marshall Wallace. Clark had been working as a clerk in an Ace Hardware store when his neighbor George Marcott, fire management officer for the Naches Ranger District, came in to shop and wound up offering him a job. Clark liked the outdoor work so much that he determined to make a career of the Forest Service. Scherzinger, another first-year firefighter, had gone home after a full day at the ranger station, watched a baseball game, and was asleep when the callout came. Tate was one of the most experienced crew members at Naches with six fire seasons under her belt; she lived at the barracks, as did Johnson, Emhoff, Welch, and Wallace, who had a season's previous experience on an engine crew. The firefighters boarded stretch pickups and drove an hour north to Ellensburg, where they were to meet Tom Craven, their squad boss.

Craven, in his thirteenth season with the Forest Service, was a former gridiron star everyone called "Big Papa" or "Crave." He was one of five brothers who had fought fire with the Forest Service, and was noted for his sunny disposition and his knack for making a fire crew feel like a family. "When we had new people, we put them with Craven—he had a gift for putting people at ease," said Mike Starkovich, a boyhood friend who had blocked for Craven in their high school football days and then, like Craven, had joined the Forest Service. "He was big and strong and safe," one female firefighter remembered.

Welch recalled: "Whenever you worked with Tom you had fun. He knew the difference between serious times and periods where joking around was appropriate. He could lead without being overbearing."

There was more than a smile and a strong back to Craven. Though he was one of the few blacks in the Forest Service in the Northwest, he was descended from a pioneer family of note. The Cravens had deep roots in the old coal-mining town of Roslyn, in the mountains west of Ellensburg. (Roslyn was the quaint setting for the fictional town of Cicely, Alaska, in the long-running television series *Northern Exposure*.) A Craven ancestor had been among a group of black coal miners recruited to break a strike there in 1888–89. Armed guards had to protect their arrival, but within a few years hard feelings subsided. Some of the blacks stayed on, joining Roslyn's ethnic checkerboard, which at one point included twenty-four groups—ranging from Greeks, Italians, and Czechs to American blacks—with each group represented by a separate area in the town cemetery. Most of the black families moved on as the mines shut down, and by 1970 the Craven family was the sole remaining link to the nineteenth-century migration. Craven's grandmother, Edith Craven, helped found the Black Pioneers, a group that honors those first black residents.

Craven's father, Will, a custodian for Roslyn's high school, won election in 1975 as the town's mayor, becoming the first black mayor in the state. He served five years and is remembered to this day as perhaps the best mayor the town ever had. Will had married his local sweetheart, Virginia, who happened to be white, and they had a daughter, Corrine, and five sons: Tom, Ted, Tim, Tony, and KC. At the time of the Thirty-mile Fire, four of the five sons were Forest Service firefighters; the fifth, Tim, had quit the agency the year before.

Craven was not merely an accepted member of the community; he was a local hero—first as an athlete but later as a hip-hop disc jockey and as a firefighter. His exploits as a high school running back for the Cle Elum-Roslyn Warriors are legendary: 3,761 yards rushing and sixty touchdowns, three kickoff return touchdowns in a single playoff game, five touchdowns during a homecoming game. Craven was known for flashing his trademark grin—joyous and open—on his many trips to the end zone. "Tom would always give credit to the linemen; he would share the glory," said his football coach, Mark Randleman.

"He was never without a smile or kind word for those who were down, or encouragement for those who needed it," recalled a classmate, Heather Mrowka. The school retired his jersey, No. 43.

Craven attended the College of the Redwoods in Eureka, California, where he set more rushing records, breaking an old one set by O. J. Simpson. There, he also met his future wife, Evelyn Yamson, a Filipina of soft beauty. After earning a two-year associate degree, Craven moved closer to home and attended Central Washington University in Ellensburg. He continued to rack up yards on the gridiron and, despite a mild learning disability, earned a degree in sociology, becoming the first member of his family to graduate from college. Craven was scouted by the Dallas Cowboys and went to training camp with the Seattle Seahawks, but an injured knee ended that career path. When he was offered a full-time job with the Forest Service, he eagerly accepted. His father, Will, counseled him to use his education to seek less dangerous employment. "I told him there is no future in firefighting," Will said. But Tom had found his home.

"No matter how miserable the situation, Tom would joke about it," recalled Tim Foss, a Forest Service fire veteran. "Once after supper on a fire in Hells Canyon we could see rain clouds rolling in. A few people were whining, but Tom piped up with a big smile, 'Hey, man, we're being paid to camp in the wilderness and watch this sunset. Who cares about rain?'" Another time the crew went to a tavern to celebrate after a fire. "I woke up the next morning to the sound of Tom throwing up on my sleeping bag," Foss recalled. "He grinned and said, 'Is this a great fire or what?' and went right back to sleep."

In his off hours Craven became a popular deejay on Central Washington University's radio station, KCWU. "He was a badass hip-hop deejay who wanted to help out a bunch of goofy college kids," said Matt Garman, KCWU program director. "He made our station better, not only through music, but through his attitude. The guy always had a smile on his face." Craven hosted a show called "Off 'da Hook," which played rap music from 6:00 to 9:00 PM every Friday. "My role models are my parents," Craven once remarked in a music magazine interview. "They taught me the difference between right and wrong, to be responsible, and that family comes first."

At the time of the fire, Craven and his wife, Evelyn, had a seven-year-old daughter, Tomisha, and a four-year-old son, T'shaun, both named for Tom. The night of the callout, he had dinner with his family and then settled on the couch to watch television. It was close to midnight when Evelyn headed for bed, leaving Tom to wait for the expected call; Tomisha and T'shaun were long asleep. "Every fire was the same with us," Evelyn said later. "I always said the same thing to Tom when he went out—this time I said, 'Honey, I'm going to bed. You come back to me safe.'"

"I'll be fine," Craven reassured her.

The call came in after midnight, and Craven met the rest of the Naches crew at a regular pickup spot, a nearby Ellensburg restaurant. Now numbering ten, they drove north from Ellensburg on U.S. Highway 97 across the flattish Kittitas Valley and into the Cascade Range, where the twisting road made it difficult for anyone to rest. Even so, after the first few miles the crew's nervous energy evaporated, and people slumped in their seats.

They pulled in at about 3:30 AM at the next rendezvous point about halfway to the fire, the town of Leavenworth, where they were to meet the rest of the crew and two supervisors. Leavenworth, which was called Icicle before a name change to honor a town elder, is ringed by snow-capped peaks, some over eight thousand feet tall. The town is built to resemble a Bavarian village, a desperate move by the business community during the 1960s to revive the town's fading economic fortunes—and a successful one. Tourists and the ski set flocked to the place. When the Naches crew pulled in at the Leavenworth ranger station, a line of sparkly gingerbread storefronts faced them from across the street.

The crew disembarked and walked around the parking lot to unlimber. A few of the other half of the crew already had arrived and were napping on their gear; the rest would trickle in over the next hour. In an echo of what had happened in Naches, where Sims could not be located, Cary Stock, who was supposed to replace Sims as crew boss, could not be found at home in Leavenworth. Stock had just moved to a new address, and his phone was off the hook following a domestic quarrel. "It's with me every day; I wonder what would have happened if I'd been there," Stock would say later, just as Sims would say.

Picking apart the buildup to catastrophe often discloses a chain of errors, of little or no importance on their own. When linked, however, the mistakes can become an unstoppable force, in the same way that a sliding pebble can start an avalanche. With the benefit of hindsight, it's easy to see many points at which the chain could have been broken. It happens every day in complex human endeavor; little mistakes are corrected or compensated for and come to nothing. But sometimes the chain of errors gains momentum to a point that the next mistakes seem "normal," and once that happens a dark tide of inevitability can descend, suffuse the event, and propel it toward a horrific conclusion. Even up to the final seconds, though, a slight adjustment, a shouted warning, a bit of luck, can often save the day. Afterward, knowledge of how easily trouble could have been avoided adds to the horror felt even by minor actors like Stock and Sims, who later tormented themselves with the idea that their presence alone would have saved the day. No one desires a bad ending—except criminals and the morally depraved. In a way, no one is to blame when so many things go wrong, though some mistakes are worse than others and worthy of punishment. An accident simply happens. An event that rises to the level of true catastrophe, by comparison, has deep roots and a long history, and sends shock waves far beyond the event. And on rare occasions, catastrophe reaches beyond itself, calls out the emotions of pity and fear, purges those emotions in a cathartic climax, and enters the realm of tragedy.

When efforts to reach Stock failed, a summons went out to the next name on the call list, Ellreese Daniels, a fire supervisor who was due for a few days' rest, having just returned from another assignment. Daniels, a cheerful soul, did not gripe about the quick turnaround. "Ellreese was one of the nicest guys you'd ever meet; he'd give you the shirt off his back," Stock later said of Daniels, a judgment shared by many. But Stock and others knew Daniels as a man with serious limitations as a supervisor.

Daniels had a reputation for being a lot of fun at a barbecue or while having a beer at a tavern after work. On the job, however, Daniels was under a cloud—a fire investigator would later describe it as "some kind of super-secret probation." There is no available record of Daniels being in major trouble. A Freedom of Information Act query to the Forest Service about disciplinary action against him brought the response "No such documents exist." The worst rap in state records is a couple of minor traffic tickets. Coworkers had complaints about him: sloughing off on work details; damaging a Forest Service vehicle in a minor accident; and according to one crew member, Matthew Rutman, "inappropriate" wrestling with female coworkers in a barracks. Most of those complaints were petty, but Daniels's behavior with women during work hours had become a serious enough matter for his immediate supervisor, Gabe Jasso, to discuss it with the top fire management officer for the forest, Elton Thomas, just weeks before the Thirtymile Fire. Thomas said later that he directed Jasso to take the matter up with human resources personnel and then never heard anything more about it.

Daniels had stuck it out with the Forest Service in the Northwest for more than two decades, no small accomplishment for a black man, and a plum for the agency. Even when a black family can be recruited to move to the Northwest backcountry, social isolation is inevitable and hostility possible. Daniels's wife, Andrea, had walked out on him two weeks after they married, on October 4, 1987. They lived apart after October 20 of that year, according to documents Daniels filed in Chelan County Court two years later, when he requested dissolution of the marriage. Andrea had simply disappeared. In the court documents, Daniels said that he had tried to find her through relatives and friends but did not know her "present whereabouts." The court granted his petition, and the marriage was dissolved.

Daniels, a native of Shreveport, Louisiana, was hired after he completed a Job Corps training program in forestry, and was subsequently sent to the Entiat Hotshots, in the early 1980s, to learn the fire trade. The hotshot supervisor at the time, Lonnie Williams, rated Daniels deficient, in part because he had difficulty with written examinations and had to be given his tests orally. But Daniels didn't quit, and he wasn't fired either. He was sent back to the Entiat Hotshots for a second try. A few years later he completed a tough, advanced fire-training course with the Redmond Hotshots, though complaints about his written skills dogged him there, too. The highlight of his career came during the massive 1988 Yellowstone Fires, when he served in the highly responsible post of division supervisor.

"Back in the 1980s, the Forest Service was fast-tracking women and blacks and pushing them into supervisory roles," said Cynthia Foster, who worked with Daniels in the Okanogan National Forest during those years. "Ellreese is a supernice guy, but he does not have a command personality. He's soft-spoken. He never wanted to lead. Ellreese is a follower. But they put on the pressure, and he couldn't find a way to say no."

Daniels was not the only special case on the crew. Daniels's No. 2, Pete Kampen, was a twenty-nine-year-old Leavenworth native, an aggressive and ambitious firefighter, who was being moved quickly up the career ladder. Supervisors later said Kampen was not on a formal "fast track." But Congress had appropriated money the year before to expand the wildland fire service, following an unusually destructive fire season in 2000, and Kampen's career, like that of many other midlevel firefighters, had been given a mild boost: he was about to become a crew boss after six instead of the usual seven years of wildland fire experience. On this assignment, he would function as crew boss trainee and would run the crew under Daniels's supervision for most of the coming day.

When Kampen's phone rang at 12:22 AM he kidded the caller, "You're late." By the time Kampen arrived at the Leavenworth ranger station at 2:30 AM, he could see the murky outlines of a couple of people sacked out on the grassy median strip in the parking lot. One of them was Thom Taylor, a squad boss, who got to his feet, reported in, and volunteered the information that he'd been in a tavern a few hours earlier. He'd be okay, Taylor assured Kampen, but he shouldn't drive. When Tom Craven checked in by radio at 3:30 AM from a few miles out, Kampen breathed a sigh of relief. Having a Craven on the crew, he knew from experience, was like "a kick in the pants." The Craven brothers got the job done and made it fun.

The combined crew, numbering twenty-one, was given the name Northwest Regulars No. 6, meaning it was the sixth crew put together in the Pacific Northwest region, which includes a broad range of fire agencies in Washington and Oregon, during this fire season. The

Northwest Regulars represented three, not just two, separate units. When the Okanogan and Wenatchee forests were merged, the Lake Wenatchee and Leavenworth district fire crews were combined and given a new name, Lake Leavenworth, though there is no such thing as a Lake Leavenworth. Crew members continued to call each other by their previous designations: "She's Lake Wenatchee," or "He's Leavenworth." When things went bad on the Thirtymile Fire, the Northwest Regulars would split along their previously established social fault lines, looking for security in a familiar face.

Once everyone had assembled, Kampen and Daniels divided them into three squads, each with its own squad boss. They tried to keep people who knew each other together and to spread the rookies around. "We were headed to a big incident; the new ones needed to stick with people they were the most comfortable working with," Kampen said later. There were eight rookies altogether, a high but not unheard of percentage, and five of those were from the Naches Ranger District: Clark, FitzPatrick, Weaver, Welch, and Scherzinger. National guidelines allow up to 60 percent of a Type II crew to be rookies, and the number of rookies on the Northwest Regulars was well within that limit.

Craven was boss of squad one, which was heavy with rookies from the Naches crew: Clark, FitzPatrick, Scherzinger, and Welch—and the veteran Emhoff.

Thom Taylor, from Lake Leavenworth, headed squad two, which had two Naches firefighters, Johnson and Weaver, and Armando Avila, Nick Dreis, Elaine Hurd, and Matthew Rutman from Lake Leavenworth.

Brian Schexnayder, who ranked as a squad boss trainee, headed squad three, with Tate and Wallace from Naches, and Dewane Anderson, Emily Hinson, and Donica Watson from Lake Leavenworth.

It was 4:00 AM by the time the Northwest Regulars were ready for the next leg of the trip, to the ranger station in Twisp, where they would be briefed on their assignment. They piled into two vans: a green government van instantly nicknamed the "Green Pickle," and a rented white van dubbed the "White Shadow," plus the two stretch pickups from Naches. They followed Route 2 from Leavenworth to the east, out of the mountains, to the Columbia River, making a brief stop at a Safeway along the way for deli sandwiches. They turned north at Entiat and from there followed the route the Entiat Hotshots had taken hours earlier, into the Okanogan side of the Okanogan-Wenatchee National Forest.

The sun was well up by the time they arrived at the ranger station at Twisp. A few people kicked around a hacky sack in the parking lot while Kampen and Daniels went inside to talk to the fire bosses, the forest FMO Thomas and the district FMO Pete Soderquist. Soderquist, whose day had begun at 6:00 AM the previous morning, had just returned to work after a half-hour catnap, the only sleep he would get until the coming afternoon, when a superior would order him home for a rest.

Soderquist had bad news. The Northwest Regulars were being diverted from the main action, the Libby South Fire, to a sideshow, the Thirtymile Fire. The smaller blaze was a mop-up job, well suited to a rookie-laden crew who had never before worked together as a unit. The job would take a couple of days at most, which meant no overtime. But the Northwest Regulars would be kept on, if possible, and eventually might make it to the Libby South Fire. "It was a big letdown; we were expecting a fourteen-day tour, not a fifteen-acre nothing," one crew member, Clark, said later.

As the supervisors talked inside, Craven's old high school football buddy Starkovich unexpectedly drove into the parking lot outside. He had been on his way to the Libby South Fire, where he was assigned as a division supervisor, when he had seen the fire vehicles and stopped to see if Craven was there. Craven was glad to see him but jealous of Starkovich's fire assignment.

"We're leaving the big fire and going to the little one," Craven remarked, downcast.

The Northwest Regulars set off from Twisp on the last leg of their journey at 7:51 AM, according to the dispatch log. Soderquist and Thomas led the way, to help with the handoff from the Entiat Hotshots. Everyone wore the same uniform: yellow fire shirt, green pants, heavy black boots, and a hard hat. But they were an odd lot of individuals, representative of firefighters today who no longer come from the ranks of the poor and unemployed, as in years past. Today, suburban athletes cut fireline alongside ranch boys; loggers' daughters work next to housewives; hunters and trappers next to "bunny kissers" and "granola bars" with graduate school on their minds. Teenage girls work side by side with men old enough to be their fathers, who can have more seasons of fire behind them than the kids have years of age.

They sign up for the adrenaline rush, for tuition money, for a break from spouses, and for the simple joy of being outdoors from the dawn of one day to the next; and some, as in the case of the Naches four, to fulfill the deepest longings. They share a hunger to step into harm's way, but with rules and always in company with others. They are team players; many were competitive athletes in school, and the ethic lingers on. They respond well to forceful, competent leadership. They take pride in being physically elite and are contemptuous of laggards in their ranks. They exhibit a striking tolerance, though, for trash talk, awful jokes, and throwing up at beer parties when off the clock, just as families accommodate quirks they would never tolerate in an outsider. They like being part of something bigger than themselves, from a fire crew to the woodland community to the natural world itself.

They respond with awe and wonder to the touch of fire, its quick heat and showy colors; its hypnotic dance of flame, smoke, and shimmering air; and its mighty roar, which everyone describes as an oncoming freight train—never a comfy passenger train—or as a jet airplane on takeoff. They love the smell of hot pine on a summer's day, the crunch of boots on a dry trail, the glint of light off running water when seen through forest cover. They wear fire shirts streaked with sweat and ash as though the marks were medals.

CHAPTER FIVE

*It is especially recommended that a law be passed, punishing,
by fine and imprisonment, all persons who leave any fire they
have made, for convenience or otherwise, unextinguished.
Nearly all extensive conflagrations of timber in the mountains
may be directly traced to negligence in extinguishing campfires.*

—Nathaniel P. Langford, first superintendent
of Yellowstone National Park, 1872

While the Thirtymile Fire cooked overnight, a gentle up-canyon breeze kept smoke from drifting down the canyon. The vacationers, Bruce and Paula Hagemeyer, awoke in the morning in their tent at Camp Four oblivious to what was happening a few miles up the road. Somehow, too, they missed the danger signal of a caravan of fire vehicles, which had to pass them by on the way to the fire. For the Hagemeyers, the day would bring one missed portent after another, which added up to one huge miscalculation: that the natural world they counted on for spiritual solace cared in turn for them.

Tired of their own cooking, the couple decided to drive the nearly twenty miles to Winthrop, a restored Old West town, for a restaurant breakfast. The Hagemeyers stowed their gear in Bruce's well-kept 1987 Dodge pickup, under an aluminum camper shell. They planned to linger in Winthrop to see the sights: false-front stores with wooden boardwalks, hitching rails, and the like. They would buy ice and then drive to the Thirtymile Campground at the head of the canyon, which they had scouted on their bikes the day before. The remote location would be a peaceful setting for the last night of their vacation.

Meanwhile, a new caravan of fire vehicles, carrying the Northwest Regulars and the others, drove into the canyon. The vehicles continued up the road until the lead pickup, with Soderquist and Thomas, the district and forest fire management officers, was halted by a burned snag across the road. "Have arrived on action number 103," Soderquist radioed the dispatcher at 9:04 AM.

As Thomas stepped out of the pickup, a spruce tree crashed into a stand of trees next to the road, sending up a shower of sparks. Thomas let out a yelp. "It scared the bejeebers out of me, and I yelled because I could see the crew buggies with the Entiat crew—not that it would ever have reached them, but I didn't know if somebody was working in there or not."

The Northwest Regulars unlimbered a chain saw and cleared the snag from the road. The commotion drew the attention of the Entiat Hotshot bosses, Brown and Cannon, who walked down the road and joined the new arrivals: Soderquist, Thomas, and the Northwest Regulars' supervisors, Daniels and Kampen. The combined overhead commenced what would be nearly two hours of talks, scouting, planning, and preparation. Brown and Cannon began with a report on the progress made overnight. The hotshots had hacked out an escape route, which they called a "rabbit trail," from the spot fires back across the river to the road and had marked it with pink flagging tape. They'd cut steps into the crossing log over the Chewuch River and extended the firelines. And at 6:26 AM, they had called the dispatch office to check the status of the personnel and equipment order made during the night; the dispatcher had noted in the log, "Double check on when he'll get equipment and crew ordered up to fire."

Cannon, using a global-positioning-system device, had spent an hour plotting the locations of the spot fires. He then had printed out a map for the incoming crew using a computer aboard one of the crew buggies. The map showed the locations of nine spot fires, the crew rigs, the fire's origin, and the crossing log. The result was far superior to the hand-drawn maps firefighters often rely on. But like many technical marvels, this one brought unforeseen consequences: the map was scaled to cover only the immediate area of the fire and thus failed to show the road's dead end to the north. The experienced local men knew this vital fact, but most of the Northwest Regulars did not learn about it until late afternoon—by which time human knowledge and all the computers in the world would be of no help.

As Brown gave his report, the fire appeared to be headed for oblivion. "The fire was flat doing nothing," Kampen said later. He and the others peered over Brown's shoulder at spot fires "no bigger than a hard hat." The fire, though, was a master of deception, a riddle wrapped in a mystery surrounded by smoke, to paraphrase Winston Churchill's famous Cold War remark about the Soviet Union. The fire already had proved impossible to contain overnight, when higher humidity, lower temperatures, and calm winds can help firefighters. Flame lengths may have been short, but they had felled big trees and extended into the upper branches of others, creating a fire of many layers and expanding possibilities. As if to underscore the point, a Douglas-fir tree near the road fell with a whoosh into a cluster of trees, which erupted in flame.

A hearty wind could transform any fire into an inferno on a day like this one, as Gary Bennett had warned at the Libby South Fire that morning. The same weather forecast Bennett had relied on for the Libby South Fire was passed along to the Northwest Regulars—nobody ever asked for a separate forecast for the Thirtymile Fire. "Dry weather pattern with hot afternoon temps and low relative humidity will stay put across the burn area through Tuesday," the all-purpose forecast warned, adding a warning note: "Expect gusty afternoon upslope-upvalley winds."

When Brown had finished his report, the supervisors broke into two groups for a "show me" tour. Cannon led Daniels and Kampen over the crossing log for a look at the spot fires. Soderquist and Thomas had started to follow, leaving Brown with the hotshots, when they ran into Dave Graves, a Forest Service law enforcement officer sent to investigate for arson. Graves was surprised to find himself there, he told the men, because he had driven the canyon road on patrol the previous afternoon and had seen no sign of fire. Whatever had started the fire, Graves said, must have happened late the previous day, after he had left. "He was amazed we had a fire because he was right there—he didn't see any vehicles, he didn't see any kind of smoke or anything," Thomas recalled.

Graves went to check out a suspicious fire ring the hotshots had discovered, and Thomas and Soderquist crossed the river to survey the fire. The scene on the far side of the river appeared almost benign. A few lazy tendrils of smoke rose into a clear sky; the air was dead calm. Thomas could see only one spot fire, a blotch of flame the size of a football. The whole fire appeared to have scorched no more than five or six acres. Thomas felt a bit cheated. He had thought the fire covered a good twenty-five acres. If he had known how small it was, he said later, he wouldn't have bothered to come along.

Thomas and Soderquist made a quick tour of the spot fires and then rejoined the other supervisors—Brown, Cannon, Daniels, and Kampen—on the road. With a river running through the fire, the first priority was to start putting water on it. "We were talking about how hot and dry we expected it to be that day," Soderquist said later. "Relative humidity was starting to drop fairly fast by ten o'clock that morning. And we thought it would be important if they got after it just as quickly as they possibly could with water." Daniels remarked that two water pumps might not be enough, and a third was ordered.

At this point, there was a major communications breakdown about the helicopter ordered overnight. "I was right there when Soderquist told Pete Kampen the helicopter was available and he had to call for it through dispatch," Thomas said later. But Kampen says he thought that the helicopter would show up at 10:00 AM, ready for work. "My understanding was that by talking to Soderquist I had ordered it," Kampen said later. "That's the difference; I thought it was an automatic."

Adding another voice to the confusion, Soderquist says that he addressed his remarks about the helicopter to Daniels, the incident commander, and not to Kampen, the crew boss trainee. But the main problem in fighting the fire, Soderquist said later, turned out not to be a tardy helicopter, which was also delayed over concerns about the Endangered Species Act; rather it was the performance of the water pumps, which had the potential to put many times more water on the fire than a small helicopter. "The Mark IIIs were the key to success," Soderquist said.

Even before the work of the day had started, errors and missed chances had begun to accumulate. The phone calls that had failed to reach crew bosses. A mounting burden of fatigue. The decision to send away water pumps in the night. The morning hours when no work was done on the fire. The mix-up over the helicopter. Taken singly, these were the kind of screw-ups that devil any complex operation. But they were also scattered particles in a kaleidoscope of tragic inevitability where actions at first appear to lack meaningful connections. As events turn, however, a pattern comes clear, as though it had been lurking in the background all along, just as a twist of a kaleidoscope turns random shards of colored glass into a coherent image.

In a tragedy, the sense of inevitable disaster builds until it overpowers the participants, who are swept along on a pathway to destruction. The audience watches with compassion and horror, aware of what's coming and as powerless as the actors to stop it. But real life is no stage play. In real life good things happen all the time. Ride out trouble, intervene and give events a nudge or a kick, take a step back, or run like hell, and everything can turn out fine. At midmorning in the Chewuch River canyon, the day held the promise of easy success. If there was a sense of overpowering inevitability, it came not from impending tragedy but from the simpler human impulses of hunger and fatigue. The assembled fire supervisors agreed that the weary hotshots would head down the canyon and "spike out" in a campground for a few hours of much-needed rest, and be prepared to return to the fireline in late afternoon. "The picture looked good—green grass, the water pump show coming," Cannon said later. "It was our impression we wouldn't have that much to do when we got back."

The picture got even better for the hotshots when they pulled their rigs into the Andrews Creek campground two miles below the fire. A Forest Service truck drove in behind them bearing much-needed fire lunches. The hotshots wolfed down the food and went, stupefied, to their tents.

THOMAS AND SODERQUIST were about to leave the scene when they again ran into Graves, who had just finished flagging the suspect campfire ring with yellow crime-scene tape. The ring wasn't much to look at—a couple of stones shoved together a couple of feet off the road. Several firefighters had walked right by it, not realizing what it was. But a closer examination told a story of careless ways and sad consequences.

Graves had discovered chunks of half-eaten hot dog and other trash near the ring. (A few light hearts on the fire crew started calling the incident the Hot Dog Fire.) He made the obvious deduction that some people, most likely motorists, had used the ring for a quick cookout. They hadn't sought out an established fire ring—there are many in the canyon—or tried to make their stay pleasant by walking the few yards to the riverbank. And they had committed the cardinal outdoor sin: they had abandoned a live campfire.

Nature pointed an accusing finger, a black scorch mark on the ground in the shape of an arrowhead, aimed straight at the fire ring. The fire had scorched the ground as it escaped the ring and widened out, driven by up-canyon breezes. Seldom do winds that fan a fire to life switch around abruptly enough to turn the flames back on themselves and obliterate those first telltale marks, which have provided clues for generations of arson investigators.

"This is where the fire started," Graves declared.

Outrage over the slovenly fire ring and its deadly consequences would fuel a hunt of many years for those who lit the fire and left behind an unintended calling card: traces of DNA on the hot dog.

Soderquist and Thomas said their good-byes to Graves and once again headed for their pickup. Along the way they noticed Kampen briefing the Northwest Regulars, but without a briefing card. "This is green, it's not going to burn," Kampen is remembered as saying. "This is basically a mop-up operation."

"Where's your briefing card?" Thomas asked, waving his own.

"Oh, I forgot," Kampen said and retrieved the card from his pack. He had covered every point on the card—weather, fire behavior, and so on. "I'm going for crew boss," Kampen said later, "and I've got the forest and district FMOs standing right there. I was just trying to do everything right." Being challenged on his briefing method in front of the crew, however, opened the door to criticism.

"Pete was being fast-tracked," Emhoff said later, "and I remember him making the comment, 'This is the last requirement I need and then

I'm signed off, I'm good to go.' It seemed like he didn't really want to do it; it was just another thing to check off."

Soderquist and Thomas wished the Northwest Regulars good luck. "Have a safe assignment and look out for each other," Soderquist said. Thomas added a caution about snags—two more trees had fallen across the road while they had been there. And then he put a hand on Craven's big, sloping shoulder, a gesture he would remember ever after. "Tom, have a good assignment," Thomas said, and with that he and Soderquist left for a planning session for the Libby South Fire.

Kampen and Daniels talked over how to divide their responsibilities: Kampen was in charge of tactics as crew boss trainee, while Daniels was to act as overseer, ready to step in if needed. The arrangements confused everyone, Kampen and Daniels and the dispatch office included. Several crew members to this day say they aren't sure who was functioning as incident commander. The official fire report has it both ways, sometimes referring to Kampen as crew boss trainee and sometimes as IC trainee. There was good reason to do so: in Kampen's statements he sometimes described himself as incident commander trainee. Today, the Forest Service position is that Kampen never filled the IC trainee role. It's clear from what happened, though, that Kampen aggressively exercised authority over the crew for the first part of the day, and may have overstepped. It's also clear, however, that Kampen was entirely out of the picture later in the day, and played no role whatsoever in the final crucial minutes.

They had a plan, appropriate for a muttering fire along a river in a time of drought. One squad of Northwest Regulars would run the water pumps and handle hose lines, couplings, and nozzles. The other two squads would use hand tools to catch the worst of the spot fires, and eventually they'd circle all the spot fires. The water would be used to control the spot fires while lines were being cut around them, and then squelch lingering flames. With the spot fires spread far apart, the work was going to be messy and take time. But they had the water pumps, and the helicopter, once it arrived, would catch spot fires beyond easy reach for hose lines.

Kampen made his squad assignments based on experience levels, a good idea that unfortunately backfired. He gave what looked like the least dangerous job—running the water pumps—to Schexnayder, who was the least experienced of the three squad bosses, but who'd been a pump instructor during fire training that spring. Everyone set off in high spirits, glad for action after hours of hanging out. Craven and his squad went directly across the river to deal with a fallen tree on the opposite bank that was sending up heavy smoke. Kampen lined up Schexnayder's and Taylor's squads, and as he started them marching up the road he looked at his watch: it read 10:22. "We spent a good deal of time sizing this thing up," Kampen said later, with understatement.

Kampen and the two squads turned off the road and crossed the river. Schexnayder's squad carried two Mark III water pumps, assorted hoses, nozzles, and couplings, and they set one of the pumps on the far bank of the river near the crossing log. Schexnayder put Tate, the veteran of six fire seasons, in charge of the water pumps, assisted by Wallace and Anderson, and kept a rookie, Hinson, with him to help handle the hoses. He posted Watson, the veteran of four seasons, in the vital position of lookout, high in the scree on the south canyon wall.

What followed would make slapstick comedy if the outcome were not so serious. The Mark III water pump is a simple, sturdy machine, but it can be balky when started and stopped, which is but one of the many things that went wrong in the next minutes. Kampen later said they couldn't get the first pump running, and so they swapped it out for the second pump, which started readily enough. But it kept conking out. According to Schexnayder, the kits for the pumps did not contain enough parts to support the pumps: pressure release valves, hose clamps to stop flowback, spark plugs, and so forth. Supply cache workers say this is somewhat unlikely. Pumps and kits are regularly inspected and must meet rigid standards.

Schexnayder and Hinson ran out hose lines only to discover that one had been rolled up backward. They had to walk out the hose and then reverse it before they could attach nozzles and couplings, which gave Schexnayder a look at the hoses. They appeared old, worn, and fuzzy, he said later, "like they'd been chewed by rats."

Water at last surged through the lines, and the show was on. A couple of spot fires died quick deaths. But water pressure caused three of the hoses to burst. Was frayed hose to blame? Were nozzles and couplings improperly closed, causing a pressure backup? A couple of things can be said for certain: hoses are carefully checked during fire season, and some fuzzing is normal with use.

Tate repeatedly called for help. "Jodie was having trouble with the one pump; she couldn't get it going," Schexnayder said later. "The draft hose wasn't tight, so she couldn't prime the pump, and then it flooded. I had to go back and help out three or four times at least." Then a Pulaski slashed through one hose, and flames burned through others. Effective water pressure could not be maintained, and Schexnayder gave up after one last try. "I didn't have time to mess around with the carburetor, or whatever it was," he said. He took the breakdown personally. When interviewed afterward by fire investigators, he sputtered: "The pump was picky—needed to leave someone there. Old hoses, several breaks, shitty pumps."

Later on, more blame and excuses further confused matters, and a reliable explanation of what caused the pump breakdown may be beyond reach. There is one point of universal agreement, however: the water operation, the helicopter included, could and should have reduced the fire to wet ash in a few hours, and it did not.

Taylor's and Craven's squads had an easier time, at the outset. Taylor's squad was to start operations at the end of the fireline cut by the hotshots, the "rabbit trail" that linked the road and the spot fires. As they formed a tool line, they peered down-canyon, where the spot fires burned. The air was still, the sun warming. The smoke, they noticed, had thickened considerably in just the last minutes.

A sawyer with a chain saw led the tool line, slashing down branches and small trees, and a swamper cleared the debris. Behind this pair came the first Pulaski, usually a big, strong firefighter, to break up the ground. The others followed with Pulaskis, McLeods, shovels, and other root ripping, ground-tearing tools shaped like medieval instruments of torture. The idea is to take a swipe and take a step, swipe and step, and not try to do the whole job yourself. Once a full squad has passed, a line has been cleared and cut down to mineral soil.

It was close to 11:00 AM by the time a chain saw came to life with a racking cough and the first tool hit the ground, and at exactly that moment the sun broke over the rim of the canyon. The fire perked right up. Flames rose, smoke churned. On a return visit to the canyon a few years later, Taylor was describing the sun's effect on the fire that morning when once again, as though on cue, the sun popped over the canyon rim. The time once again was a minute or two before 11:00 AM.

Taylor's squad had barely started cutting line when a nearby tree torched up. He and his squad beat a hasty retreat and started over a dozen yards back, picking up the hoses that by now had been run out along the trail: a large hose branched at a wye gate into two smaller hoses with nozzles, one for each squad. Taylor picked up his hose and nozzle and directed a stream of water into smoking brush.

Morale soared. "We're kicking butt!" Rutman, who was working as a swamper, chortled to his sawyer, Dreis. They slapped high fives. What this crew needed was a catchy nickname, they remarked, to celebrate their outstanding performance. Rutman, who considered himself something of a writer, wracked his brain for inspiration. When Rutman had joined the Forest Service in the spring, his mother, Patricia, who wrote poetry, had given him a blank pocket journal to encourage his literary aspirations. Within a few hours, Rutman would use the journal to write a story beyond his or his mother's wildest imaginings. But at the moment his mind was as blank as the pages of the journal, and he couldn't come up with a nickname.

Tall, thin, and thoughtful, Rutman was possessed of an independent spirit even by fireline standards. After graduation from the University of Oregon in Eugene, with a degree in environmental studies, he had taken a volunteer job in Costa Rica, intending to "make the world a better place." When the job ended, he found himself on the loose in Central America. He wandered into an Internet café one day and discovered he could apply online to become a firefighter. He had been around fires when he had worked one summer for the California Conservation Corps. Firefighters helped people, which he found appealing. The work was exciting. And it paid well. "Firefighting is the Gold Rush of my generation, the last frontier," Rutman said later. He sent an electronic application to the Forest Service, was accepted, and at the beginning of the 2001 season signed on with the Lake Leavenworth fire crew. The Thirtymile Fire was his first fire. As he had stepped forward to fight it, he had passed the lawman Graves, who was holding up a chewed hot dog.

"Want a bite?" Graves said.

Graves had picked the wrong man to kid around with; Rutman, a vegan, recoiled in disgust.

As the fireline progressed, someone shouted and held up a Pulaski handle with a missing head. This event was followed by a boom, and the hose line out to Taylor's squad went limp. Taylor alerted the pump handlers by radio to the burst hose. He told them he was going to shut down the wye gate and replace the blown section, and they should watch out for a pressure buildup. If they failed to activate a release valve, the water pump would back up and flood, which is one possible explanation for how the "picky" pumps broke down in the first place.

With the water flow stopped, heads went up and the crew sensed the smoking landscape shrink-wrap around them. "We never had an idea of the full dimension of the fire," Taylor said later. "It was one dimension at first—a flat map with circles. And once you started to fight the fire, it was two-dimensional. All you could see was the brush in front of you—vine maple six to ten feet tall—and puffs of smoke."

Flames bristled in a light wind, and sparks swarmed into the air. Grass wilted and became yellow flame. The ground was littered with "dead and down"—fallen trees, branches, and brambles piled on duff—all of which readily ignited. The flames cooked living vegetation and made it, too, ready for burning. Thickets of brush morphed from green to red and orange.

The Northwest Regulars' happy mood vanished. Cutting fireline had turned from a familiar, reassuring activity into a frustrating, hateful chore. The grass, duff, and dirt were knitted together by a spider's web of roots and had to be chopped out in blocks, like peat. Taylor thought it was the worst digging he'd ever encountered. Those with Pulaskis sliced the ground cover into squares, and those following pried them out. Pulaskis bounced as often as they sliced; after the handle broke on one, the heads flew off three others.

Meanwhile, Craven's squad had finished with the smoking tree they had crossed the river to extinguish and had started to cut a line along the bank on their side of the river, circling other spot fires along the way and heading for a hookup with Taylor's squad. The job wasn't going well.

"We changed strategy and tactics several times," Kampen said later.

"The initial strategy was that the two Toms would line the two most crucial spot fires, the ones we identified as the greatest threats, and use the hose lay to cool things down. The helicopter would show up and hit the spots. Fairly rapidly, the strategy began to fail. Fire activity picked up. We couldn't get a line around the spot fires before they spread."

Kampen noted that Taylor's squad had done a "monumental" job putting in line and weren't far from the river. He called Craven and told him to stop what he was doing and bring his squad over to the "rabbit trail" and start a line in the opposite direction from Taylor's squad, toward the far canyon wall. If they could establish a continuous line across the canyon bottom ahead of the fire, from the river to the far canyon wall, they still had a chance to stop flames from spreading up-canyon. Craven brought his squad over, passed through Taylor's squad, and started to extend the line toward the far canyon wall. The heat had become so intense, though, that Craven's squad had to back off and start over farther up-canyon, in a dense aspen grove. As the two squads worked, they were close enough to mix, and at one point Rutman wound up next to FitzPatrick. It may have saved his life.

Rutman was tossing branches aside with such gusto that he failed to notice when one caught the holder of his fire shelter and flipped it open. The shelter slipped out. Rutman didn't register the loss until a smiling FitzPatrick caught up to him holding out the lifesaver in her hand. This was the sort of thing FitzPatrick had signed up for, making a difference for others.

As progress slowed on the fireline, worries grew about a stand of spruce trees along the riverbank. The lowest branches swept the ground, making it easy for flames to catch and race upward, setting the crowns ablaze. The spruce trees were packed together, and even a light wind could send flames cascading from one to another in a classic crown fire. The flames then would draw in fresh oxygen and sweep ahead on a wind of their own making, and the fire would be lost.

Disturbing, too, were weather updates from Watson, the lookout. She was taking humidity and temperature readings every half hour from her post in the scree. By noon, the humidity was 10 percent and the temperature eighty-nine degrees. With the sun beating down, the humidity was certain to slip into single digits and the temperature to rise into the nineties—unmistakable signs of extreme fire danger.

Even so, the situation at noontime was not desperate. True, the promised helicopter had not shown up. The water pumps were failing. The ground pounders were in slow march, and the fire was cooking up. But with a little luck and a lot of energy, the firefighters could turn the tide. Kampen, the soul of energy, repeatedly called Schexnayder by radio and asked, "What's up with the water?" He went from squad to squad, offered encouragement, and sometimes grabbed a tool himself.

He also repeatedly tried to reach the dispatcher in Okanogan to ask the whereabouts of the promised helicopter. He got through scratchily once in a while. He made the first request shortly after looking at his watch at 10:22, he said later, and was told, "Status unknown." The dispatch log does not record the exchange; according to Kampen, the dispatch office showed little interest initially in running down the helicopter. Most of his transmissions, he said, were blocked by the steep canyon walls. The problem was partly solved by having Daniels, who had better radio contact—he could walk out to the road while Kampen stayed with the crew—act as relay. That system, though, created an automatic delay in passing messages. And it resulted in a muddy log record because Kampen occasionally got through and those messages are attributed to the IC, or Daniels; it took weeks before the dispatch center realized the designation "IC" in the log referred to both Kampen and Daniels. But perhaps worst of all, Daniels became focused on the radio link to the exclusion of other duties, which had serious consequences later in the day.

The first request for the helicopter was not logged until 12:08 PM: "Daniels: Launch 13N to this action w/bucket."

Helicopter 13N, or One Three November in radio jargon, had been on standby beginning at 9:00 AM at Pangborn Field in Wenatchee, aircraft records show. The ship had to undergo preflight checks and did not depart the airport until 9:53 AM. The pilot, Paul Walters, landed the helicopter at 10:30 AM at the airstrip at the North Cascades Smoke-jumper Base, five miles south of Winthrop and a short hop to the Thirtymile Fire.

Walters thought he was supposed to be over the fire at 11:00 AM, an hour later than Kampen was expecting, and he was on time to meet that deadline. If this hourlong delay were the only one, it might not have made much difference. But instead of heading straight to the fire, helicopter 13N sat on the tarmac at the smoke jumper base, awaiting a dispatch.

The helicopter was still there at 11:52 AM when dispatcher Ed Hutton alerted Daniels that it was available "if needed," according to the log. It was there when the Daniels-Kampen relay team requested it, in the message logged at 12:08 PM. And it had not moved by 12:30 PM, when a second call was made from the fire to ask about the continuing holdup.

Why the long wait? Why not simply dispatch the helicopter as soon as it was ready to go? Hutton, the dispatcher who handled most of the radio traffic on the fire, said later that when he had arrived at work at 8:00 AM, the night dispatcher, Tina Stoddard, had emphasized the hotshots' request for water pumps, not the one for the helicopter. "There was no specific time it was ordered for," Hutton said.

Only minutes from the fire, helicopter 13N sat idle for hours.

CHAPTER SIX

From the forest and wilderness come the barks and tonics
which brace mankind.

—Henry David Thoreau, 1851

B ruce and Paula Hagemeyer left Winthrop about noon refreshed by their brush with urbanity and headed for the Thirtymile Campground, where they intended to spend the last night of their minivacation. They drove up the Chewuch River canyon, past the dozing Entiat Hotshots, and on until they came to a cluster of Forest Service vehicles parked along the roadway. Bruce slowed the Dodge pickup.

Antic flames did a jig in tree branches fifty yards off the road. Coils of dark smoke rose in the middle distance. There wasn't a soul in sight. Perhaps the Forest Service was deliberately burning to clear brush, the Hagemeyers thought. No one flagged them down to offer an explanation or warning. Nothing blocked their way; Soderquist had ordered road barriers put up before he left the fire at midmorning, but at this hour the road was still open.

"That was the green light," Bruce said later. "Whatever was happening, the Forest Service was taking care of it."

The Hagemeyers drove past the visible flames to the Thirtymile Campground, about three miles farther on. After crossing a bridge over the Chewuch River, they took an immediate left at a fork in the road, following a sign for the campground. The road made a teardrop loop, through the campground, to the trailhead, and then back to the bridge. The Hagemeyers pulled into an established campsite in sight of the river and shut off the Dodge's engine, which ticked off-rhythm as it cooled. Forest sounds became audible. The erratic pulse of the river. The brush of wind on leaves, needles, and branches. The buzz of fly-ing insects—there seemed to be an awful lot of bugs, far more than at their previous campsite. But the seclusion put the Hagemeyers at ease.

"I was finally at peace after three days," Paula said later. "I had recon-nected. I could go back and see patients."

Not wanting to break the mood, Paula found a rock in the river to perch on and dipped her feet into startlingly cold water. The flies wouldn't leave her alone, though, and after a minute she went back to the pickup, where she settled inside the protection of the camper to read.

Bruce made lunch for himself; Paula, petite and high-strung, some-times skipped meals altogether. The flies bothered Bruce, too, but two people in a camper make a crowd, so he set up a backpacker tent and crawled inside, wearing shorts and a T-shirt for the heat. He opened a book on Buddhist meditation, one of several he had brought along. Bruce had taken the formal vows of a Zen Buddhist and made a daily practice of "mindfulness," a clearing of the mind in order to concentrate on being "fully present in the moment." The food and quiet, though, were making him drowsy.

The Hagemeyers were California dropouts advancing into middle age—Bruce was fifty-three, Paula fifty-one. Like many California dream-ers, they had abandoned the Golden State for the presumed paradise of Montana, in search of less stress and a closer spiritual tie to nature. They moved to Bozeman, but like other seekers before them, they dis-covered that the stupendous beauty of Montana comes at the price of isolation, long winters, and a spotty economy. The Hagemeyers even-tually moved to Thorp, Washington, a few miles west of Ellensburg, where they could live near mountains and both be fully employed.

As they settled in at the Thirtymile campsite, Bruce and Paula were unaware of being caught up in a twisted parody of their dream of an intimate bond with the natural world. Isolated inside the tent and camper, they missed nature's clarion warning signals: below them in the canyon arose a plume of smoke, stained scarlet and orange by flames and reflections of flames, driving swarms of insects up the canyon to escape the flames. The Hagemeyers were about to feel nature's touch— the furious embrace of wildfire—turning their dream relationship with nature into waking nightmare.

AS NOONTIME CAME and went and the day grew hotter and drier, Kampen realized the fire was getting away from him. "It would be the first fire I ever lost," he said later, as though he had bossed many a fire. Kampen's hopes for the helicopter were fading. With an empty sky and failing water pumps, he couldn't count on water to solve his problems. "Craven was calling and saying that they needed the water now; trees were candling, numerous new spots," he recounted later. "Taylor notified me that he had spots across the line. At this time I had the feeling we needed at least two more crews and wanted to get the 'shot crew up to help."

Kampen's request for more resources went through the Kampen-Daniels relay at 12:30 PM, in the same exchange in which the helicopter's status was requested for the second time. "Need to chat on ETA [estimated time of arrival] 13N—Also need 1 or 2 more crews," the dispatch log notes.

Kampen got none of the resources he asked for, and again no explanation is logged for the helicopter delay. The dispatcher said that no extra crews would be available until nightfall, at the earliest, but promised to wake the Entiat Hotshots early and send them back to the incident. The dispatcher also offered a substitute for the helicopter, a single-engine air tanker, or SEAT, a small tanker with a payload perhaps a mere third that of a big tanker. Using any kind of aircraft, though, raised another environmental issue. Federal regulations require aircraft to drop water rather than the more effective retardant when operating near waterways because retardant, made up mostly of fertilizer, contains chemicals that are potentially damaging to aquatic life. In addition, drops must be made at least three hundred feet from a waterway, a severe limitation when a fire is burning on the banks of a river in a narrow canyon, as was the case here. Kampen decided that a SEAT wouldn't do much good, a judgment that time would confirm. He thought, too, that putting a

SEAT and a helicopter together without an air supervisor was asking for trouble.

"No need for SEAT at this time" was the message from the fire logged at 12:46 PM, though that was not to be the final word on the matter.

"We were kind of hung out," Kampen remarked with hindsight years later. "I've since heard in classes that if you're standing there playing the 'if' game—we can hook this IF the hotshots show up, IF the helicopter shows up—then you're already too late. That's exactly where we were. We were fighting a losing battle."

Before long, though, an air armada including the SEAT would converge over the canyon. An air attack supervisor, by chance Daniels's regular boss, Gabe Jasso, would arrive in a piloted light observer plane and act as an "eye in the sky" while managing aircraft operations. Jasso would order up not only the SEAT but also two heavy air tankers and a lead plane, while a third tanker waited on standby. The air fleet would do little to dampen the fire, though; and in a near-disastrous finale, two Air Force jet fighters on a training mission, and perhaps drawn by the smoke, would zip unexpectedly over the canyon and nearly collide with one of the fire planes.

Jasso was an incident commander's dream, a man with long experience fighting fire from the ground as well as from the air. The role of "air attack" is vital, providing not only an overview of a fire but also a communications link for the dispatcher, pilots, and ground crews; in addition, a veteran like Jasso can help with tactical decisions. Jasso was on familiar terms with two of the fire's supervisors: he was Brown's immediate predecessor as superintendent of the Entiat Hotshots as well as Daniels's current boss. Jasso in fact had served two tours as Entiat superintendent, the first from 1992 to 1993 and the second from 1995 until 1998, when he turned the job over to Brown. At the time of the Thirtymile Fire, Jasso was serving as assistant fire management officer, or AFMO, for the Lake Wenatchee Ranger District, the position that made him Daniels's supervisor. In that role, he was acting as a kind of mentor for Daniels, helping him sort out personal behavior problems, such as the complaint Jasso had made about Daniels's excessive familiarity with women on the job. Jasso's ties to Daniels and Brown could have contributed to smooth teamwork on the fire. Instead, it was another boomerang. Daniels became so dependent on his radio link to Jasso that at times he ignored his crew and the Hagemeyers. His 12:46 PM message turning down the SEAT, for example, was his last direct communication with the dispatch office for many hours; subsequent messages were passed through Jasso. Using air attack as a communications relay can be a good thing, but in this case major developments on the fire went altogether unreported, by Daniels, Jasso, or anyone else. And once things turned bad, Daniels and Jasso talked almost constantly, which diverted Daniels's attention from his crew during the crucial buildup to the fire's climax.

Jasso had begun his day with air attack on the Libby South Fire. Heavy smoke made air operations there impractical, and Jasso and his pilot were reassigned to the Thirtymile Fire. Jasso called the dispatcher at 12:42 PM, four minutes before Daniels turned down the SEAT, and reported that he was on the way to the Thirtymile Fire.

En route, Jasso listened to radio chatter about the SEAT, and upon arrival over the fire, shortly after 1:00 PM, he asked the dispatcher if the SEAT was still available. "Dispatch responded that the SEAT would be available with water only!!!!" an exasperated Jasso remarked in a later, written statement.

Minutes after that, at 1:12 PM, the dispatcher at last responded to Daniels's request for helicopter 13N. "Can not use heli until we get permission," the log reads, acknowledging a second delay, this one apparently caused by confusion over requirements of the Endangered Species Act, which caused a political controversy at the national level after the fire. That problem began around 12:30 PM when the dispatch coordinator, Sally Estes, started a lengthy process to get the helicopter launched. Recognizing that this would take time, Estes offered the SEAT, which could be dispatched immediately.

She then turned to the problem of finding a district fire official to identify a dip and operations site for the helicopter. She reached Barry George, Soderquist's AFMO. George later acknowledged that it was he who questioned the environmental propriety of dipping water from the Chewuch River, habitat for a remarkable variety of endangered species of fish: Chinook salmon, steelhead, bull trout, and red band trout. George said he asked the dispatch office to get confirmation from the "fish folks" that it was okay to dip water from the river. George's question, he acknowledged, "delayed the estimated time of arrival of 13N to the fire." Indeed it did, though the earlier delay, when the helicopter sat idle during the quiet morning hours, when the fire was most vulnerable, was probably the crucial one.

Estes also contacted the forest's FMO, Thomas, but not until nearly 2:00 PM. "There was a lag," Estes acknowledged later. It was a busy day; it took time to make contacts and get answers back; personnel were scattered. Thomas, when reached by telephone, was sitting across a table from Soderquist at the Libby South Fire camp, so Soderquist made the decision about launching the helicopter. "My first reaction was to go ahead and get started," Soderquist said later. He had plenty of people at the table to advise him: John Rohrer, the district wildlife biologist, and John Newcom, the Methow Valley district ranger, were both there. But the 1973 Endangered Species Act is the third rail of environmental politics, a hot item for anyone who touches it. While the act specifically allows federal agencies to respond immediately to wildfire, they are advised to make contingency plans beforehand, in the off-season, in consultation with the U.S. Fish and Wildlife Service.

Soderquist said later that forest personnel had an internal agreement "to go ahead with bucket work and then involve our fish biologists later." But lower-ranking personnel were either unaware of the policy or unwilling to stick their necks out. Even Soderquist took a second to buy insurance before giving the go-ahead. He asked someone to contact the district *fish* biologist, Jennifer Molesworth, "for diplomacy purposes," though the district *wildlife* biologist was an arm's length away. Molesworth, a quick check showed, was out of reach, and at that point Soderquist gave a thumbs-up to launch the ship.

The dispatcher radioed the happy news to the Thirtymile Fire at exactly 2:00 PM, but the helicopter had one more stop to make first. It flew to an operations site set up at the Eightmile Ranch, a Forest Service facility a little more than fifteen miles south of the fire, to put on a water bucket. The helicopter did not take off from there for the fire until 2:38 PM, according to log records. The first water drop, then, was made about ten minutes later, just before 3:00 PM, or about five hours later than expected, at least by Kampen. By then the Thirtymile Fire was no longer a handful of scattered spot fires exactly suited for a helicopter with a smallish one hundred thirty-five-gallon water bucket. By that time the fire was on its way to becoming a "major rager"; even a workhorse helicopter carrying 2,500 gallons of water can't do much with a fire that size. "It's like spitting on a stove," one veteran remarked later.

Soderquist, meanwhile, grabbed a sack lunch at the Libby South Fire camp. When Newcom, the district ranger, got a good look at Soderquist's exhausted face, sagged over a crumpled paper bag, he ordered him to go home and rest. On his way home, Soderquist stopped by the ranger station at Twisp and told his AFMO, George, to drive up to the Thirtymile Fire and see if anything more needed to be done. "I did not realize at that time that things were starting to build," Soderquist mournfully said later. He arrived home and showered, and when he sat down for a chat with his teenage son, he nodded off in seconds.

HELICOPTER 13N APPEARED over the fire just as Jasso, the air attack supervisor, was preparing to leave to refuel. The fire was growing, but Jasso had no choice: the fuel gauge was headed to E. He had spent the last hour and a half directing a vigorous but ineffectual air show. When he had been told the SEAT was available "with water only," he figured something was better than nothing. He ordered the plane at 1:15 PM.

Ron Smith, the SEAT pilot, took off from Omak Airport north of Okanogan in timely fashion at 1:28 PM. By the time Smith reached the fire, it had become an alarming sight. He noted the fire's advance a quarter of the way up the south wall of the canyon. With steep terrain driving the fire, it would be difficult if not impossible to catch. But perhaps it could be slowed, giving firefighters on the ground a better chance to stop it.

Jasso and Smith established radio contact and talked over potential targets. Through breaks in the smoke Jasso could see a rash of spot fires in the canyon bottom ahead of the main body of flame. He asked Smith if he could hit them. The light wind was pushing a column of smoke over the head of the fire, obscuring the view. "There was no way to get under the column," Smith said later. He flew the SEAT in a figure-eight pattern above the fire, scouting for a better target. They decided at last to make a water drop on the fire on the canyon's south wall. The SEAT let loose with several hundred gallons of water, to no discernible effect.

Smith said he would fly back to his base for a refill, return, and try again. When Smith touched down at the Omak Airport at 2:36 PM, however, he was reassigned to a new fire elsewhere and never returned to the Thirtymile Fire.

Two minutes later, at 2:38 PM, the dispatcher gave Jasso the welcome news that helicopter 13N had left the operations site at the Eightmile Ranch and would be over the fire in minutes. At almost the same time, an order was placed for more help, but in another perverse twist this order would become the catalyst for disaster. The importance of the order was well understood afterward, though to this day no one, not even those involved, is certain who made it.

"Sometime I remember calling dispatch or dispatch asking if we wanted any engine support and dispatch said they did," Jasso later recounted, providing a confused account of a confused situation. The log, however, records a 2:27 PM request directly attributed to Jasso: "get couple engines." The idea of sending more engines to the fire may have developed during the discussion between Jasso and the dispatch office and had no single sponsor. No matter how the idea started, the dispatcher followed up and ordered two engines, Nos. 701 and 704, to start for the fire. As it turned out, the most significant issue was not who had the idea for engines or who made the order, but rather the lack of communication and supervision once the engines arrived.

According to the log, Jasso also asked the dispatcher to send a lead plane and heavy air tankers, which were quickly found. The dispatcher reported two minutes later, at 2:40 PM, that a lead plane was on its way to the fire and the first heavy tanker to become available would follow.

When helicopter 13N at last showed up, the pilot, Paul Walters, took a hard look at flames he had been ready to fight since midmorning. Trees torched in every quarter. The fire extended from one side of the canyon nearly to the other. Heaps of dead trees and brush lay in the fire's path. The sight was daunting, but Walters dipped his water bucket into the river and set to work.

"He dropped one or two buckets and said he wasn't doing any good," recounted Jasso, who remained over the fire long enough to observe the first drops. As Jasso prepared to depart for refueling, he offered a piece of advice to the pilot of the approaching lead plane, Greg House. The advice, like the order for engines, had unintended consequences, becoming a strategy that would drive events toward catastrophe. Jasso told House to direct the heavy tankers, when they arrived, to drop water to keep flames from crossing the road. And with that Jasso left—at 2:54 PM by the dispatch log—to refuel at the North Cascades Smokejumper Base.

Jasso's "suggestion," as he later called it, to keep the fire from crossing the road was meant to give shape to the air attack. But with Jasso gone for the next hour, the "suggestion" took on a life of its own. No one debated the pros and cons; no one challenged the idea. By the time the two engines, Nos. 701 and 704, showed up about a half hour later, the "suggestion" had become the guiding strategy for fighting the fire.

It was midafternoon, the time of quick change on a fire. The Northwest Regulars chopped away in the thick vegetation, but with flagging energy. When a spruce tree exploded in front of Taylor's squad, cutting off the lead saw team of Rutman and Dreis, Taylor had had enough. He yelled for the saw team to head for the river, where they would be safe. Then he radioed Kampen and said he wanted to pull the entire squad out.

"There was no water at this time," Taylor said later. "I did not know where the spot fires were. And I knew that minute by minute the fire activity was increasing."

"Keep going," Kampen told him, "and I'll come over."

As Kampen trotted down the fireline, flames erecting over the exploding spruce near Taylor's squad formed a gloriole of blazing color that framed the tree. The flames soon left the tree a smoking skeleton.

"This is not a go; this is not going to happen," Taylor told Kampen.

"We need to hook this thing," Kampen replied. He thought: I bet Thom and I can bust this out. The hose is coming around. The hotshots are on their way back. We can tie the line in and make it to the river.

But several years later, standing in the same place on a return visit for this account, Kampen had a different perspective. "I thought we could make a line that would hold," he remarked, "but I look at it now and see that no, we couldn't hold it."

At the time, he told Taylor: "You take the saw, and I'll run your squad. I'll swamp for you, and we'll hook it."

Taylor thought: You know, Pete's right. There's time for one last try.

Taylor grabbed a chain saw and began to slash right and left. He had felled two trees in quick succession when his saw ran out of gas and died. As Taylor knelt to fill the tank, he glanced back over his shoulder—and freaked out. Kampen, who should have been right behind him, was nowhere in sight. The squad had scattered like lost children. Taylor had started the day using Avila as a squad boss trainee, or No. 2, but Avila had not been aggressive enough in taking charge. Taylor had talked it over with Kampen, and they had agreed to relieve Avila, who accepted the move without protest. As a consequence, Taylor was left without a No. 2. The squad had begun to split up even before Kampen joined them: Taylor had directed two firefighters, who appeared exhausted, to sit down and take a break. But Taylor had expected Kampen to be the anchor and know where everyone was.

Taylor had to make a quick decision. He could round up the squad, or he could extend the fireline to the safety of the river. Presented with the choice, he tried to do both. First, he gassed up the chain saw and cut a hasty line to the river. Then he turned back to gather his squad and get a look at the fire along the way. As he walked back along the fireline, embers the size of match heads snapped to life on every side, expanded into necklaces of golden flame, and torched low tree branches, which in turn sent ribbons of fire slithering upward into the crowns of trees. The forest seethed and rocked with flame. Taylor counted thirty new spots of fire within a hundred yards.

Above the fire's growing din, Taylor heard the metallic whop of helicopter rotor blades and watched as 13N dropped a load of water on a torching tree. The fire had become a hydra: as the chopper drenched one tree, two or three others candled up nearby.

"The fire was a lost cause," Taylor said later.

Kampen, it turned out, had walked away from Taylor's squad in order to meet the hotshots, who were coming back to the fire after being rousted from their resting place earlier than planned, though even here there was a delay. The designated messenger had begged off waking the hotshots, and Kampen had been obliged to send a Northwest Regular to do the job.

"We were nearly tied to the river," Kampen said during the return visit to the site. "Things were going good. I grabbed Avila and said, 'You take over swamping for me.' I didn't make contact with Thom, though, and I should have."

As Kampen returned to the road, he came upon an improbable situation. A vacationer was driving a huge pickup truck, towing a trailer, up the road, which still had no barricades. The truck and trailer blocked the way for the hotshots.

The vacationer leaned his head out the cab window. "Can we still camp out up here?" he called out to Kampen.

According to his later statement to fire investigators, Kampen told the driver it was "not wise" to continue up the canyon, though at the time his language was more vivid. "I'm standing there getting my butt kicked across the river," Kampen said years later. "I'm not given to cursing, but I may have made a strong statement."

Whatever was said, the message got across. As the vacationer struggled to turn the pickup and trailer around, the hotshots managed to squeak their vehicles past. Brown had been awakened at 1:30 PM, after less than an hour's rest, with the request to return early to the fire. Worried about the exhaustion level of his crew, Brown had held off waking the hotshots for a while. Once rousted, the hotshots climbed into their rigs, eventually worked around the pickup and trailer, and parked in a wide turnout, which would become the gathering place for the entire fire crew and be called the Lunch Spot. Brown and Cannon got out, crossed the river, and confronted a different fire than the one they had left a few hours earlier. The far bank was littered with burned-over hoses and Mark III water pumps. The main fire burned smartly up the far south wall of the canyon.

And there was no lookout. Kampen and Daniels had decided to withdraw Watson from her lookout post in the scree shortly before 3:00 PM and rely on Jasso to act as lookout from the air. This would not be the first time an "eye in the sky" was substituted for a ground lookout, but it violated safety regulations and, worse, Jasso was preparing to leave to refuel at that time. Watson had left her post by 3:00 PM, six minutes after Jasso reported his departure. This meant that at midafternoon, as the fire transformed into a different creature, the crew had no lookout anywhere, not on the ground and not in the air.

Watson, though, had observed major changes in the fire's activity before she had to pull back. "The first blowup occurred at two to two-thirty," she told fire investigators later. "It started to burn toward the timber and steeper slopes, to torch trees, and got really hot. I could feel the heat from where I was sitting in the rocks." She hadn't felt personally threatened, she said, but when told to retreat she did not linger.

She came down from the scree, joined Craven's squad on the fireline, and made a 3:00 PM weather check from there. The wind was a light three to four miles an hour, she noted, gusting to ten to twelve miles an hour. Though the gusts were significant, the heavy afternoon wind warned about in the weather briefing that morning had so far failed to materialize. The humidity was a chalk-dry 7 to 8 percent, Watson noted. The mercury stood at ninety-seven degrees, but she was close to flames and that likely raised the reading.

The fire's buildup was apparent even to lookouts on faraway mountaintops. "Everything seemed pretty quiet until about 2:30 PM," said Bill Austin, the lookout on Goat Peak, about eighteen miles southeast of the fire. Mort Banasky, Austin's counterpart on First Butte, a dozen miles south of the fire, had an eye on the smoke—and her weather gauges. She could not remember humidity readings this low. Banasky said the smoke column was getting larger at this point. "It never really backed down much at any time, except for a few times when they were putting some retardant or water on it. They kept asking for retardant. Dispatch seemed to have trouble getting more air tankers."

The firefighters worked in a fug of smoke and heat. Eyes watered; noses ran; throats grew raw and parched. "For a lot of people, this was their first real fire, and the heat was getting to them," recounted Emhoff. "People hadn't figured out how to hydrate themselves, and they were sucking down a lot of water. Things were getting pretty heavy."

Someone managed to get one of the water pumps running again, but it was too late. Emhoff picked up a hose and aimed the nozzle at a torching pine tree about ninety feet tall. "I had this little stream of water going twenty feet in the air," he said later. "It was ridiculous."

Everyone realized it was time to quit the fire. For Taylor, the moment arrived when he saw the rash of spot fires on his walk back along the fireline. He radioed Kampen and, leaving no room for argument this time, said he was pulling back. For Craven, it came when trees torched and spot fires ignited *behind* his squad. "Let's get out of here," he shouted, and his squad broke for the river.

Kampen, after meeting up with the hotshots, went back over the crossing log, ready to go another round with the fire. The water pump was working again, though lamely; the hotshots were back; the two squads had put in a lot of good fireline.

"I was standing there, and another tree torched up in front of me," Kampen said later. "There were embers across the scratch trail. I turned around, looking up the canyon, and suddenly I saw fires breaking out all over—*behind the squads.* The fire was getting huge fast—it was just rippin' up the far side of the canyon. It hit home that we got spot fires we can't pick up, the fire's going up the hill, everybody's beat up—and people still want to camp up the canyon!

"I said, 'I'm done.' I called all the people back to the water pump, and Ellreese came on the radio and said bring all the crew back to the road."

As Kampen withdrew, he met Brown and Cannon on the far bank of the river and made them a surprising offer.

"This is too much for us," Kampen told Brown, tempering his aggressive nature for the moment. "It's a lot bigger than we can do anything with. Do you want to take this over?"

Brown would look back in sorrow on this moment; his years of experience could have saved the day. But the Northwest Regulars were walking—and trotting—away from the fire. Helicopter 13N was the only unit left in the fight.

"No, I don't want it," Brown told Kampen. "Call the district and see what they want to do with it." Veterans say fighting a fire is like asking a lady to dance: you listen to what the lady says, and sometimes you step forward, sometimes you back off. In this case, everyone on the fire crew made a successful, injury-free retreat to the Lunch Spot.

"We were golden at this point," Taylor said later. "We had cut line that didn't hold. But we were out of it, on the road, drinking water."

Kampen congratulated the Northwest Regulars on a job well done. "He said there was nothing to be done to stop the fire; it would have jumped our lines anyway," said one crew member. As if to underscore the point, flames flared up in spruce trees on the riverbank opposite the Lunch Spot, the same bunch of trees that had caused worry earlier about a crown fire. Suction from the burning on the south slope of the canyon drew smoke away from the Lunch Spot, so the flames in the spruce stood out in high relief. The sun bore down with midafternoon intensity. A near-cloudless sky gleamed cornflower blue, as brilliant as a Montana Yogo sapphire. The flames were a siren call for firefighters, who drifted back toward the river with cameras in hand, unmindful that a wind shift could send flames plunging onto their side of the river.

Some sprawled on the ground and opened food boxes, picked out the fruit and cookies, and left untouched the sandwiches with "mystery meat," instead eating the deli sandwiches they had brought with them. The food acted like a sleeping potion. They slipped into what scientists call a circadian trough or postprandial dip, or to put it simply, a midday slump. Welch snuggled up against a log and fell into a drowse.

CHAPTER SEVEN

Care with small fires is the best preventative of large ones.

—from *The Use of the National Forest Reserves,*
U.S. Forest Service, 1905

As Barry George, the district AFMO, drove into the Chewuch River canyon, he saw a heavy smoke column building ahead and, as he drew closer, flames running up the canyon's far south wall. This was no mop-up operation, George thought. The fire was "probably beyond the capabilities of the resources that we had there on the ground, just due to the terrain and the field conditions," he later told fire investigators. As George parked at the fire scene, a truck drew up behind him with a supply of drinking water—and the third Mark III pump, the extra one Daniels had ordered in the morning. The pump arrived too late to do any good; in an unhappy epilogue it would be found unopened in its container after the fire.

Nobody was in sight. George radioed the dispatcher at 3:07 PM and said he was going to look for Daniels "to see about taking IC." George's assignment was to do whatever needed doing, from taking over as incident commander to providing an extra set of eyes. Daniels would suffer no loss of face if he gave up the fire; George was much the senior man, and it was his turf.

George crossed the log over the river. Before him the charred, smoking landscape had an abandoned look, as though a battle had just swept by. In the middle distance, a helicopter with a bucket made persistent but futile stabs at torching trees. George raised Daniels by radio and learned that the Northwest Regulars had quit the fire and were gathered, along with the hotshots, at the Lunch Spot. George recrossed the river and joined Daniels and the hotshot supervisors, Brown and Cannon. Daniels was almost apologetic about having abandoned the fire, George recalled, though he couldn't understand why.

"There was no way we were going to keep up," George said later. "Coming back to the road they'd done the correct thing, in my mind." The best to be hoped for, George told Daniels, was to keep flames from crossing the road, the same strategy Jasso had recommended before he left to refuel. George, though, sounded a note of caution.

"Barry said, 'Let's stand back and watch,'" Brown said later. "He did not want anyone in there. He did state that it would be nice to keep fire south of the road, but that was a 'nice to do' rather than a 'have to do.'"

George asked Daniels if he felt comfortable continuing as incident commander, and Daniels indicated that he did. Daniels was not the man to manage a runaway fire, which this one had become. But in truth there wasn't much firefighting activity to manage. Everyone had disengaged from the fire except helicopter 13N, which could fly away if the fire blew up. "I felt comfortable there just above the cross log with our location and fire activity," George said later.

George had spent years as a smoke jumper at the North Cascades Smokejumper Base before taking the AFMO job. Studious by nature and quiet to a fault, George made a hobby of digging up old fire reports, which had earned him a reputation as the region's fire historian. "We counted on Barry for his depth of knowledge," said Steve Dickenson, manager of the North Cascades base.

George let Daniels continue as incident commander, but he passed along a lesson from the past. The Chewuch River canyon, George said, had burned out before: the Remmel Fire had scorched 40,000 acres in the Chewuch River watershed in 1929. The canyon had been threatened again during the terrible fire season of 1994, the year of the South Canyon Fire. The Thunder Mountain Fire, one of several large fires in the North Cascades that summer, had spread over 4,780 acres and dipped into the Chewuch River canyon. Nearly four hundred firefighters had fought the blaze; the smoke became so intense at one point that every-one was forced to withdraw. Flames burned along the south ridge of the Chewuch River canyon and sent stringers of flame backing down into the canyon. When that happened, the fire bosses picked out a safety zone where the river, the road, and the rocky wall of the canyon formed a broad, semiprotected opening, about two miles short of the end of the canyon road. The safety zone wasn't used in 1994, but it would be on this fire.

George added a remark that would ring in memory: "This is history repeating itself."

George asked if anyone had checked up the road for hikers or camp-ers, and became alarmed when not everyone seemed aware that the road dead-ended. Brown and Cannon volunteered to drive up the road and make the check. George described for them how a side road forked off along the way, and remarked that a vehicle parked there would be nearly invisible. They should look there on foot, if necessary.

George radioed the dispatcher at 3:58 PM, nearly an hour after his arrival, and reported that the crew had been ordered back from the fire. He also said an effort would be made to stop the fire from crossing the road. How those contradictory directives were to be achieved he did not explain. The log reads: "Barry G.—pulled crews to road—trying to keep from crossing road—torching spruce—subalpine."

George had another assignment for himself. Now that the fire had escaped the initial attack, it was headed for "extended attack," which means fresh supervisors, crews, and other resources would have to be brought in. George was responsible for putting together a Wildland Fire Situation Analysis, or WFSA, which would script the upcoming cam-paign. This was the sort of job George liked best, going off on his own and scrounging data.

George drove up the canyon road for more than a mile trying with-out success to find a good place to scout the fire. On the return drive he met the two engines that had been ordered coming up the road, after they had passed the Lunch Spot. He didn't stop to question the crews; after all, George was not the incident commander—Daniels was. George drove on down the road, passed the Lunch Spot, and parked at the heel of the fire. He climbed up the rock scree on the near north side of the canyon and snapped a few photos but was frustrated by a curtain of smoke that obscured flames.

The best view of the fire at this time was from the air. The pilot of the lead plane, Greg House, told the dispatcher at 3:31 PM, about the time George was conferring with Daniels and the others, that the fire appeared to cover fifty acres. Flames were leaning away from the road. Smoke was drifting upward and not churning. House decided to have the arriving air tankers make their drops ahead of the flames advancing up the south wall of the canyon. The first tanker, T-62, made two runs, dropping half of its three-thousand-gallon load each time; the second tanker, T-12, tried to extend the line started by T-62.

The drops had little effect, as far as House could see. The air tankers departed by 3:45 PM with plans to refuel, reload, and return. In the brief time House had been there, the fire had changed character dramatically. He radioed a disturbing update to the dispatcher at 3:54 PM, less than a half hour after his first report: the fire had doubled in size to a hundred acres and was almost to the ridge on the south canyon wall. Flames rose 100 to 150 feet above the crowns of trees and sent up a mushroom-shaped cloud of smoke. House told the dispatcher he would need a lot more than two air tankers to slow this fire.

At that moment he received an urgent "heads-up." The helicopter ground crew at the Eightmile Ranch had spotted two A-6 Intruder jets—headed straight for him.

House had no time to dodge. "My first sighting of the two military aircraft was as the first aircraft appeared flying out from beneath my left wing," he said later. The second jet flicked past a few hundred feet under his right wing. The two jets banked to skirt the smoke column and sped off. House called the dispatcher at 4:03 PM, directly after the near miss, and asked for the imposition of a temporary flight restriction, or TFR, to warn nonfire aircraft to stay at least five miles from the incident, a normal precaution that had not yet been taken. The letters *TFR* are written large and underlined twice in the log, so it's fair to assume that he made the request with vigor.

House had been talking during this time on air-to-air radio with his counterpart at the Libby South Fire, Jamie Tackman, the lead pilot there. House said his air show wasn't having any effect. Tackman said he, to the contrary, faced a critical situation—the Libby South Fire was threatening homes—and he could sure use more air tankers. With no such threat at the Thirtymile Fire, House asked the dispatcher at 4:18 PM if the two air tankers assigned to him wouldn't be put to better use at the Libby South Fire. "Looks like the fire's going strong," House remarked, "not going to help throwing tankers at it." The dispatcher agreed, and the two air tankers that had been assigned to the Thirtymile Fire were diverted to the Libby South Fire.

As the Thirtymile Fire grew unchecked, House radioed Daniels and told him that the smoke column now extended from one canyon wall to the other. "It was becoming a catastrophic fire, but there wasn't too much urgency or concern on the part of the IC," House later told fire investigators.

Jasso, meanwhile, had completed his refueling mission at the North Cascades Smokejumper Base, where weather conditions had become extreme: the temperature hit 101 degrees, and the humidity fell to 5 percent, levels that take fire danger into the stratosphere. On his return flight, Jasso heard the radio chatter about diverting air tankers to the Libby South Fire and called the dispatcher to voice his agreement. "Move air tankers to Libby," he directed, according to a log entry at 4:20 PM. That meant there would be no air traffic at the Thirtymile Fire left to direct, except for helicopter 13N. Jasso said he would stay around anyway to keep an eye on things. Below him, flames boiled under a blanket of smoke.

THE MORNING HAD passed quietly for Tim Schmekel and the others assigned to Engines 701 and 704. Schmekel had reported back to work at 8:00 AM, only five hours after he had arrived home following his release from the Thirtymile Fire. His engine, No. 704, drew a laugher of an assignment for the morning: taking down Fourth of July "No Fireworks" signs across the forest. He might as well have stayed in bed, Schmekel thought. Big engines aren't supposed to go on little assignments, but after working into the early morning hours, he wasn't going to complain about light duty.

At least the regular foreman, Dave Laughman, was back on the job, which relieved Schmekel of the unwanted responsibility of being engine boss. Schmekel took the wheel of a chase pickup and, following behind Laughman in Engine 704, spent the morning scouring back roads for fireworks signs. At the noon hour, the engine crew drove into Winthrop for a restaurant lunch. They were settling down to eat when a call came from the dispatch office with a new assignment: to pick up road barriers and block access to the Thirtymile Fire—about two hours after Soderquist had ordered the closure. The barriers were kept in a warehouse in Twisp, ten miles south of Winthrop. It was midafternoon before the engine crew finished lunch, drove to Twisp, and loaded up the hefty orange and white boards, sawhorses, and "Road Closed" signs. Engine 704 was reported heading for the Chewuch River canyon, with barricades aboard, at 2:22 PM.

The engine crew had gone only a few miles when they heard the dispatcher assign another engine, No. 701, to go to the Thirtymile Fire and check for spot fires. That order went through quickly: though there is no log entry to confirm it, Schmekel remembers hearing the broadcast about 2:30 PM, three minutes after Jasso's 2:27 PM request to the dispatcher to "get couple engines."

It was the best-sounding assignment the crew of Engine 704 had heard all day, and Laughman broke in on the radio and volunteered his unit to help out. He was told to place the barriers first and then go to the fire and assist with spot fires. As the two big engines headed up the Chewuch River canyon, they drew together the elements of catastrophe as surely as a magnet draws metal filings—from the fumbled water show, which was the reason they were called in, to major screwups yet to come. History was repeating itself, as George had warned: the Chewuch River canyon was about to burn out. But at least the hotshots and Northwest Regulars were out of harm's way at the Lunch Spot, where flames provided them a living laboratory of fire behavior.

Craven gathered several young firefighters around him for an impromptu lecture. Never before, the veteran told them, had he seen flames burn with such intensity. "This is extreme fire behavior," he said.

Weaver, Rutman, and others began snapping photos. One image shows the Northwest Regulars seated on the ground, half of them with their hard hats off. Food boxes are scattered around in what might be a picnic scene, except that all heads are turned to the sight of the flames on the far bank of the river. Minutes before, the crew had been right where flames now raged. In another image, half a dozen firefighters wearing hard hats have walked toward the river for a closer look. Several of them aim cameras.

While the fire crew took its ease at the Lunch Spot, Engine 704 with Laughman, Schmekel, and the road barriers pulled up at the Eightmile Ranch to the south. The engine crew had begun to wrestle the barriers into place when the second engine, No. 701, pulled in behind them with the captain, Harry Dunn, at the wheel. Dunn appeared frazzled. But Dunn always appeared overexcited at the start of a fire. After twenty-nine years in the fire service, he was known as a competent hand, but one who couldn't escape his roots.

Dunn had been a California Earth child, dreaming of becoming a subsistence farmer on his own five acres of ground, until he discovered the drudgery of agriculture. He joined a fire crew in northern California instead and never looked back. In a salute to his past, he kept his blond hair long and often sported a cowboy hat on the job. He was well liked, but his quirks made him a favorite target for coworkers.

"'Scuse me, sir," someone shouted at Dunn, "but you can't go by. This road has been blocked for traffic!"

Dunn was not in a kidding mood.

"There's spot fires across the road; we've got to get up there," Dunn yelled back. Indeed, the smoke plume from the canyon, visible in the distance, was becoming heavier by the minute. Schmekel nudged his crewmate Andy Floyd. The plume signaled the kind of extreme fire behavior they had predicted the night before.

Dunn drove Engine 701 past the barricades and on up the road. He tried repeatedly to contact Daniels by radio, but the steep canyon walls once again stopped radio signals. "I remember Harry attempting to radio Daniels before the entrapment, but he couldn't get hold of them," Bill Austin, the Goat Peak lookout, told investigators after the fire.

Dunn called the dispatcher at 3:24 PM to report his arrival at the fire. He had the briefest of encounters with Daniels, under circumstances that remain controversial to this day. Daniels waved him on, according to Dunn. But Daniels later maintained that Dunn never checked in, a charge that nearly got Dunn fired.

"Did you know that the engines had arrived on the fire?" an investigator later asked Daniels.

"No, the only thing I knew they had just showed up," Daniels replied. "They didn't stop to talk to us. They [were] just kind of doing their own thing. They never contacted me."

Others there at the time, however, remember Dunn stopping long enough to yell at Daniels. Emhoff, who had to get up from the side of the road to let Dunn's engine pass, recalled: "The engine wasn't going fast. The engine crew saw us—there was a big pile of forty people in that little area; we were pretty hard to miss. They pulled by, slowed down, and said something. They spent not much more than a minute talking—it obviously wasn't a briefing."

The answers to what actually happened at the check-in would be years in coming.

Dunn drove on searching for spot fires, and Laughman and Engine 704 pulled in at the Lunch Spot minutes later, at 3:27 PM. Laughman reported his arrival to the dispatcher but not to Daniels, figuring he was following the leader, Dunn. He called Dunn by radio and asked him what to do next, and Dunn told him to stay put for the moment.

With time to kill, Laughman gave his engine crew a safety briefing. He reminded them to keep an eye on the weather and maintain communications, and identified the road as an escape route and the Lunch Spot as a safety zone. When he had finished, he and Schmekel walked up the road for a look around. "The fire was starting to pick up," Laughman said later. "I could hear it start crowning."

"So that's the fire over there," said Schmekel.

"Yep," Laughman said.

"And this is all unburned here, between us and the fire?" Schmekel asked.

"Yep," Laughman replied.

"And we're supposed to hold the road? *Riiight*," an unbelieving Schmekel drawled.

At that moment Dunn called on the radio and told them to bring their engine up to help with a spot fire. The job, Dunn said, was big enough to require recharging the big engines with water. They should find a place along the road where Schmekel could run a draft hose from his pickup, which carried a slip-on pump, into the river.

After leaving the Lunch Spot, Dunn drove more than a mile up the road without seeing any spot fires. He stopped at the place where the river, the road, and the rock scree formed a large open space, which he remembered as a safety zone during the 1994 Thunder Mountain Fire.

He turned around and was halfway back to the Lunch Spot before he discovered his first spot fire, about fifty yards off the road in the direction of the river. Flames were a moderate foot to a foot and a half high, outlining a circle perhaps ten yards in diameter. "We figured that if it got any bigger, it would jump across the road," Dunn said. He and his crew rolled out hose and began to spray water to take the heat out of the flames. But somebody would have to cut a fireline around it too, to fully contain it.

Dunn raised Daniels by radio and asked for help, but within minutes the engine crew had so thoroughly soaked the spot fire that Dunn decided he didn't need help after all.

"I can handle it," Dunn told Daniels, in an exchange overheard by Laughman.

"I have the personnel; I'm going to kick you down a squad," Daniels replied.

Daniels later told the story of what happened next in different ways. On one occasion, he told fire investigators that he sent help because Dunn had asked for it. "We got a call from Engine 701 saying they had a spot up the road, needed some help." In another interview, he said he made the decision when he saw an engine crewman walking down to the Lunch Spot seeking help. "It was more of a verbal thing, not a radio," he told another fire investigator.

Struggling to understand, the investigator asked, "Why is it that you went up there to help them out?"

"Because we were just sitting there," Daniels replied, to explain the most fateful decision of the day. "Just sitting there when there's work to be done, and people have had lots of rest and it's for them to choose, you know. Might as well be busy than just sitting there."

Kampen got the ball rolling. In one version, told by witnesses, Kampen called out, "Who wants to go get some hot spots?" There was a moment of silence. Then Craven slowly got to his feet.

"Okay, I'll do it, I'll take my squad," Craven replied.

In an only slightly different version, told by Kampen, he went to Craven and asked, "How do you feel about heading up the road?"

Craven replied, "Sure, we'll do it."

Others, too, rousted themselves. Emhoff gave the snoozing Rebecca Welch a friendly kick in the side. Emhoff liked to pick on Welch—she was round, solid, and self-confident, just like him.

"Wake up, lazy ass," he called out cheerfully.

"Hey! What?" Welch replied sleepily, taking no offense.

"We gotta go," Emhoff sang out. "Craven's squad has got to go."

CHAPTER EIGHT

> *Fear. The fine line you walk where what you have to do drives*
> *you to do it up against what your better judgment tells you not*
> *to. A firefighter cannot be a coward. He can be a lot of things,*
> *a prick, a thief, a liar, but he cannot be a coward.*
>
> —Larry Brown, author and firefighter, from *On Fire*

The sun had cooked the canyon for hours, and flames had magnified the effect near the ground, wicking moisture from the air and boosting temperatures. The heat turned the upper atmosphere unstable, spawning fresh winds and crosscurrents, and by afternoon the fire itched to break loose—the only missing ingredient for a full-scale blowup was a wind. The weather's effect on the firefighters, however, was exactly the opposite. Heat, dryness, and hours of physical activity had sapped human energy and awareness. Tunnel vision set in, and the ability to make thoughtful adjustments ebbed to a low mark. Under these conditions, inexperienced supervisors blindly follow plans hatched in the cool and calm of morning. Experienced firefighters, keenly aware of the opposing trends, employ countermeasures that range from packing a canteen with extrastrong coffee to setting "trigger points" that mandate defensive actions to planned "timeouts" to look things over and make adjustments. Even so, late afternoon, when the day hangs heavy, is the time for big trouble on any fire, from a mop-up show to a "major rager."

At the Lunch Spot, Craven's squad rose from the ground and swung back into action in slow motion. Their bodies were stiff, their limbs creaky, their brains shut down. A few may have harbored a dim sense of dread about returning without discussion to a fire they had quit by universal agreement an hour earlier. But Dunn's spot fire was just up the road, which was a natural escape route. They had a vehicle—the "Green Pickle" van—if a speedy exit became necessary. The main body of fire was being drawn away from them up the far side of the canyon. And the presence up the road of two big engines, Nos. 701 and 704, provided reassurance that it was okay to go there.

There was no shortage of volunteers, once Craven had struggled to his feet. By the time Wallace picked up a chain saw and headed for the green van, he was too late. Craven stuck a forearm out the van window and blocked him. "No, we've got enough," Craven said.

Tate jumped enthusiastically to her feet and buckled on her gear, and was headed for the van when Emhoff stopped her short. "You aren't on this squad. You're on my squad back home, but not here," he said.

"No, I'm not," Tate acknowledged, in a small voice, and turned away crestfallen.

Kampen took the wheel of the green van, and Daniels sat beside him. In the back, in addition to Craven and Emhoff, were Welch, FitzPatrick, Clark, and Scherzinger. As they began the short drive, Emhoff noted several spot fires on the side of the road nearest the river.

"I made the comment to Tom, 'Why aren't we getting these along the way?'" Emhoff said. "There was almost a thousand gallons of water ahead of us in those engines. They could have taken care of their own spots."

The van kept going and in a minute pulled up next to Dunn's Engine 701, about a half mile above the Lunch Spot. As Craven's squad stepped out, a pickup with the hotshot supervisors, Brown and Cannon, came down the road toward them, returning from the scouting mission to the end of the road at the Thirtymile Campground. Their way was partially blocked by the traffic, and needing to report in, they stopped to talk to Kampen, Daniels having headed off for the spot fire.

Brown and Cannon had found three vehicles parked at the trailhead but hadn't seen any people or other vehicles. The parked vehicles probably belonged to campers or hikers who were off in the woods; the hotshots had noted license numbers for further checking, but there wasn't anything more to be done. How two veteran fire supervisors managed to overlook the vacationing Hagemeyers and their Dodge pickup has never been satisfactorily explained. Granted, the Hagemeyers were inside the truck camper and the backpacker tent. But the Hagemeyers remember parking the Dodge in plain sight at a designated campsite just off the road, not down some hidden spur.

Brown and Cannon say they drove the entire loop of the road, up one side to the trailhead and back the other side through the campground, and shouted hellos along the way. There's no question that they reached the trailhead because that's where they took down the license numbers, which were later traced to people who indeed were safely off in the woods. One possible explanation is that after Brown and Cannon reached the trailhead they doubled back down the road by mistake and missed the half of the loop with the campsites and the Hagemeyers. But the road to the campsite was obvious, the sign marking it was prominent, and the hotshots insist they explored the full loop. Two things are certain: Brown and Cannon should have found the Hagemeyers, even if they were parked out of sight; but they were so worn down that they had chosen to run an errand—checking the trailhead—instead of running the fire.

No matter how the oversight came about, the hotshot supervisors declared the road ahead clear of people. This was the last chance to break with the fire. What was left to fight for? No one was aware of the plight of the Hagemeyers—not even the Hagemeyers. There were no homes to defend. The skimpy amount of timber to be saved by keeping the fire from crossing the road would be no loss to anyone. The fire was going to burn out the canyon anyway, in a much-advertised repeat of history.

The ensuing brief talk among Brown, Cannon, and Kampen, however, set a new strategy for the fire. The word *decision* is too strong for what happened; matters went forward in a kind of trance, like a blind man groping toward the edge of a cliff. Brown and Cannon had misgivings about the worsening fire situation, and Brown remarked that nobody should go any farther up the canyon, beyond Dunn's spot fire, until all the spot fires were under control.

Kampen remarked that he had one squad with him and could summon the other two and spread them out along the road. "Marshall and

Kyle bought off on that," Kampen said later, indicating their agreement. In addition, Brown agreed to move the hotshots a short way up to help. In retrospect, the question stands out, Why did no one consult about these important matters with Daniels, who was fifty yards away attending the spot fire? Why did Brown and Cannon not report directly to Daniels, the incident commander, on their scouting trip to the upper canyon? Ascribing these oversights to fatigue and lack of concentration, as happened afterward, avoids another possible but more unpleasant conclusion, namely, that Brown, Cannon, and Kampen did not take Daniels seriously. Kampen said later that he's pretty sure he walked over and told Daniels what had been decided, and Daniels replied, "That's fine." But that was after matters had been settled.

The new strategy was this: Daniels was to stay with Craven's squad and finish off that spot fire; the rest of the Northwest Regulars would be brought up by van to deal with spot fires now blossoming along the roadway; the hotshots would tackle spot fires just slightly up the road from the Lunch Spot and thus provide an anchor point; and Engines 701 and 704 would independently engage spot fires. In fairness, the participants thought of it only as a holding action. With hindsight, however, they had just recommitted over forty firefighters to a running fire, along a dead-end road, on a scorching day in a time of drought, at the most dangerous time of day for a fire, in a narrow canyon with a history of burning out, after quitting the fire because it had grown too dangerous. "Things kind of evolved," Kampen said later, plaintively. "There was an unfortunate chain of events."

Kampen hurried things along. He called Taylor by radio and told him to get his people into the white van and up the road. As Taylor herded his squad—Avila, Dreis, Hurd, Johnson, Rutman, and Weaver—toward the van, Brown and Cannon drove their pickup back to the Lunch Spot. The hotshot bosses parked there and were joined almost immediately by George, who had just returned to the Lunch Spot after his frustrating attempt to scout the fire from the north wall of the canyon. Taylor, watching George and the hotshots from afar, wondered what the senior men were talking about. But he couldn't linger. He got into the white van and started to drive his squad up the canyon.

George, leaning on the hotshots' pickup, could see plenty of signs of a reengagement. Taylor's squad was driving off in the white van. Craven's squad, Daniels, and Kampen were nowhere to be seen. But George said later that he did not discuss these developments with Brown and Cannon. Instead, he asked the hotshots if they had found anyone at the Thirtymile Campground, and accepted the list of license numbers for further checking. George also asked for a humidity reading, and Brown passed along the most recent figure he had, 14 percent. For the moment, George said later, he still thought all was well.

Taylor, meanwhile, drove the white van a few score yards beyond the Lunch Spot to Engine 704 and Laughman's crew, who were wetting down a spot fire. Taylor assumed they knew he was coming, but nobody had told the engine crew anything and they said they didn't need help. As Taylor started to drive up the canyon again, the green van came down the road with Kampen alone at the wheel. What's this? Taylor thought. Kampen had left Craven's squad without a ride if the fire took off. As the green van passed by, Taylor muttered, not loud enough for Kampen to hear, "What the fuck are you doing going down by yourself?"

Taylor became further alarmed when he reached Dunn's Engine 701 and saw, mounting into the cab, a disheveled figure with yellow fire shirt unbuttoned and long yellow hair flying free—a vision of General George Armstrong Custer in his last moments!

"What are you doing?" shouted Taylor. But Dunn ducked into the cab and rumbled off down the road.

Taylor and his squad tooled up and followed hose lines, which Dunn had left behind intending to pick them up later, into the woods. They soon found Craven and his squad and worked in with them. "Let's get this wrapped up so we can get out of here," Taylor yelled. He was in such a hurry that he grabbed embers in gloved hands and crunched them out, which reminded Emhoff, who was working nearby, that he had left his own gloves back at the Lunch Spot. As a fire instructor, Emhoff had preached to rookies to wear gloves at all times, but in practice he liked to work bare-handed, to keep his hands calloused. Emhoff normally clipped a pair of gloves to his pack. But he'd gotten up quickly back at the Lunch Spot, and he'd forgotten them. I need to get back down there and find the gloves, Emhoff thought, not realizing how right he was.

Kampen, meanwhile, drove the green van back to the Lunch Spot, passing Taylor along the way, and loaded up the last of the Northwest Regulars: Schexnayder and his squad—Anderson, Hinson, Tate, Wallace, and Watson. He didn't have far to go. He drove back up the road about five hundred yards, came around a sharp bend, and there were Dunn and his engine crew, who had driven down and stopped to fight a spot fire at a new location. Kampen stopped, turned the van around, and stepped out to talk to Dunn. The time was just after 4:00 PM.

At 4:03 PM the First Butte lookout, Mort Banasky, reported to the dispatch office that smoke from the Thirtymile Fire had formed a thunderhead. Under the smoke, the fire was growing in two directions, as photographs and witness testimony would later confirm. The main arm of the fire went up the south side of the canyon, as it had for most of the day. At the same time, flames were making a strong move straight up the canyon floor. Kampen and his firefighters thought they were safe on a flank of the fire, and they were right, until Kampen drove the green van around the sharp bend and stopped. The turn had put the van square in the path of the flames raging up the canyon bottom. "The vegetation was really thick; you couldn't see into it," Kampen said years later as he stood at the same place, which the fire had made barren.

The wind turned gusty, and sheets of flame flapped in the trees. The smoke column was cut by amber slashes, as gasses inside the column ignited or as sunlight broke through. The fire growled like an advancing thunderstorm. As Kampen and the others put on their gear, a wave of pine needles glowing like fireflies swept over them. In seconds, bigger stuff followed: flaming pinecones, twigs, and branches that rattled when they struck the green van, hard hats, anything solid. Embers stenciled freckles on exposed skin.

"Harry Dunn was pulling his hose reel out as I pulled my pack on," Kampen said. "I was walking across the road to touch base with Harry; that's when the smoke column shifted and it got dark."

On the far side of the river, now directly down-canyon from Kampen and his crew, trees bent, swayed, and sent balls of flame from the crown of one to another, driven by the gusting winds generated by the fire. The crown fire progressed in stately fashion, bowing and rising, bowing and rising, until it reached the river. There it paused, drew in oxygen, and recharged itself. Then in a moment, as though ignited by an unseen torch, a mass of flame came alive on the firefighters' side of the river.

"Here it comes!" someone shouted.

The flames sent forward an invisible vanguard of superheated air that scalded exposed flesh: necks, hands, faces. "It was starting to burn us; it was *hot*," Schexnayder later recalled. "Pete said, 'Let's go,' but we were already halfway back to the pickle van by then. By the time I buckled on my pack, I was taking it off and throwing it in the van; it happened that fast."

When spot fires flared up on both sides of the road, for the second time that day Kampen took the signal to get out. He ran for the van. "It took me five steps to get to the van, and they were already inside when I got there," he said. "It was the fastest load-up I've ever experienced. It was very obvious we were in the wrong place. The fire was spreading faster than I have ever seen fire spread. It just got up and ran on us."

The radio sounded a babble of warnings.

"You need to get out of there," Brown said in a controlled voice. Others picked up the chant, with urgency: "Pull out. Get out of there now. Down the road! Get out! Get out!" Calls went out by name to Daniels and others, but for long, anxious minutes no one answered.

Kampen slid into the driver's seat and gunned the engine. Dunn and Engine 701 had already disappeared down the road. As Kampen started the drive, the crew huddled back from windows too hot to touch and yanked up fire shirts to shield their faces. "The fire was bumping up against the road, trying to cross over," Schexnayder said. "Every one of us covered our faces."

Just ahead, flames bent over the road. "All we could see was red everywhere," said Hinson. "Flames were curling right over the top of us." Kampen never thought about stopping. (In fact, he remarked later, he never thought; instinct told him he could make it.) "Flames were starting to come out on the road," he said. "I decided to go for it. We weren't driving through fire, but I remember being scared."

Others, too, raced to escape. When Dunn had driven away from Taylor, with his hair flying, he had not been running off, as Taylor had feared. Confident that he would be able to come back and pick up his hoses, Dunn was on his way to deal with spot fires farther down the road, which is where Kampen found him.

Dunn and his crew had finished with one spot fire and were dousing another when Dunn felt "a large momentum" building up in the air. Dunn jumped into the engine cab and yelled at his crew to get aboard. With flames bending over the road, Dunn drove until he came to the hotshots' fire rigs, which had been moved up a few score yards from the Lunch Spot. The hotshots were just getting out. Dunn braked to a halt in the middle of the road and shouted, "You got spot fires by your rigs!"

As the hotshots watched in disbelief, an engine with a frazzled driver bolted out of the flames, and the driver, leaning out of the cab, yelled something about spot fires. One hotshot grabbed a shovel and started to throw dirt, but it was too late for that. Another hotshot shouted, "Load up!"

At this moment, the green van with Kampen at the wheel shot out of the closing curtain of flame—and kept going, right through the traffic jam. Kampen did not stop until he came to the site of the offending campfire. Improbably, the green van escaped without a scorch mark. Kampen dropped off Schexnayder's squad and pondered his next move.

"The radio was going crazy," Kampen said. "My thought was, There are fourteen people up there in a ten-person van. I needed to get back up there with the green van."

Kampen drove alone back to the Lunch Spot. By then Dunn and the hotshots had moved their vehicles down the canyon, and the place was empty. What do I do now? Kampen thought. Make a rescue run for Daniels and the others? Looking up the road, though, was like peering into the mouth of a fire-breathing dragon.

Kampen tried to raise Daniels by radio, but there was no response. "I had no idea how far up the road that wall of fire went," Kampen said later. "I really, really wanted to be with them." When flames reached the edge of the Lunch Spot, Kampen, his body shaking, got back in the green van. He turned the van and drove away.

Daniels and his crew had their eyes on the ground working the spot fire when they heard the first radio warning. "Butt out of there, the fire is crossing the road," a calm voice said. The only fire they could see was the spot fire in front of them, and it was going nowhere. The radio voice did not sound alarmed. Daniels and Emhoff started to walk together the fifty yards back to the white van. The ten-passenger van was going to have to hold fourteen, they remarked, unless somebody wanted to walk.

"Get out of there!" the radio blared.

Taylor's head went up; it was the message he had been waiting for all afternoon. "We need to get out of here," Taylor told his squad.

Nobody moved.

"Let's get the fuck out of here!" Taylor yelled.

He and the others started to run for the white van. By the time they got there, Daniels was behind the wheel. Taylor slid in beside him. Packs and tools were tossed inside, people piled onto bench seats, and a second later the van was headed down the road—leaving four people stranded: Clark, Emhoff, Craven, and Welch.

"It was my second fire; I had no idea if it was dangerous or what," said Welch. "Tom Craven was pretty calm, and we all started out of there. We were on the road, and the fire was ripping through the trees. It was like, 'Holy crap!' because it was really ripping. And there was four of us who couldn't fit in the van—me and Tom and Jason and Beau—running on the road."

Emhoff began to trot, joking that this was one reason they trained so hard, so they could run away from fires. "There was no panic or yelling; we just humped it," said Emhoff.

Taylor leaned his head out the van window and yelled back, "Double time! Double time it!" feeling like an idiot because the four were already making the best time they could. Daniels kept the van at a deliberate speed, but the gap widened with the four.

Dead ahead, flames formed an archway over the road; in seconds the one avenue of escape would be cut off. Daniels and Taylor locked eyes. They had time, barely, to gun the engine and pass under the flaming arch. But the four people on foot would never make it. Without a word, Daniels spun the wheel and ran the vehicle to the side of the road, jammed the transmission into reverse, and made a 180-degree turn. When the firefighters on foot saw the van's brake lights flash red, an unbelieving Welch turned to Craven.

"Is it like this every day?" she asked.

The four spun on their heels and began to jog back the way they had come. Emhoff, a map buff, knew the road dead-ended farther up the canyon, but they had no choice except to head that way. The van overtook them—and kept on going, which caused a moment of sheer terror. The van stopped a few yards ahead, and the doors burst open. FitzPatrick grabbed Clark by his shirt and half dragged him inside. "We're going to make room for you," FitzPatrick assured him.

The van was halted only a few seconds, but it seemed like an eternity before they were moving again, away from the fire. Bodies shook with the electric rush of adrenaline. Hearts pounded. Brains accelerated to hyperalert. "Oh my God, we're going to die!" FitzPatrick cried out. The fire-choked canyon heightened intimations she had felt for several days, of a youthful death and early glory, a romantically satisfying end to her religious quest. The feelings had come and gone, she had told others, but now she felt justified.

Taylor yelled for everyone to shut up so he could hear the radio. The near panic subsided. People barked questions like "What's going on here?" and "Are we going to be safe?" But the flames were behind them and mercifully were not following them up the road. Daniels drove slowly, searching for a likely place to ride out the fire's inevitable passage. They had been granted the precious gift of time—time to make an escape, time to find a safety zone, time to prepare for the worst.

Watching the scene from above in the air attack plane, Jasso radioed the dispatcher that he could see firefighters trying to get away. "Fire pushing road at bottom—crews moving down road," begins a log note at 4:34 PM, and continues with startling news: "Fire crossed road [north] side 1 acre."

Jasso said nothing—or at least the log records nothing—about anyone being cut off or trapped, perhaps because he did not yet realize the scope of what had happened. Far more disturbing is the lack of any mention of an entrapment in the log for another fifty minutes, though everyone on the fire almost immediately became aware of what had happened. In fact, there was almost no communication of any kind logged between the supervisors on the incident and the dispatch office during those fifty minutes. (There was plenty of radio chatter, but it was mostly people at the fire talking to each other, and none of that was logged.) An exception is one cryptic note in the dispatch log at 5:01 PM recording a message from Jasso, who reports that the fire has grown to five-hundred-plus acres and is "still moving." That note is followed by the ambiguous phrase "crews pullout."

When investigators later asked the dispatcher, Ed Hutton, whether someone should not have reported the entrapment immediately, and what difference it might have made if someone had, he replied: "For sure the IC should be communicating to dispatch. That is common sense. In this case the IC was talking with air attack." The dispatch office could have alerted forest officials and medical and emergency services earlier, he said. But knowing there was an entrapment would not have changed the outcome, Hutton concluded, and it's difficult to argue with that judgment. He added, "I just wish they would have gotten the heck out of there fifteen minutes quicker." The long delay in reporting the entrapment raises the suspicion, however, that very little would ever have been said if Daniels and the others had escaped unscathed.

Daniels, meanwhile, continued driving, on the lookout for the best place to ride out the fire. The road along this stretch hugged the north side of the canyon, which was steep and rocky but also held patches of timber. Daniels checked out three possible safety zones, each time asking Jasso what they looked like from the air. All three were rejected on grounds of being too small or too cluttered with timber.

Then the van came to the old Thunder Mountain Fire safety zone, where the river curved away from the road in a horseshoe bend and created a broad opening. An unbroken stand of trees grew along the far bank of the river, on the outer rim of the horseshoe. Inside the river bend was a sandbar, bounded by water and by the road on the north side. The road ran hard against the north wall of the canyon, whose rocky slope rose abruptly more than three thousand feet to the canyon rim. Just before reaching the place, the canyon took a dogleg turn to the left, or north, which was marked by a ridge of scree that extended down the north side of the canyon to the road. This ridge appeared substantial enough to deflect flames coming up the canyon, before they reached the broad opening.

The combination of rock scree, road, sandbar, and river bend created the largest open space anywhere in the upper canyon. Daniels asked Jasso what it looked like from the air, and Jasso replied that it was the most likely place he could see. Later analysis by investigators would confirm this judgment: Daniels and Jasso had picked the best available spot.

Daniels halted the van, and the fourteen firefighters stumbled out, their legs wobbly from excitement and the cramped quarters. Everyone from Daniels to the greenest rookie knew what was coming next. The fire was going to sweep the canyon. Yet most felt a rush of relief after being imprisoned in the van. They had been close enough to a raging fire to feel its lethal powers. But they had gotten clean away, without damage or injuries. They knew they were lucky the flames hadn't raced them up the road, and the luck felt sweet. They had a good place to ride out the flames and time to get ready for what was coming. "There was pretty unanimous agreement this was the best spot," Emhoff said later. Here they would take their stand.

Taylor lit a cigarette and let it dangle from his mouth. He did not share in the general giddiness. "I wonder if anyone's done any thinning around here," he said to Emhoff, "because if a fire ever came through, you know . . ." His voice trailed off.

CHAPTER NINE

*There aren't any fires alike, and you have just got to follow
them through as they come and keep ahead of them—to
outguess them.... [T]his fire was burning at very slow speed
and we were apparently in safe territory and not in any
danger because the wind wasn't very strong at that
particular time and it was carrying the fire away from us.*

—from the testimony of Jack F. Herndon, a crew
supervisor injured on the Hauser Fire of 1943, which
killed eleven men and injured seventy-two others

FitzPatrick laughed with relief. "This is so cool," she said. "We're trapped by a fire. I'm going to remember this." She took out her camera and held it above her head for a self-portrait.

Rutman stepped back and saw a tableau worth a photo. He took out a disposable camera and shot an image that would become an icon of the fire. The time is seconds after the crew stepped out of the van; in the image, the white van points upriver, its doors and rear hatch open. The crew is spread across the road but not scattered. At this point a stern word would have brought them together. Down the canyon a light column of purple-gray smoke rises from the arm of the fire that cut off their retreat. Taylor stands closest to the river, a cigarette stuck in his mouth, and his hands stuffed in his pockets. He casts a grim look across the river at the main body of fire, not visible in the photo, which has progressed up the far side of the canyon to a point directly opposite where everyone is standing.

Another firefighter, probably Dreis, stands next to Taylor and gazes at the same arresting sight. In the middle of the road stands a tall, straight-backed figure, his hands on his hips and his back to the camera, a pillar of stability; almost certainly Weaver. Emhoff, his hands gloveless, walks toward the camera as though on a purposeful errand. Just behind Emhoff stands FitzPatrick, holding up her camera with both hands and smiling gleefully into the heavens for the self-portrait. Daniels is not visible; he has moved away from the crew, perhaps to talk by radio to Jasso.

The tableau didn't last. Moments after the photo was snapped, Daniels turned the white van and parked it facing down-canyon for a quick getaway, when the time came. The van now pointed to a broad, tunnel-like opening just below the entrapment site, the same place where the canyon took the dogleg turn. There, the river and road ran side by side, creating the opening in the otherwise dense forest, and projecting mixed visual signals. The running river and the tall trees along its far bank were an image pretty enough for a postcard. But flames were visible far in the background. The opening pointed like the barrel of a massive gun straight at the entrapment site, where the firefighters had taken refuge, and already visible in the opening were fingers of smoke.

Daniels told everyone to stick together and stay close to the road. No one has a clear memory of exactly when he first made those remarks. For sure, he never gathered everyone together, addressed them, and issued a firm set of orders to prepare for a burnover. Daniels was soft-spoken, and ordering people around was not his way. Many people, though, remember Daniels remarking repeatedly: "Everything's going to be fine. Stay near the road. The fire's going to go past us." He spent most of the next half hour or so, however, on the radio with Jasso.

"You guys are in a good spot; that's the spot to be," Jasso reassured Daniels, over and over.

LYING IN HIS tent in shorts and a T-shirt, Bruce Hagemeyer had cleared his mind of useless mental debris and centered his thoughts on the present moment. The Buddhist meditation technique of "mindfulness" sounds simple enough. One smiles the half-smile of Buddha, breathes quietly, and exercises firm but not abusive control over errant thoughts; the technique applies to daily life, by turning ordinary actions into meaningful rituals. "Washing dishes is meditation," a Zen master has written. "If you cannot wash the dishes in mindfulness, you cannot meditate in silence." Bruce's longtime practice of this technique had taught him to let the past slip away like a worn-out garment, to put aside worries about the uncertain future, and to be conscious of the moment at hand. Meditation brought him an inner sense of well-being, as though he were bathed in warm, golden light.

A brightening inside the tent made Bruce look up from his book. Something was afoot. The walls of the tent had taken on a yellow radiance, and it had nothing to do with inner glow. Bruce poked his head out of the tent flap and felt a knot tighten in his stomach. A smoky haze drifted across the sky, and through its filter passed rays of sunshine that gilded the objects they fell upon, his tent included.

Bruce called to Paula to come take a look. Paula peered out of the camper, but she was in a holiday mood and saw no reason for alarm. The scattered flames they had seen on the drive up to the campground could easily account for the smoke. They hadn't been afraid before. Why worry now?

Bruce persisted. There was too much smoke for the small amount of fire they had seen, he said. The timber around them was so thick that flames could close on them without warning.

"What does your gut tell you, honey?" Paula asked.

"Let's get the hell out of here," said Bruce, who seldom used such language.

Paula dropped her book and swiftly gathered her things. Bruce pulled down the tent and threw it in the back of the pickup. In minutes, they were driving down the canyon road in expectation of speedy deliverance, but this was not to be. Ahead in the road several figures in hard hats, yellow shirts, and green pants waved them to a stop.

"We've been cut off," one of them told the Hagemeyers, stunning them with the news.

A dozen or so firefighters milled around on the road. One burly firefighter—Taylor—broke from the others and marched toward their pickup in a determined, almost scary manner. Peering into the cab, Taylor saw what looked to him like "a couple of middle-aged, burned-out hippies" in light clothing, completely out of place at a fire scene.

"Hey, where does this road go?" Taylor asked.

"It goes up about a mile, and there's a trailhead," Bruce replied. "It's a dead end."

"Where's the fire?" Paula asked nervously. "Oh my God, there's a fire! Where's the fire?"

Taylor leaned into the vehicle.

"It's right there, lady," he said, pointing across the river. "The fire's THERE." But Paula kept repeating in a shocked voice, "Where's the fire? Where's the fire?"

Taylor was disgusted. "The mountain's on fire, and this lady is asking me where the fire is," he said later.

"What should we do?" Bruce asked.

"Stay with us," Taylor replied, "or if you know a better place up the road, you can go back there."

Taylor stepped back from the pickup. It was his turn to feel stunned. Nobody had said anything to him about a dead-end road until this moment. The situation was worse than he had thought. Taylor made a beeline for Daniels.

As Taylor departed, FitzPatrick bounced up to the Hagemeyers's pickup bubbling with excitement. She seemed to the Hagemeyers like a girl on a summer adventure. FitzPatrick asked the Hagemeyers where they were from, and when they said Thorp she enthused that she was from Yakima, so they were nearly neighbors. She told them she had just completed fire guard school and found firefighting "totally exciting." But it was a serious business, too, she said; her instructors had put much stress on safety first. "These guys are good," FitzPatrick said, reassuringly.

She pointed to the sun, which had turned bloodred.

"Oh! This is so beautiful, look at the sun. If you've got a camera, you should take some pictures. You'll never see anything like this again in your life!"

Paula felt an instant "parental connection" to the girl, who seemed "like an angel" sent from heaven, she would remark later. Paula began to calm down. FitzPatrick gave them both a big smile and dashed off.

The Hagemeyers got out of the pickup and asked one of the firefighters, Avila, which one was in charge.

"That's our IC, the guy in the red hat," Avila said, pointing out Daniels. The Hagemeyers walked up to him.

"We're civilians," the Hagemeyers said. "We have no clothing. We don't know what to do."

"Just don't panic," Daniels replied, but he offered nothing in the way of further advice or protective clothing. Daniels was holding on to a radio as if it were a lifeline, the Hagemeyers noted.

Why is everybody spread out? the Hagemeyers wondered. Why aren't we all together in case something goes wrong? As they walked back to their pickup, they again encountered Avila.

"Does that guy know what he's doing?" Paula asked, motioning toward Daniels. Avila offered no reply.

"Honey, we're on our own here," Paula said.

Bruce scrounged in the pickup and found an old canvas work jacket and long pants for himself. Paula put on sleek cycling pants and a polar fleece jacket, anything to cover bare skin. They had no gloves, but in an inspired moment Paula grabbed a gallon of water, a towel, and a leather backpack, not knowing exactly what use she might make of them. Nobody paid them the slightest attention.

CHAPTER TEN

Things looked bad. I slipped into my tent and strapped on my gun. As I stepped out a red glow was already lighting the sky. Stepping before the men I delivered an ultimatum with outward confidence. "We'll stay by this creek and live to tell about it. I'll see you through. Every man hold out some grub, a blanket, and a tool." The men did not hesitate.

—Joseph B. Halm, forest ranger, recounting how he saved his fire crew during the Big Blowup of 1910

Taylor walked away from the Hagemeyers and their pickup with his mind racing. The news they had brought that the road dead-ended changed everything. If he had been aware of the situation earlier, Taylor later came to believe, he never would have allowed his squad to reengage the fire. As he marched down the road heading for Daniels, Craven swung in beside him, and they approached Daniels together.

"We're trapped here. Let's get some saws out and see what we can do," Taylor said. They could clear trees and brush on the far bank of the river, he told Daniels, and take down a small stand of trees nearby in the rock scree.

"No, it's okay. We'll be fine here," Daniels replied.

"Are you sure?" Taylor said.

"Yes, we're safe here. Stay near the road."

"*Ellreese,*" Taylor said, his voice rising, his finger pointing, "Tom and I have two saws. We could do work here. We could do work there."

The encounter started to draw a crowd. A voice in the background remarked that the sandbar would make a good place to ride out the fire. Taylor replied that the sandbar was too small to hold everyone, and besides it would put them too close to the timber on the far bank of the river. Another voice said why not simply jump in the river and ride out the fire there? Someone else responded that the fire could turn the river to steam and poach them like eggs—unmindful that the water was deep and cold and that the river flowed into the fire, not from it, which meant the river had a constant source of cooling.

Taylor felt lost. Daniels took no part in the group's discussion. "Stay near the road," Daniels said, and then went back to talking on the radio to Jasso. Somebody had to do *something*, Taylor thought. He decided to head up into the scree for a better look at the fire, but as he started for the scree, Craven blocked his path. Craven smiled his trademark grin, ear to ear, but his eyes flashed heat. Craven gathered the lapels of Taylor's fire shirt into his powerful hands, braced him up, and locked eyes. "We're fucked," Craven said, matter-of-factly.

FARTHER DOWN THE canyon, the wind began to rock helicopter 13N with gusts of twenty to forty miles an hour. "The fire was drawing me in," Walters said later, and he was forced to pull back. Unwilling to give up completely, he flew the ship around the edges of the fire where the air was calmer. At one point, he heard Jasso on the radio talking urgently to Daniels, who replied, "We're fine." That remark was followed by an electronic rush as though someone was holding down a transmission button. A moment later Walters heard a voice in the background remark, "We're fucked."

THE ENTIAT HOTSHOTS and the rest of the Northwest Regulars wound up scattered along the road below the fire, from its heel to several miles down the canyon. Away from the fire, the sky was a summery blue. Those who had escaped had trouble believing that their trapped comrades faced mortal danger. "I heard there were people surrounded by fire, but it didn't register that it was my crew," said Tate. Some took photos of the billowing smoke, and others found a patch of shade and hung out. Hinson tried to lighten the mood by remarking that at last they had the big fire they had wanted in the first place. Nobody laughed. The thundering pillar of smoke was a sight to behold, and the realization spread that Daniels and the others might not make it. Hinson joined Watson, and they began to pray for the missing.

Anyone with a radio could track the progress of events, as Daniels and Jasso exchanged remarks. At one point Jasso told Daniels, "You have fire all around you," and Brown threw down his shovel in disgust. "He was pissed about the whole thing," Cannon said later. Brown and Cannon began to pick out the emergency medical technicians from their crew.

BARRY GEORGE, AFTER accepting the license numbers collected by Brown and Cannon, had headed to a staging area several miles below the fire, where contractors had begun to set up portable toilets. George, too, became aware of the entrapment, but he continued work on his analysis for the next stage of the attack. "I felt as though we had a bad situation, but Daniels kept saying they were in a good position," the AFMO told fire investigators later, to explain his continued absence from the scene of the action. George radioed the dispatch office at 4:58 PM and asked if arrangements had been made yet for a fresh team to take over the fire. According to George, he also reported at this time that they "had a predicament starting, but . . . would wait for things to cool down and then would pull everyone out of there." The log notes his question about the fresh team but contains no mention of a "predicament," let alone an entrapment.

"George was putting a bug in our ear and saying, 'Are you guys thinking about [bringing in] a team?'" dispatcher Hutton said later. "And we were already thinking about it. I had no information at this time about an entrapment."

DANIELS AND THE others at the entrapment site, meanwhile, finished the discussion about where to ride out the fire and began to break up.

"Hey, Ellreese, I'm going up in the rocks to get a better look," Taylor called out.

"Okay, but stay close to the road," Daniels replied.

The rock scree, a mishmash of shattered rocks and boulders, offered no easy path. As Taylor picked his way up the scree, he could hear Daniels and Jasso over his radio reassuring each other about the "fine" situation they were in. Things sure didn't feel fine to him, Taylor thought.

Craven, too, put distance between himself and Daniels. His squad was loaded with rookies and teenagers, several of whom were anxious and jittery. It wouldn't take much to trigger a panic and send someone screaming down the road. Craven needed an activity, a focus of attention, to take people's minds off their situation.

Craven was big and strong and safe, a haven in time of trouble. As he started to walk up the road, he attracted people to him like a pied piper, drawing in his wake Emhoff, FitzPatrick, Johnson, Scherzinger, Weaver, and Welch. The group walked about thirty-five yards up the road and then a few steps up into the rock scree, where they settled in a cluster of boulders, out of Daniels's immediate range but not too far away.

Emhoff perched on a boulder with a depression that exactly fit his ample rear end. People "did their own thing," Emhoff said, and stayed or left as they wished. Somebody got a laugh when they mimicked the civilian woman and cried out, "Where's the fire? Where's the fire at?"

"The fire seemed long gone," Welch said later. "You couldn't see it, taste it, or feel it."

Scherzinger asked Craven what they should do if the fire came their way. Craven told him they could go to the sandbar or jump in the river. Something about the answer unsettled Scherzinger, and he turned and made his way back to the road.

As FitzPatrick climbed into the rocks, gaily waving her arms, Clark watched from a few steps behind her. "She turned around and smiled at me, and her face shone like an angel," recalled Clark, who followed her for a few more steps and then, for no particular reason, drifted back to the road.

FitzPatrick shot photos until she ran out of film and asked Welch if she could borrow her camera. Welch, who was too anxious to be taking photographs herself, readily handed it over. Welch's anxiety went up another notch when Johnson remarked to her that they ought to consider deploying fire shelters.

"We should mentally deploy our shelters, go over the whole thing in our heads," Johnson said.

"What!" Welch said with alarm. "We don't have to do that. What are you talking about?"

"Yeah, we might have to," Johnson remarked.

Welch had started to feel freaky the moment that the Hagemeyers passed on the news about the road coming to a dead end. She had walked up and down nervously asking everyone, "What am I supposed to do? Are we going to be okay? It's coming! It's coming!" The only reply was "Be calm, be calm," which made her even more jittery.

When Craven and the others had started to walk up the road, Welch had followed because that was her squad, the people she knew best. But nobody gave her answers. Nobody called a play. Johnson's remark about getting ready to use fire shelters was unnerving. The shelters are supposed to be used only as a last resort in times of greatest peril. Emhoff called her over to his rock and tried to calm her down, but she couldn't sit still. After a minute she turned and took about ten steps from the boulders back to the road—a distance of thirty feet by later measurements. The road was the place for her, she figured, close to Daniels, the designated leader. "It was instinct, just instinct" that drove her from the rocks, she said later.

Craven told those who remained—Emhoff, FitzPatrick, Johnson, and Weaver—to settle down and focus on what the fire was doing. Weaver, the physics buff, asked Craven if he could explain the fire's explosive behavior, and Craven gave it a try. The fire's move trapping the crew had surprised everyone, and is still studied and debated to this day. There is general agreement among the experts that the trap was sprung by an offshoot or smaller arm of the fire that worked its way up the canyon bottom, while the main arm of the fire went up the south canyon wall. It's indisputable that the smaller arm made a sudden leap across the road. But there is no consensus about how and why this happened. Was there a "mass ignition," a complex and rare event that would help excuse everyone's failure to see what was coming? Did flames from a crown fire bend over the road? Did fire ignite simultaneously on both sides of the road, when embers fell like rain? Or some combination of those elements?

No matter how it happened, after the flames crossed the road they settled down and burned steadily, in a stand of timber shaped like a mixing bowl on the north side of the road. At first the bowl kept the flames from spreading up the canyon, which helps explain why the fire did not immediately chase the retreating firefighters up the road. The mixing bowl effect, however, sent embers sailing up into the rock scree, where fresh fires sprang up in duff, brush, and scattered trees. The sight of flames apparently springing out of rocks was hidden from the trapped crew, by now far up the canyon. If they had realized early on that the fire could get above them, ignite in the duff in the scree, and in effect surround them, they might well have done more to prepare for its arrival.

The main body of fire progressed along the bottom of the canyon at a stately pace of a mile to a mile and a half an hour and made faster runs up the canyon's south wall. In places flames reached to the ridge top. This was the fire visible on the opposite canyon wall to Taylor and the others when they arrived at the entrapment site. It sent aloft a thickening plume of smoke and debris, as different from a smoke column as a tornado is from a dust devil. A smoke plume can draw aloft everything from smoke to entire flaming logs. A twisting coil of smoke and fire can rise tens of thousands of feet until it becomes "buoyantly stable" and hovers overhead in brief equilibrium, like impending doom. If the plume becomes big enough, it creates its own weather. Air is sucked in from the bottom, compressed inside the plume, and then shoots up the core of the plume in the same way that exhaust shoots out of a jet engine. A cumulus, or more appropriately, "pyrocumulus," cloud forms atop the plume, in the anvil shape familiar from thunderstorms. If the plume holds enough moisture, it can form rain or hail or a mixture of both. A plume extending far enough into the upper atmosphere, with its freezing temperatures, can actually form an ice cap.

As the fire dies down, the plume cools and sheer weight takes over, and then the whole thing collapses. The effect is similar to a downburst in a thunderstorm and can be spectacular, and potentially deadly, in its effects. When Delta Airlines Flight 191 flew into a thunderstorm in 1985 while on approach to the Dallas/Fort Worth International Airport, a sudden downburst drove the airplane into the ground, killing 136 passengers and crew and one person on the ground. There is no record of a smoke plume causing a similar disaster. But in 1990, a thunderstorm over the Dude Fire in central Arizona created a sudden and dramatic downburst. Blasts of wind sent flames racing in unpredictable patterns, a Forest Service analysis later concluded, trapping eleven firefighters and killing six of them.

When the smoke plume first appeared over the Thirtymile Fire, it was a positive development. The phenomenon helped draw flames up the far side of the canyon and away from the firefighters, and became a principal reason that everyone, with varying degrees of confidence, thought that the fire was going to pass by harmlessly. "I've been in some hairy situations before, and we're going to get out of this," Daniels told the crew at the entrapment site at one point, recounting how he had survived the famed Yellowstone Fires of 1988.

Rutman, for one, was not completely reassured. He had not been around long enough to be part of a group or "comfort clique," and so he stayed close to Daniels. Deeply uneasy, however, he pulled out his journal and began to write in large, hurried letters, no more than a couple of sentences to a page.

> *Blackened pine and fir needles are falling on our heads. We've been cut off from our escape road, backed into a dead-end road (needles and ash are bouncing off my shirt, off this notebook).*
>
> *The roar of the fire is getting louder, louder. The column twisting, several fires joined, it sounds like a tidal wave is coming our way. The sun is a bloody red, the smoke dark and high. The falling needles sound like hail on a cold Northwest morning. The wind rips through the canyon. I watch the top of the trees swaying violently from the high winds that the fire is creating. It's changing and twisting all around us.*
>
> *The beach and the creek are our last stand: we may be jumping in soon.*

Rutman's note jotting was interrupted when Daniels shouted to someone, apparently Taylor, to come out of the rocks. Taylor stayed where he was. If Taylor had been one of the rookies, Rutman thought, Daniels would have made the order stick. But Taylor was a squad boss "so you don't yell at him or order him around."

Taylor said later that he never heard Daniels call to him, though he acknowledged it could have happened. Daniels's voice might not have carried the distance; he had a soft voice, and the fire was roaring. After Taylor climbed into the scree, he had had only one direct contact with the others, when Avila had climbed up and joined him.

"Thom, I'm scared," said Avila, his face pale and strained. "I don't know what we should do."

Taylor said something reassuring.

Avila asked if Taylor planned to deploy his fire shelter where he was, in the scree. Taylor wasn't comfortable with the idea, though fire manuals recommend rockfalls as possible deployment sites. In the Mann Gulch Fire of 1949, one of the most famous wildland fires in history, two smoke jumpers in jeans and cotton shirts raced up the side of the gulch and then took shelter in a rockslide, on the far side of the gulch, as flames crossed the ridgetop and then flapped around them. They survived while thirteen others perished. Taylor worried, however, that the rock scree would make it difficult to seal the shelter, which has no floor, to the ground.

"You can stay in the rocks with me, or you can go to the road," Taylor told Avila. "Do what you want."

Avila turned for the road.

Taylor was left alone to watch the oncoming fire. The canyon bottom had become an angry sea of smoke, heaving and rolling. Here and there the smoke parted and disclosed writhing flames. Just downriver, the wisps of smoke in the tunnel-like opening above river and road had turned heavy and gray-black.

Something made Taylor turn his head and look up the canyon wall. Just above him in the scree was a spot fire: one little puffer. Then another and another broke out, and he realized that the fire was surrounding him, and there was nothing he could do to stop it.

On the roadway below, Rutman scribbled:

> *I hear a chopper, or is that just the roar of the fire rapidly coming upon us. It's changing, rolling, screaming!*
> *I feel the heat. I smell the smoke. The sun is free of the tall column, sending dusty rays our way through the haze. Its close now, its close now!!!*

Craven's squad huddled among the boulders just off the road. Fitz-Patrick, alternately gay and emotionally spent, sank down beside Emhoff and gripped one of his sturdy thighs. "She was starting to freak out," Emhoff recalled, "but she wasn't screaming. Just really, really worried." He put an arm around her shoulder and gave her a rub, and it seemed to settle her down.

Weaver had his camera out. He shot a photo as a shower of embers blew toward him across the scree. The sky became a velvet backdrop for red, purple, and golden spots of fire, which seemed to sparkle with celestial intensity. The embers hung in suspended animation during lulls, then swirled on fresh blasts of wind, and then became fixed again on the next lull, as though someone was turning a gigantic kaleidoscope. Johnson stared transfixed by the sight of the embers as Weaver's camera flashed behind her. In one photo Johnson, her hands at her sides, faces the ember storm with apparent composure. The flash illuminates a bush directly in front of her and makes the green leaves sparkle; just beyond the bush are scarlet specks, the coming fire, easily mistaken for red leaves from the bush. In another shot, Johnson has moved a hand to protect her face.

The main body of fire had marched steadily up the canyon bottom until it reached a massive rock slump a half mile below the entrapment site. Blocked by the slump, the fire churned at its foot, eventually reducing entire trees to white ash. The rock slump had formed thousands of years earlier when the last of glacial ice melted and the canyon walls, compressed like a spring by the enormous pressure of the ice, were suddenly released. The walls snapped back in a process called "isostatic rebound," which caused huge blocks of stone to split off from the canyon wall like a calving glacier and slough to the canyon bottom. The falling rock came to rest in a slump in the bottom of the canyon eight hundred to a thousand feet long—the length of three football fields at its longest point. Over the millennia the slump had become covered with lichens but almost no other vegetation, which meant that there was no ready place for flames to take hold. Runoff and melting ice had eroded a channel through the slump, and that channel had become the Chewuch River.

In theory, the slump was too long to be crossed by unsupported flames. Safe separation from a fire is often estimated at four times the length of flames, which in this case was at most two hundred feet. Even the shortest stretch of the rock slump at eight hundred feet was four times the length of those flames and should have provided an effective buffer. The fire could have curled around the slump, in scattered timber and brush, and almost certainly did so. But that was a slow process. The slump should have stopped any swift advance by the main body of fire, and it did not.

One possible explanation is that the fire churning at the foot of the slump preheated the air above the slump and created unsettling winds. Waves of embers cascading over the slump provided the physical equivalent of a fuel source for the advance of flames. An oscillating wave of embers and superheated air then may have defied the basic physical law that hot air rises and instead, propelled by an up-canyon surge of energy—a combination of wind and heat—stretched horizontally the full length of the slump. As it turned out, flames did pass over the rock slump and surge into the timber directly ahead, setting off a string of spot fires. From the point of view of the trapped firefighters, the flames appeared instantaneously, and with a power no one had imagined possible.

Jasso, flying in circles above the fire, had taken out a camera when Daniels told him two civilians had turned up at the entrapment site out of nowhere. Jasso shot photos as the expanding fire forced him to fly wider and wider circles. Smoke thick as fleece blanketed the canyon and swept upward in a plume. Ahead of the smoke a walking barrage of spot fires advanced step by inexorable step.

Meanwhile, the smaller arm of the fire had escaped the mixing bowl and sent up its own smoke column, though it lacked the heft of a fully developed smoke plume. That's where real trouble lies, Jasso thought. He watched in horror as the smaller column bent over and began to roll toward the entrapment site.

"The column's coming down," Jasso called to Daniels.

"I see it. It's just above us," Daniels replied.

Spot fires flashed in the rock scree high above the road, and as the two arms of the fire drew together, flames appeared to be everywhere. Rutman described the moment:

> Rolling right by us now, just across the little creek, the creek that may end up saving our lives.

Here it comes. Again the sun is covered, bright orange, then yellow, then red.

There is a strange calm, coolness in the air amongst the crew. For the first time, we can see the flames. It's licking, its rolling, its alive, its screaming at us!!!

There's a spot fire in the rock scree, just above us.

And now it's gray, here comes the flame again. It's snowing.

Rutman dropped his journal and began frantically to swat embers from his neck and hair.

Taylor, in his exposed position in the scree, may have been the first to take decisive action. "You look up and see two separate columns," Taylor said years later, standing in the same spot where he had stood that day. "Starting to get pretty hot. It's pretty much pitch-black, hot, pretty good wind bursts coming up the drainage."

Flaming needles rained down. A cluster of trees in the scree erupted in flames. Swirling embers the size of baseballs made fat blobs of illumination in the enveloping darkness.

Taylor broke for the road, mindful that one false step would end his race. The temperature ratcheted upward. Embers slipped down his shirt. He flipped down a cloth shroud from inside the back of his helmet to stop embers from scorching his face and neck. He would be clear of the rocks in a few steps, and then he'd confront choices: whether to jump straight in the river or to deploy a fire shelter on the sandbank or on the road. He was a couple of steps from the road when an invisible wave of heat slammed his chest. The next thing he knew he was on his back like a bug with his legs kicking air.

Taylor struggled to his feet, but going on, he thought, would be like walking into a shotgun blast. As he turned back up the scree, the temperature rose in pulses as the invisible wave of heat pursued him. He had a lead of a few steps, and he drove his legs until the muscles burned. But where was he racing to? he wondered. The very rocks seemed to be aflame, as duff in the rock crevices ignited. Taylor fell to his knees and hunkered into a ball, but it was no protection. The heat rose without mercy.

He yanked out his fire shelter and was spared having to shake it open when the wind nearly tore it out of his hands. As he struggled to climb inside the shelter, he looked under the crook of his arm, and there, racing up from below, he saw Craven and four or five others.

"Deploy! Deploy!" Taylor screamed.

"Deploy? Deploy!" they shouted back, as though it were both a question and an answer.

Craven's group came to a halt in the slightest of depressions, about twenty feet across, in the midst of jagged rocks not big enough to offer real protection. They bunched up in a horizontal line, just below and slightly up-canyon from Taylor. He could make out five of them now, almost in a row, side by side, all madly struggling with their fire shelters.

Taylor pulled down the side of his shelter like a closing curtain. I can't believe this, he thought. I can't believe I'm in this shelter. I can't believe any of this is happening.

He was close enough to the others to hear their heavy breathing. Someone screamed. Someone recited the Lord's Prayer. Someone cried out, "I'm burning!"

When the wave of superheated air had vaulted the rock slump in the canyon bottom, the bulk of it had continued on up the canyon, as everyone had expected. A small portion of the fire, however, had separated from the main body, made a left hook, and headed straight for the entrapment site. The Chewuch River canyon was burning out, wall to wall, just as it had in the past.

On the road, the fire's sudden moves caught everyone off guard. Daniels told people to take out their shelters and use them as shields. "A few of you, get out your shelters and cover your buddies," Daniels was heard to say. At least one crew member recalled hearing Daniels use the word *deploy*. Then other voices cried out, "Deploy! Deploy!"

"All hell broke loose," Daniels recalled later. "People deployed their shelters, I was telling people to stay calm, and they were deploying their shelters, and I was talking to Gabe. Then I could hear people screaming, 'I'm being burned!'"

Circling above, Jasso called in news of the entrapment to the dispatch office. Sensing the importance of the moment, he asked the dispatcher for the exact time: it was 5:24 PM, exactly fifty minutes after he had reported "crews moving down road . . . fire crossed road"—and virtually the same moment when Kathie FitzPatrick in Yakima was try-ing to reach Karen by cell phone and Tom Leuschen in Twisp was leav-ing his office for home. The log notes the 5:24 message, with a note of reassurance: "Danials [*sic*] and crew deployed shelters—everybody fine—going back to air ground."

Afterward, Jasso said Daniels had "sounded apologetic" when he told him shelters had been deployed, as though "we didn't want to, we had to." Daniels at this time was on the road with nine other people: the Hagemeyers, Avila, Clark, Dreis, Hurd, Rutman, Scherzinger, and Welch.

Clark saw people around him getting into their shelters and took the cue. "There was no instruction about what to do," Clark said. "Some-body yelled, 'Deploy!' and I tossed my pack and got into my shelter."

"You all right?" Dreis called from the shelter next to Clark's.

"I feel like a baked potato wrapped in tinfoil," Clark yelled back, and they both barked laughter at the oldest fire shelter joke of all.

A firebrand whacked the side of Clark's shelter with enough force to knock off his hard hat, inside the shelter. Clark gritted his teeth. Orange light peeped through pinholes in the fold lines of his shelter. He drew scant comfort from having been told during training exercises that pinholes in fire shelters were normal and not a cause for worry. Inside a shelter during a burnover, pinholes were terrifying.

Avila, Scherzinger, and Hurd huddled inside the shelters they had set up in the roadway; Avila had been among the first to deploy. The wind blew so hard that Scherzinger had to try three times before he made it under his. Once inside, he held down the sides of the shelter with all his might to keep the wind from tearing it away. Hurd had so much trouble getting into her shelter that she lost track of time. She thought she was under the shelter for four or five minutes, though the deployment was many times longer. She kept up her spirits by yelling to the others.

As Rutman fumbled for his shelter, he thought, I'm going to be one of those who gets a shelter out because if I don't I'm dead. Rutman kept his backpack on, contrary to safety training: A backpack can protect a firefighter's back during a burnover, but backpacks often contain fusees, the firefighter's tool for igniting fire. (Rutman's pack did contain fusees.)

If the fusees ignite while the backpack is on, they can melt the pack and the firefighter's shirt down to bare skin. Wearing a backpack also makes it clumsy to get inside a shelter, as Rutman was about to discover. He could not fully extend his shelter, and at six feet two inches tall he needed every inch of that shelter. He rolled on the ground trying to kick the thing open, knowing that if he tore the fabric he was finished.

Finally, he was inside. Just before he pulled down the sides of the shelter, Rutman took time for one more photograph. He pointed the camera at the far bank of the river where a pocket of flame, red at the edges and white-orange at the center, was framed by dark, unburned trees. The framing is oval-shaped, and it doesn't take much imagination to see in the image an open throat uttering a fiery scream.

Rutman tucked down the shelter sides and told himself, It's not going to get better from here on. A blast of heat set his shelter rattling. His lungs burned; his head spun dizzily.

Oh God, this is how you die, he thought. I can't believe this is happening. I can't believe we're in these shelters. This is going to be hard for my dad and mom. She just lost her mother, and now she's going to lose me.

He felt Death approaching, and he began silently to talk to it, aware that he was screaming out loud at the same time. *What are you doing here, Death? You're not supposed to be here. I'm not ready for this. I have things I'm supposed to do with my life.*

Rutman hoped for one of those white light experiences, a beckoning illumination calling him home, but this was not to be. He stopped screaming when he finally ran out of oxygen. Desperate for a breath, he put his lips to the earth and drew stabbing sips of air. He quickly exhausted the paper-thin layer of oxygen at ground level and shoved his face into the dirt. Deeper, he thought, I must go deeper. He took a Leatherman tool from a holder on his belt and began stabbing the dirt with the pliers end of it. He hacked, took a breath, and hacked again, wishing he had spent the money for the heavier, top-of-the-line model. The work was slow and frustrating, but after a while he realized that he no longer was conversing with Death.

The Hagemeyers, who were standing near Daniels, were dumbstruck when they heard Daniels call out, "Get out your bandannas, if you have them. Get out your shelters!" They weren't exactly sure what a shelter was. Daniels seemed calm, so maybe he was going to hand out shelters or something. Daniels, though, was obviously fully occupied in getting out his own shelter.

The Hagemeyers screamed for help.

Glowing needles whirled past them. Welch, who was near Daniels and the Hagemeyers, thought it must be raining. This is awesome, she thought. We're going to get an afternoon shower, and this will be over. Her mistake became clear to her when flaming debris banged against her hard hat.

Welch knelt at the side of the road and groped behind her in her backpack for her fire shelter. She couldn't reach it, but she didn't panic. She had turned calm the moment she heard the word *deploy*—someone at last had given an order, and she knew how to follow orders. She called to Daniels, "Can you get my shelter?" and he came over and helped her take it out. Then she shrugged off her backpack and let it go—and somehow dropped it right on her feet. Still acting with deliberation, she kicked away the backpack, pulled on her gloves, and shook open the fire shelter.

Next to her the Hagemeyers screamed and swatted embers as though under attack by hornets. Daniels called out, "Wipe the ash off their legs so they don't catch fire." In despair the Hagemeyers turned to Welch.

"You've got to help us!" Paula called out. "Nobody else is going to help us."

Who are you? Welch thought. Why should I help you?

Welch got inside her shelter and curled up with her face in the dirt for the oxygen. The shelters, designed for one person, have successfully protected two people during burnovers on several occasions in the past, though it's rare and does not always work. In at least one case and possibly two during the South Canyon Fire, two firefighters tried to use the same shelter, though they perished. Never in recorded history had three people survived a burnover under the same shelter.

The Hagemeyers had no more options. Flames were erupting on the far bank of the river. Smoke, noise, and heat mounted past the point of mental endurance. "Somebody help us!" Paula wailed, but the fire's roar drowned out her cry. The Hagemeyers dove for Welch's shelter.

"We have to share this with you," Paula said as they began to crawl inside with her. According to Paula, Welch gave them a dirty look as they struggled in. "We did what was instinctive," Paula said later. "Every firefighter was under their shelter. We were pretty much on our own. We dove for whatever was available."

Welch was strong enough to have kicked them both out, and she later acknowledged that she was not overjoyed to see them. But she decided that the three of them would make it through together, or they would not make it together. "All or nothing," she said later. "I was the last resort. Nobody else would help them. People later came up and apologized for not putting one of them in their shelter."

Amazingly, the Hagemeyers found they could huddle at one end of the shelter and everyone was covered. Welch claimed afterward that she was not touching the Hagemeyers, and even drew a stick-figure picture to show how it was done: Welch was scrunched in the shelter's upper-right-hand corner and the Hagemeyers were together at the bottom.

At the time, Welch told the couple to stay calm and hold down the shelter sides. Then there was a ripping noise.

"Do you have to pull down so hard?" Welch yelled.

"We're not! We're not!" the Hagemeyers chorused.

Welch had set her shelter in a brush patch next to the road, and the brush had promptly caught fire. Flames slipped under the sides of the shelter. Paula pulled out the towel she had had the foresight to bring and slapped out the flames.

Welch, who by now had her yellow fire shirt over her mouth as a filter, was able to breathe. But the Hagemeyers kept raising their heads and quickly ran short of air. Paula had put on an allergy mask and could breathe more easily than Bruce, who tried to use his canvas jacket as a smoke mask, while holding down the shelter side at the same time.

Paula told herself, We are not going to die like this. We have animals at home, two dogs and a cat. There are animals waiting for us.

"What should we do?" Paula asked. "What are we going to do? How long do we have to stay in here?"

"You've got to stop talking and get down low in the dirt," Welch told them. She started the Lord's Prayer, and Paula, a Roman Catholic, joined in.

The shelter filled with sooty smoke, and the heat became almost too much to bear. Welch felt a burning sensation on her right side as the rubber middle layer of her belt melted, and she shifted her body around, no mean feat in the cramped space. "I was praying the whole time," she said later. "I was praying *I would pass out before I burned*, before I felt anything."

Bruce felt intense heat on his backside and lower body. The soles of his tennis shoes began to scorch. In desperation he scuttled forward and lifted up the side of the shelter, trying to get out. The outer world was a nightmare of coal-black smoke and liquid orange flame.

"Don't get out! Don't!" both women screamed.

Bruce pulled the shelter side back down and struggled to regain his self-control. He turned his mind to his Buddhist training and concentrated his thoughts on the present moment and what would naturally come next. Meditation was like life, he was fond of saying; you simply took things a step at a time. The next inevitable thing to happen, he figured, was his own death. After all, it wasn't as though death was a now-or-never thing; it was going to happen sometime. His time had come. The reflection brought him a kind of peace, and he settled down and did not try to raise the shelter flap again.

IN HIS FIRE shelter up in the rock scree, Taylor felt a searing pain in his rear end and his left elbow. He was under the shelter in the fetal position, with his feet pointed toward the flames. The shelter was fresh out of its plastic wrapper, but bright orange light came through pinholes in the fabric. That wasn't his biggest worry. His fear about getting a seal between his shelter and the rocks unfortunately had proved well founded. Waves of heat came into the shelter, though he was trying to hold down the sides of it with both his hands and his elbows.

Taylor had no idea how much time had passed. Time was being measured now not in minutes or seconds but in racing heartbeats, rasping breaths, and prolonged screams. Maybe one minute had gone by, maybe more, before his shelter began to disintegrate. As the inside layer of the shelter started to flake off, the interior gradually grew brighter. Woody debris under his body ignited. Even with his nose down low,

Taylor's lungs throbbed with pain; he could not seem to draw a full breath. It came to him that he no longer heard screaming.

I just heard them burn to death, Taylor thought. And I'm next. I am not going to die like this. I am not going to die in the rocks—I am going to die trying to get out of the rocks!

He took a breath, figuring it was his last, and in a single motion he threw the shelter off and rose to his feet. He entered a furnace of Halloween horrors, of black smoke, scarlet-orange flames, and bellowing winds. In a miracle of good timing, just as he stood up there was a pause between waves of superheated air. He took a giant step Superman-fashion, half flying through the air, and his boot landed with a thud that knocked the wind out of him. By lucky chance he had landed on a flattish rock and was able to keep his balance. He recovered and took another giant leap, and landed on another rock with another painful "umph." But this time he never paused, and he never slowed, and he never looked back until he hit the road.

The air was clearer down this low, and he could make out the white van. Next to it was a red plastic gasoline container, swollen by the heat into the shape of a fat, evil pumpkin. He grabbed the thing and sent it flying, then jumped over a log and threw himself into the river. He came up shocked from the cold water—his lungs bursting for air—and drew an enormous breath, and if in that moment the heat wave had dipped down to water level it would have killed him. Superheated air would have entered his throat and nasal passages, seared the delicate tissues down to his Adam's apple, and he would never have taken another breath. Instead, he gulped from the layer of sweet, cool air just above the surface of the water.

Oh my God, Taylor thought, I've fucking made it. I was going to die, and then I was going to die trying, and now here I am. The next ten minutes, he said later, were the happiest of his life.

CHAPTER ELEVEN

The Lord was good to me. He put wings on my feet and I ran like hell.

—Walter Rumsey, survivor of the 1949 Mann Gulch Fire

It was a pretty neat sight, thought Emhoff from his perch on the boulder. You couldn't see much flame on the far side of the canyon because of the trees and smoke; the fire was putting up a good, thick column. Every now and then, though, the smoke parted up on the far canyon wall, and you had a real good picture of a bunch of trees torching. There was a smaller column of smoke on the near side of the canyon, but it wasn't doing much. You could sit there and watch the two smoke columns grow darker and more intense. That was pretty neat.

He and Craven had talked it over and figured the fire would creep past them. When the fire arrived, though, things were going to get pretty tense. They had a couple of options. If flames crossed to their side of the river, they could go farther up in the scree. If flames somehow circled behind them they could head for the road. The scree wasn't the perfect place in the world to be, but there was plenty of room to dodge around. Folks were getting a little freaky—not screaming, just tightening up.

"Don't worry, be calm," Craven had told everyone. "Do I look scared? When I'm scared, then you can be scared." Emhoff had trusted Craven from the first time he met him, which is why he had followed him into the rocks. Now he and Craven worked as a team to steady the others.

While Craven explained fire behavior to Weaver, Emhoff thought he would lighten the mood—by tossing his jacket over Johnson's head, just for laughs. Rubbing FitzPatrick's arm had stopped her chattering, but it hadn't drawn off the tension. She had a vise grip on his leg.

The fire was going to make a spectacular sight as it passed by, Emhoff thought. The sky was dark enough that embers and flames would show up brilliantly against it. They would take some heat, but there was no need to move, at least not yet.

Then everything seemed to stop. A hush fell on the canyon. The darkness became almost liquid, and the air drew back like a wave gathering strength. Sudden gusts of wind broke the stillness. Then out of the darkness a vanguard of embers in purple, orange, and pink swept prettily across the river. A shimmering wall of flame arose above the trees along the far riverbank and sent big chunks of fire whirling across the river and into the scree.

"Hey, what's going on?" somebody asked. "Are we going to be all right?" Emhoff and the others swatted bits of flaming debris off their shirts and pants, and off each other.

Farther down the canyon, flames began to roll in the tunnel of air above road and river. Emhoff thought it couldn't be a true horizontal vortex, thank God, because those things had trees flying around in them. It looked, though, like a clothes dryer or cement mixer gone crazy.

A rash of spot fires ignited across the scree; the fire was here, not safely across the river. The fire was everywhere. They could hunker down and take it, Emhoff figured, or they could get moving. The time had come. Nobody gave an order, but Emhoff, Craven, FitzPatrick, Johnson, and Weaver arose as one.

They had barely gotten to their feet when they were slammed by a blast of heat, as though from an open furnace. The road, a mere ten strides away, might as well have been a mile off. They turned and began to scramble up the scree. Emhoff put both hands on FitzPatrick's rump and shoved her forward, but nobody needed urging. They stumbled and scrambled with furious determination, using their hands as well as their feet.

"Deploy! Deploy!" Taylor screamed at them from above.

"What's going on?" Craven shouted.

"We need to deploy!" someone yelled.

The five of them came to a halt in a horizontal line, about a hundred feet up the scree and about twenty-five feet in elevation above the road. Hot ash and embers swirled in the darkness around them, but there were no flames, not yet. The heat was not unbearable.

Emhoff's boot slipped on a rock and hit something soft.

"Hey, my head! Who kicked me?" yelled Johnson.

"I did," Emhoff said, and they broke into high-pitched giggles.

The leading edge of the heat wave flashed over them, and the temperature soared. People yelled, "Deploy! Deploy!" but the wind scrambled their words. Even so, everyone reached for a shelter. Emhoff thought: Why am I doing this? This isn't a blue practice shelter; this is a real silver one, and I'm getting into it. Something isn't right here.

Emhoff fought the wind as he tried to shake out his shelter. He was slightly above the others, and by the time he was ready to crawl inside the shelter he could see that they had already deployed their shelters in a neat row. They had done well for their first time out, Emhoff thought with pride. He had a firm grip on his shelter but couldn't get it to seal with the boulders. The lower-right corner of the shelter kept coming up. Chunks of fire the size of coffee cups slipped inside, and he twisted and turned to kick them out.

Then he heard Weaver cry out, "I'm burning!"

Wow, things are not going so great, Emhoff thought. If Weaver's burning, how am I doing?

Embers slipped under his shelter from every side. Emhoff grabbed them bare-handed, and as he lifted the shelter side to throw them out he took a quick glance outside. Four silvery shelters sparkled in a row amid a rippling sea of black smoke and orange flame. Someone screamed. Female voices cried out, "Oh, God—Oh, God, no!" and he heard snatches of the Lord's Prayer. Emhoff yanked the shelter side back down.

The heat would not let up, and he could not let go of the shelter. He refused to think about what was happening to his gloveless hands. When the pain became too much for him to bear, he picked up his elbows and shifted them around but kept a grip on the shelter.

After a minute or so he realized the screaming and praying had stopped, or maybe the roar of the fire had drowned them out. This is way too much to handle, he thought. I might as well close my eyes and take one deep breath. It'll be easy. I can drift off, just like going to sleep. I'll wake up in an hour, and this will all be over. Okay, okay, I know I won't be waking up. But I can tell myself that's what will happen.

Emhoff felt a scorching sensation on his right side. Was the shelter touching his shoulder? Was the shelter breaking up? He couldn't be sure, but something on that side of the shelter wasn't working anymore. And he was running out of oxygen. He closed his eyes and prepared to take that one deep breath. Then he thought: Why am I doing this? I made it this far, to this place. If I did that, I can make it to somewhere else.

Leaving his shelter under these conditions was unthinkable, a violation of the basic dictum that once inside a shelter you stay there until the flames have passed. But it was his only chance. Emhoff jumped to his feet and threw off the shelter. The four shelters below him were silent, but he told himself the people inside them could be perfectly all right—except that he was close to passing out. Maybe they were already unconscious. They had sheltered up before he did, and they had gloves for protection. They could be alive, he told himself. There was no time to kick their shelters to find out, but he couldn't leave without a word.

"I'm getting the hell out of here," he shouted at the shelters.

The heat drove him farther up the scree. He dodged and scrambled, hopping nimbly from one rock to another despite the pain in his hands, until he found a boulder big enough to hide behind. The protection it offered was more psychological than physical: the heat made an oven of the scree, and no place was safe.

Emhoff climbed higher, dodging from rock to rock. Minutes passed. Finally he found himself far enough above the heat blast to have a moment for reflection, and for the first time he could check the damage to his hands. He looked down. His fingers were too long for his hands, he noted; the sight reminded him of melted cheese. His lucky silver bracelet had melted into his wrist, and when he shook his wrist the bracelet didn't budge. Wow, thought Emhoff, that's not cool.

The initial flame front had passed, but another wave of heat was sure to follow. I'm not going to make it here, Emhoff thought. I've got to get off the scree and into some sort of safe place.

He could see the white van, apparently intact, on the road straight down from where he was. There was no obvious safe route down the scree. A flaming log blocked him to the right, a burning patch of trees to the left. He darted back and forth for a few moments and then picked a roundabout path between the burning log and the trees. He was half-way down to the van when he tripped and his sunglasses went flying. He debated for a moment whether to stop and pick them up—they were pretty nice sunglasses, and he had gotten them on sale—but the thought didn't last and he continued on his way. In a random act of sparing, the sunglasses would be found intact after the fire had passed.

Emhoff's race to the road fixed itself in his memory in signpost images. The flaming log. The flying sunglasses. The door of the white van smeared with blood. Patches of blood on his hard hat. And the dizzying realization that all of the blood was his.

He got the van's passenger door open, on the side away from the coming fire, and somehow shrugged off a water pack and radio harness before getting inside. He left the door ajar for air.

The van's not going to explode, he told himself. This isn't the movies where cars explode for no reason. This is the best place for me for a while.

He got his breathing under control. Hyperventilating at this point would not be cool, he told himself. A fresh wave of heat swept over the van and then another, and Emhoff thought each one was the last, and each time another wave followed. Embers slipped through the open van door and landed on his pants, which began to steam.

I'm too tired to wipe my legs off, he thought. I'm going to sit here and keep my hands on my thighs and let the fire do its thing. I'll keep my head still because otherwise I'll get dizzy and pass out. And I'm going to look straight ahead because whatever happens now, no matter what, I am not going to look at myself in the rearview mirror.

CHAPTER TWELVE

> *We were all very anxious about what had happened but were*
> *uncertain as to what the outcome might be. The whole canyon*
> *at this time was just a mass of hot smoldering embers and snag*
> *and brush fires—just a mass of red glow.*
>
> —Lee Thomas, Mendocino National Forest supervisor,
> describing the aftermath of the 1953 Rattlesnake Fire
> that killed fifteen firefighters

Flames swept the entrapment site, scorching and sparing in random fashion. Brush along the river and roadway was left green with a layer of brown at the top. The worst damage to the white van was a melted license plate holder and slightly damaged tail lights. A little foam ball on the radio antenna survived. Grocery receipts on the front seat did not even curl. Up in the rock scree, flames jumped around, charring only one side of a tree or scorching one fallen log and reducing another nearby to white ash. But in the horizontal zone, the slight depression about twenty feet long and five feet high, where Craven's group deployed their shelters, nothing was spared. Temperatures there rose above 1,600 degrees, perhaps in spots close to 2,000 degrees, perhaps for minutes. Granite rocks bleached, snapped, and flaked off, leaving behind a ghostly imprint that would mark the place for years.

A big fire in a narrow canyon, where intensity is magnified, often reaches temperatures in that range, which is the upper limit for wildfire. Entire canyon walls can be bleached. What is extraordinary is that in this case the extreme heat was confined to a well-delineated area of about a hundred feet square, as though a giant blowtorch had been held there and nowhere else. A few feet away temperatures reached to no more than 500 or 600 degrees, later examination and the experience of Jason Emhoff would show, the upper limit at which fire shelters can be effective.

Down on the roadway, Daniels took comfort from hearing people call from shelter to shelter. "We just lay there, and I started talking to Gabe on the radio telling him everything is okay," Daniels said later. "He asked if I had all my folks, and I said yes, everybody's here."

After he first reported the entrapment to the dispatcher at 5:24 PM, Jasso called in regular updates. At 5:26 he reported the fire covered more than a thousand acres and was crowning. At 5:28 he gave a rundown on the scattered firefighters: Daniels and his group had sheltered up; the Entiat Hotshots, the rest of the Northwest Regulars, and the engine crews were out of harm's way; and Barry George was at a campground far down the canyon.

The main body of fire moved off up the canyon, leaving in its wake an echoing stillness. At first, no one trusted the quiet; there had been moments of calm like this before, followed by more waves of fire. This time, though, rays of sunshine penetrated the darkness and danced without flaming heat on the silver sides of the fire shelters. The worst was over. Daniels poked his head out from under his shelter.

A shroud of gray smoke draped the blackened trees and ashy ground. A lingering orange flame or a green bush made a smudge of color here and there on the dismal landscape. Coils of hot smoke arose from smoldering logs. Every now and then a tree cracked with a loud report and thudded down. Daniels called for everyone to get out of their shelters and into the river. Shelters twisted and squirmed as their occupants struggled to emerge, like chrysalises shedding cocoons. "It was like a war scene—everything was smoky, gray, and foggy," said Rutman, who got tangled in the straps of his shelter as he tried to stand up.

The Hagemeyers and Welch emerged from their cramped quarters and drew deep breaths. Paula started to thank Welch for saving their lives but realized the danger was far from over. The acid bite of wood smoke was pervasive.

"Get in! Get in!" Taylor yelled from the river. "Come to the river and bring your shelters."

Paula looked around for someone she could help and saw the struggling Rutman, his face white "as though he had been blown up." Paula made sure Rutman could walk, and then she started for the river. There was one last obstacle, a burning log between the road and river, but someone had thrown a shelter over it as protection. As Paula put her hand down to straddle the log, someone jerked the shelter away and she grabbed live fire. In her shocked state she did not notice that her hand had been seriously burned.

The river felt wonderfully cold, but waves of hot air swirled over the water as in a fevered dream. Welch and others held their shelters over their heads for protection, and in a repeat of the deployment scene the Hagemeyers once again tried to get under Welch's shelter with her. Welch wasn't going to refuse, but she had had enough of togetherness.

"Here, you take my shelter, and I'll go in with someone else," she said.

Fire shelters bobbed in the river like capsized silver boats. Welch didn't have time to count them, and it was impossible to tell who was under each one. She worried about Craven and his little group—had they made it from the rocks into the river?

"Jessica?" she called out. "Jessica!"

Welch felt a surge of relief when a girl's voice answered. If Jessica was in the water, it meant Craven and the others probably were there too. The time had come for Welch to think about herself. In a quiet voice she asked Rutman, who was nearby, "Can I get in with you?"

Rutman lifted his shelter, and Welch slipped under. At first they hugged just to make themselves small, but the water was icy, they were drained of strength, and in a minute they were holding each other for warmth too.

"You know what's good about this?" said Rutman, not one to pass up a captive audience. "Let me tell you about my favorite book." It wasn't a conversational gambit Welch had expected, but she figured anything would be better than thinking about the mess they were in.

Rutman's favorite book, it turned out, told the story of the Shackleton Expedition of 1914–16, one of history's most harrowing cold-weather misadventures. Rutman related how Sir Ernest Shackleton's ship, the

Endurance, had been trapped in Antarctic ice for five months and then crushed. Shackleton had drifted hundreds of miles on ice floes with his men, led a small party in an open boat across eight hundred miles of the world's stormiest ocean, and then trekked overland across daunting terrain to a whaling station—after that, he returned eight hundred miles to rescue the remainder of his party. As Rutman related the tale, he comforted himself with the thought that Shackleton had brought every one of his men home alive. He couldn't finish the story, though, because he began to shake uncontrollably in the first stages of hypothermia—and likely shock.

After a few minutes, Daniels called for a head count. Taylor tried to make one, but some people were sharing shelters and others were moving around, eager for the ordeal to end. "I'm going to a bar and getting a beer now that it's over," someone shouted with glee.

"Shut up!" someone else shouted back.

Some people did not respond when their names were called, and Taylor's numbers came up short. The stay in the water lasted long enough for everyone to get bone-chilling cold. When they finally dragged themselves onto the bank, they wrapped the metal shelters around their shoulders like blankets. "Everything was gone," Hurd said later. The roar of the fire had been replaced by a "crazy quiet," as Taylor remembered it, with billows of smoke deadening sound.

Then an explosion ripped the air.

"Turn your back—there's shrapnel coming!" Taylor shouted.

"Get up in the rocks, get away from it!" Daniels called out.

"Your truck's on fire!" someone yelled at the Hagemeyers.

A tire on the Hagemeyers's pickup had blown up after it was set on fire by a burning bush next to the road. One after another, all four tires exploded. Everyone watched with a mixture of alarm and curiosity as flames swallowed the pickup, the aluminum camper unit melted, and fingers of molten metal spread out on the road.

"Honey," Paula said to Bruce, "we're still on our own here. Look for a place for us to run if we need to get out of here in a hurry."

As if a melting truck weren't enough, a big tree crashed down about this time and landed in the river right where the survivors had been sheltering moments before. One euphoric firefighter cried out that now they had survived everything. "It's over! We're alive! ALIVE!" Others joined the celebration.

"Listen up, people, this is not a party," Daniels said. "We've got a serious situation. I want to see everyone's face. Did anyone get burned?"

"Yeah, I did," Welch responded.

"Are you okay?" Daniels asked.

"Yeah, but I got burned on my right side."

Taylor made another count, this time of faces, but again his number came up short. As the smoke haze thinned, a metallic glitter from the scree caught his eye. He made out a blurry, crumpled mass of metal in the scree and instinctively knew what it meant. But things were happening too fast for him to fully digest. He ignored the heat radiating from the rocks and clambered up the scree, not stopping until he was a few yards below the mass of crumpled metal. From there, he could distinguish four separate bundles of scorched aluminum lined up in a row, almost close enough to be touching.

"Tom!" he cried out. "Tom!"

The bundles lay mute and unmoving. Taylor saw no point in going closer. It wasn't the fierce heat that held him back, though it would keep others out of the rocks for hours, but rather the solemn finality of the scene. He turned and headed back down to the road.

Emhoff, from his seat in the white van, saw Taylor coming down from the rocks and tried to get his attention by shouting. It was like a nightmare, Emhoff said later, where you yell for help and no sound comes out. Somehow, though, he caught Taylor's attention. Taylor came over to the van and told Emhoff he should get out and join the others at the river. But Emhoff thought he meant get *into* the river. Forty-five-degree water would about finish him off, Emhoff figured, and he stayed where he was.

Others began to circle the van and peer in at Emhoff. I'm a fish in a fishbowl, Emhoff thought, and maybe I'm warped, but this is kind of amusing. Emhoff kept his breathing regular, his hands on his thighs, and his eyes straight ahead.

Taylor went to report to Daniels, who was standing on the sandbar clutching his radio. Taylor told Daniels that visual inspection of the crumpled shelters indicated that four people had been lost. Emhoff was in the van and appeared to be severely burned.

Daniels, his voice trembling, radioed Jasso. "Gabe, I am missing four."

Jasso told him not to give up hope and that he should try to reach the four by radio. Jasso then passed on the bad news to the dispatcher and requested an ambulance for the injured. The message "missing 4 people" was logged at 5:48 PM, twenty-four minutes after the first report of shelters being deployed, at 5:24 PM.

Daniels tried again and again to raise Craven over the radio, but there was no answer. He fell sobbing to his knees. "Goddammit, why? Why?" he cried out, and pounded his fists into the sand.

Taylor realized that Daniels shouldn't be talking on the radio in his condition, though someone had to start making calls. "It got pretty ugly," Taylor said later. "Ellreese was a wreck. My radio was wet. I grabbed the radio away from Ellreese—we struggled—and called Marshall Brown." The road from the Lunch Spot to the entrapment site was blocked by fallen, burning timber, but Taylor and Brown agreed that the survivors were in no shape to be using chain saws to clear it. Instead, the hotshots would cut their way in.

Word of Taylor's report about four missing people spread quickly among the survivors at the entrapment site and had a sobering effect. A ring of people gathered around Welch, who started a prayer. "Thank you for letting us survive," she said, and asked God's mercy for those who had not been so lucky.

Thoughts turned to the living. When someone opened the van door to get to Emhoff, smoke puffed out. "When we looked into the van, I could have sworn Jason was on fire because he was smoking," Rutman said later. "We had to fan smoke out of the van. I thought, Who is this guy? He looked like an old man." Emhoff was moved to a more spacious seat in the van, and someone started the engine, which fired up without hesitation, and turned on the air conditioner.

At the Lunch Spot, the hotshots gathered sleeping bags and emergency medical gear in preparation for the trip to the entrapment site. When Brown and Cannon first tried to break through, they were turned back by the heat and the mess on the road. On the second try, Kampen insisted on coming along, though Brown and Cannon tried to keep him back. The exchange became heated. Kampen argued that he was an experienced emergency medical technician, it was his bunch up there, and he was determined to go.

The rescue party, Kampen included, started up the road in Brown's pickup. "I could hear that Ellreese had lost control and knew it was going to be a bad deal," Brown said later. By 5:58 PM Jasso was able to report to the dispatcher that he could see the rescue party "heading that way—very slow." Three minutes later, at 6:01 PM, they were reported to be at the entrapment site assessing the situation.

Kampen hadn't imagined the site to be so far up the road. He looked in on Emhoff, who was the most obviously injured. Without prompting, Emhoff rattled off the answers to the questions usually asked to determine if someone is in deep shock: "My name is Jason Emhoff. It's Tuesday," he said, and so on. One of the hotshots began to work on Emhoff but became unsettled by the sight of his shredded hands and scorched face. "People freaked out," Emhoff said later. "I think I was the most relaxed of anyone." When the hotshot tried to wrap a wet, dirty headband around Emhoff's hands, Emhoff told him to stop. "Your hand is pretty much ruined if they do that," Emhoff said later. The hotshot then settled down and did a proper job, placing gauze between Emhoff's fingers and wrapping his hands in clean bandaging.

Kampen tried to talk to Daniels, but the incident commander was incapable of making a report. Kampen went looking for the squad bosses, Taylor and Craven, and saw Taylor standing in the road.

"You've got four people missing?" Kampen asked Taylor, not realizing that Taylor had been burned.

"No, they're not missing," Taylor replied, solemnly.

"Where are they?"

Taylor pointed up the scree at the crumpled metal.

"Are they alive?"

"No, they're dead."

"Where's Craven?"

Again, Taylor pointed. Kampen grabbed a trauma kit and started up into the rocks but was stopped by the heat. He and Brown then tried to approach the site from a flank, with the same result.

There was little useful to be accomplished at the entrapment site, but the pull of disaster held everyone in check. The horn on the Hagemeyer's truck was stuck and made a constant blare. Paula Hagemeyer's burned hand had begun to throb; she and Bruce repeatedly asked when they were going to get out of there. Others walked around in a daze "like zombies," Kampen said later. Kampen took some photos of the scene, thinking they would aid fire investigators.

Finally Brown said, "We need to leave now," and the trance was broken. As survivors filed into the white van, Taylor took a last glance around. There's nothing in this drainage worth any of this, he said to himself.

Taylor wanted to drive, but his buttock had been scorched and he couldn't sit comfortably in the driver's seat. A young firefighter took the wheel and gunned the engine, frantic to get away. Smoke obscured the roadway. More trees had fallen across the road. The van raced on a slalom course around big trees and over small ones, lurching from side to side.

"Slow down," said Daniels, in a lucid moment. "There's no hurry."

The van came under control. Inside, it was quiet except for stifled sobs. People offered each other comfort as best they could: Avila held Paula Hagemeyer's hand; Bruce turned in his seat and touched Welch— she was tending Emhoff.

Then in a moment everything changed. The air cleared, trees turned from black to green, and glinting sunlight replaced the darkness. The intense heat faded into memory, and instead of acrid smoke, a warm breeze with the smell of summer blew over the van. Wow, thought Emhoff, I've been looking for this for a while. The van pulled to a stop below the fire, where the lucky ones had gathered, and the survivors piled out, to be met with hugs and tears.

"Did you guys know we had to deploy?" Rutman asked.

"We thought you were all dead," someone answered.

Rutman, Welch, and others got out of their wet clothes and scrounged dry ones. The adrenaline rush was long gone, and everyone had the shakes. Rutman asked if anyone had seen Jessica Johnson. He had been with Welch when she called out Jessica's name and a woman's voice answered. So where was Jessica?

"I was having convulsions and started crying," Rutman said later. "We had been through hell; everyone was breaking down. They didn't know what to do with us. It was hours before we got out of there."

Welch put on dry shorts and a sweatshirt and found a place to go to the bathroom. Then she sat in the road wrapped in a sleeping bag. Word of her exploit in saving the Hagemeyers began to circulate, and Kampen came by, congratulated her, and asked if she was okay. Welch couldn't stop crying.

Kampen questioned Taylor and some of the others and made yet another head count. Then he called for everyone to listen up. "There was no easy way to say it," Kampen said later. There were four dead, the Naches four, and Kampen read out the names: Tom Craven, Karen FitzPatrick, Jessica Johnson, and Devin Weaver. The voice answering for Jessica had been one of the other women.

Fire investigators were on their way to the scene, Kampen said, but it would be a long time before they arrived. He handed out pens and paper and told everyone to use the intervening time to write down their account of events, while memories were fresh. Avila wrote, "Fourteen of us deployed. Four didn't make it."

The injured were given attention. Emhoff was put aboard helicopter 13N and flown to the operations base at the Eightmile Ranch, where a medical evacuation helicopter picked him up for a flight to Harborview Medical Center in Seattle. Once he arrived there, doctors started what would become a monthslong series of treatments and operations to try to save his hands.

Scherzinger and Welch, who had the least serious injuries, were taken to Dr. Ann Diamond's clinic in Winthrop, treated for second-degree burns, and released. Taylor and Paula Hagemeyer, whose burns were more serious, were driven to a hospital in Brewster, where Hagemeyer was treated for smoke inhalation and the burn on her hand and then released. The burn on Taylor's buttock had formed a blister the size of a saucer. He was treated for second- and third-degree burns and smoke inhalation and kept at the hospital overnight.

It was growing dark by the time the rest of the survivors were taken from the canyon to Winthrop, where they assembled at the North Cascades Smokejumper Base. The base manager, Dickenson, called in a cook and set up the mess hall. "They could have had anything they wanted," Dickenson said. But they opted for take-out pizza and a motel for the night.

THE THIRTYMILE FIRE was the worst loss of life for wildland fire-fighters since the fourteen deaths on Storm King Mountain on July 6, 1994, seven years earlier almost to the day. The Thirtymile Fire grew in less than a day from a backcountry smoke into a towering spectacle with fatal powers. Once flames passed the entrapment site, they burned into a stand of heavy timber up-canyon. The most violent action of the fire occurred there, in the stretch from just above the entrapment site to the Thirtymile Campground. The smaller arm of the fire, which was lying nearly horizontal when it passed over the entrapment site, then went vertical and created a second smoke plume alongside the already existing plume, with each plume spinning tornadolike in the opposite direction. A double fire plume of counter-rotating vortices, as the phenomenon is called, is known for its destructive powers—imagine the consequences of two tornadoes with counterwinds sweeping along side by side. The double fire plume tossed trees about like pickup sticks and flattened whole swaths of timber.

The fire roared on, swept the Thirtymile Campground, gutted the parked vehicles there, and then burned into the Pasayten Wilderness. Over the next two weeks, the fire would draw in more than a thousand firefighters, dozens of helicopters, engines, bulldozers, and water tenders. By the time it was declared 100 percent contained on July 23, almost two weeks after it started, it had scorched 9,324 acres and cost $4.5 million to suppress. The Libby South Fire, which had been considered the big fire, was contained a week earlier, on July 16, with less acreage burned, 3,830 acres. It cost slightly more to fight the Libby South Fire—$4.8 million compared to $4.5 million—because more aircraft were used, to protect homes.

The Thirtymile Fire left behind a host of unanswered questions and lingering mysteries. The main lesson of the 1994 South Canyon Fire was to back off when conditions become too dangerous. No patch of timber or home or other structure is worth a human life. Why had that simple lesson been ignored and the Thirtymile Fire reengaged?

How were fire supervisors to be held to account? After the South Canyon Fire, some managers who had failed to adequately support firefighters publicly congratulated themselves on a job well done and accepted bonus pay increases for their efforts. Reaction to that display had helped fuel a movement to make wildland fire managers more accountable. How would the new attitude be applied in this case?

Why did the Thirtymile Fire take the fatal left hook and blast a tiny area that became the fatality site, when everyone thought it was going to pass safely by?

Those questions were important but predictable. What no one saw coming was the accusation that Craven, FitzPatrick, Johnson, and Weaver were to blame for their own deaths. All four had made their lives more meaningful by joining the fire world—some for a career, some for a summer—and then had lost their lives to the very element, wildfire, which had called them out. That seems irony enough. In the coming weeks, however, they would be placed in the dock, unable to answer for themselves, and stand accused of disregarding a direct order that likely would have saved their lives.

CHAPTER THIRTEEN

> *The Forest Service sounded the note of progress. It opened the*
> *wilderness with road and telephone lines, and airplane landing*
> *fields...and poured in thousands of firefighters year after year in*
> *a vain attempt to control fires. Has all this effort and expenditure*
> *of millions of dollars added anything to human good? Is it possible*
> *that it was all a ghastly mistake?*
>
> —Elers Koch, legendary forest ranger and fire supervisor,
> "The Passing of the Lolo Trail," 1935

Two investigators from the North Central Washington Narcotics Task Force were on undercover patrol near Twisp when their radio broadcast a sudden flurry of traffic. Detective Steve Brown and Sheriff's Deputy Dave Rodriguez listened to excited reports of a fire that had blown up in the Chewuch River drainage; firefighters had been injured, some seriously. When Rodriguez asked the dispatcher if they should assist, a paramedic broke in on the radio and replied that anyone available should respond. The two investigators drove north from Twisp and into the Chewuch River canyon.

"I could see the plume of smoke as we drove up the road; it continued to get larger as we got closer," recalled Brown, who once had been a firefighter. The plume was "white as a cloud" at the top, darker in the middle, and glowing red and orange at the bottom, which Brown recognized as signs of fire burning "at a rapid pace."

It was 7:38 PM by the time Brown and Rodriguez pulled in below the fire, where survivors were gathered. Forest Service law officer Dave Graves had arrived a few minutes earlier and was able to pass on the news that four survivors with minor burns had been evacuated by ambulance and a fifth, in serious condition, had been airlifted to Seattle. Four others were missing. Kampen, who was standing nearby, told them there was nothing to be gained by going to the entrapment site. No one could have survived "in that environment," he said.

The lawmen checked with their dispatcher and were told to proceed to the entrapment site and confirm any fatalities. They were given yellow shirts and hard hats and switched to a sturdy Forest Service pickup. Graves, a paramedic, and several smoke jumpers sent to help followed in another vehicle. They had to cut their way through a fresh fall of trees, and it was nearly 8:00 PM before the search party reached the site. "As we rounded the last corner I could see where the incident had taken place," Brown recounted. "I didn't need anyone to explain to me what it was."

The wind had picked up, fanning old spot fires into new life. The heavy smoke brought on an early twilight. Boulders the size of small cars crashed down slopes; trees cracked and thumped to the ground. The gutted hulk of the Hagemeyers' pickup partially blocked the road. "The scene looked extremely unsafe to me," Brown observed laconically. The road was littered with fire shelters, packs, fire tools, and "black smoldering items" no longer identifiable. Brown picked up a Pulaski from the road so no one would run over it, but left everything else where it was.

On the sandbar was a set of clues inviting a detective's attention: an intact fire pack, a wet fire shelter, and boot prints. The sight that compelled their immediate attention, however, was a clump of scorched metal up in the scree. From the road the clump appeared to be four bulky fire shelters in a row and two others, slack in appearance, just above them. Brown, Rodriquez, and the paramedic picked a path up the still-smoking scree, trying not to burn themselves or disturb anything. They took extra care once they reached the shelters because flames continued to sputter around them. "I checked for signs of life at each shelter," Rodriguez noted. But there were none.

Meanwhile, the Okanogan County sheriff, Michael Murray, the county coroner, Karl Sloan, and several deputies had arrived and joined the survivors lower down the canyon. Sheriff's Sergeant Dan Christensen was the first outsider to question Daniels, who provided a sketchy account of events in which he made one notable claim: he said that he had tried to get the four missing firefighters to come down from the rocks long before the flames had arrived. As Daniels described to Christensen the moment when "the fire column came down," he became emotionally upset and could not continue. Christensen had no tape recorder, but within minutes he dictated a summary of the interview into a recorder brought by the sheriff.

About this time Rodriguez radioed the sheriff from the entrapment site and reported finding the lifeless fire shelters. The road had been cleared to the site, he said. But as the sheriff and others started the drive a tree toppled over and struck one of their vehicles, slid across the hood, and tore off the front bumper. The driver, Detective Kreg Sloan, a brother of Coroner Sloan, was unhurt. He managed to drive the vehicle back to the campground, where he scrounged a chain saw, work gloves, and another vehicle and set off to clear the road. It was getting dark by the time Sloan made it up to the entrapment site. He took some photographs but had to stop when the light failed.

In the meantime, Graves and a couple of smoke jumpers had driven up to the Thirtymile Campground. There, they found three gutted vehicles but thankfully no more victims. "Trees were rattling down all over; it was the spookiest thing I've ever been involved with," said one of the smoke jumpers, Tim Lum, several years later, just after he'd returned from a combat tour in Afghanistan, as an Army sergeant. As Graves, Lum, and the others headed back down the road, the bridge over the Chewuch River was burning behind them.

With the canyon in full darkness, Sheriff Murray ordered everyone to pull back for safety's sake. The road was cleared and closed for the night by 10:24 PM. The fire remained visible as a red halo over a bed of orange flames along the rim of the upper canyon. In the scree at the entrapment site, the ruined fire shelters, dimly illuminated by flickering flames, kept a lonely vigil.

WHEN THE PHONE next to Dave Leitch's bed rang about 2:00 AM, the West Valley fireman knew it couldn't be good news. Deputy fire chiefs don't get happy wake-up calls in the middle of the night. When he answered, Leitch heard the familiar voice of George Marcott, the

FMO for the Naches Ranger District, with whom he had worked many times.

"We lost four firefighters, and two of them are yours," Marcott told Leitch, and read him the names: Jessica Johnson and Karen FitzPatrick.

"No, that's not right," Leitch said. True, Johnson had been a West Valley Fire District cadet. FitzPatrick, however, had never joined West Valley because, as she had once explained to him, drill meetings were held on the same night as her prayer meetings. Strictly speaking, notification of families in cases of fire fatalities is a police responsibility, and neither Marcott nor Leitch was eager to take on the job. They agreed, however, that the alternative of an anonymous telephone call or a visit from a uniformed stranger was unthinkable.

"What should we do?" Marcott asked.

"We'll do it together," Leitch said.

They met in a church parking lot about 3:00 AM and decided to go first to the FitzPatrick home. It was a hot night, and the FitzPatricks had left the outside door open for air, giving the house a hollow, empty look. When they knocked, Kathie appeared out of the gloom. "It was the knock on the door you hope you never get," she said later.

"There's been a terrible accident," Leitch told her. "Your daughter is one of four firefighters killed on a fire. Is there someone you can call, a pastor or a friend?"

Kathie was joined by her husband, John, and as the news sank in they both collapsed into chairs at the kitchen table. Leitch and Marcott passed along the few facts they knew. After the two men left, the FitzPatricks sat in silence with the lights out. About daybreak, Kathie went to Karen's room and looked around at her things. One of the inspirational sayings posted on the wall seemed hauntingly appropriate to the moment: *Come Away My Beloved*, a quotation from the Bible's Song of Songs. Karen had often turned to the biblical poem for inspiration, copying down its lush imagery to describe herself: "I am a Rose of Sharon, a lily of the valleys, as a lily among brambles, so is my love among maidens." She had titled her senior English thesis, an account of her spiritual journey and its tribulations, *Lilies Grow in Difficult Places*.

Kathie went into the garden and gathered a bouquet of tiger lilies. As she placed them in a vase next to a photograph of Karen, she remembered another verse from the Bible, this one from Psalm 30: "Weeping may endure for a night, but joy cometh in the morning." She felt her heart rise. "I have never looked back since," she said years later. Karen's death, she believes, raised her daughter to a new and better life.

At Jessica Johnson's house, Leitch had not finished knocking when the door opened and Jody Gray appeared. "No, no!" she cried out, as though she already knew their errand. She had been lying in bed half awake when she heard the rumble of a diesel engine in the driveway, and, upon rising, she'd seen the flashing lights of a fire truck through living room curtains. She went to the door with a heavy sense of Jessica's presence. She had spent the evening in Jessica's room patching holes in a wall. (She later realized she had been there at 5:30 PM, during the entrapment.) She had been filled with delight over Jessica's decision to turn her life around. "I was having joyous memories of her and went to sleep thinking about her," she said.

She woke in the night when the telephone rang, as someone else tried to contact her. The call had come in on a line she used for business and she hadn't picked up, but the ringing left her troubled and restless. In the twilight world between sleep and waking, she began to make worrisome connections between the telephone call and news reports about dangerous fires in the region; she later learned the telephone call had been from someone trying to notify her of Jessica's death. When she opened the door to Leitch's knock, fear and fact came together.

"I'm very sorry to tell you, but Jessica was killed in a fire," Leitch said. Jody wanted every detail: Where did it happen? What time? *How* did it happen? Did Jessica suffer? And more than anything else, she wanted to go instantly to wherever Jessica was. Leitch and Marcott could offer sympathy, a telephone number for her to call in the morning, and not much else.

Painful as were these scenes, the Cravens and Weavers received notification of the deaths of their loved ones in telephone calls from strangers, which became a source of enduring outrage. When Evelyn Craven heard the news, she was alone with her children. She fell screaming to her knees.

For Ken and Barbara Weaver, the call ended many a happy dream. Barbara, shaking and bent over in pain, woke Ken at 1:07 AM, a minute that would fix itself in their memory. "Ken, there's a man on the phone, and he says Devin is dead. You have got to talk to him and tell him he's alive."

"I instantly knew those words were true," Ken said later. He would relive the next minutes over and over, telling and writing the story and eventually testifying about it before Congress. "Hello, Mr. Weaver. My name is Randy. I am with the Forest Service. Devin's crew was over-run by a fire at about five-thirty yesterday afternoon, and Devin didn't make it."

"My son could outrun any fire. It's not possible for a fire to overtake Devin; he is in too good a shape."

"I'm very sorry, Mr. Weaver, but the ID is positive. We know for sure that Devin was one of the casualties."

"One of the casualties? Are there more?"

"Yes, there were three more. We are trying to reach their families now."

"Was Jason Emhoff one of the other casualties?"

"No, Jason was burned. Let me give you some numbers that you can call for . . ."

"Why do I need numbers? You killed my son, that's plain enough. Don't think I need to have that repeated." Ken hung up the phone.

Barbara refused to believe what had happened. "We'd always been a family that could fix things," she said later. "Somebody, hit the undo button. I thought, My God, I might live another forty years."

Amid the disbelief, rage, sorrow, and resignation lay a common conviction among the families that their loved ones had been badly served by their supervisors and by the Forest Service. Ken Weaver became so outspoken on the subject that he alienated other families.

"They said it was no one's fault, an act of God," Weaver summed up at one point. "The picture that emerged was something quite different from an act of any God I know. The fire was indeed out of control but had been for more than four hours. This crew was led down a dead-end road with a plan of attack that was later determined to have no chance of success. In all, the people who were supposed to protect Devin's life violated every single rule of safety on the books. They ignored every single warning sign present, abandoned all common sense, and could not exercise even minimal command authority after they were entrapped. All the training Devin received stressed safety first. As it turned out, it was all a fraud."

Telephones rang from coast to coast as the fire world mobilized for catastrophe. Forest Service chief Dale Bosworth took one of the calls at home in Washington, D.C., while the entrapment was under way. "We didn't know whether they were alive, just that they were trapped," said Bosworth.

One of Bosworth's top deputies, Jim Furnish, had just dropped off to sleep at home in suburban Washington when his phone jangled. Furnish knew it was bad news when he heard the name of the caller, Caroline Deaderick. Deaderick was the agency's head of safety and health, the one responsible for putting together investigation teams for wildland fire fatalities. Furnish, deputy chief for the national forest system, had limited experience with wildland fire, but under a new setup inaugurated after the South Canyon Fire, all senior Forest Service executives were required to place their names on a rotation list to head a fatality investigation. The system, designed to break down old-boy alliances and improve the quality of investigations, included training for team leaders.

The South Canyon Fire investigation had been a political nightmare, and the Forest Service was determined that nothing similar would happen this time around. Two of the South Canyon investigators had refused to sign the final report on grounds it wasn't accurate or balanced. One, Dick Mangan, added his signature after additions he had requested were made; the other, Ted Putnam, never did sign it. The South Canyon Fire report's charge that the fourteen deaths came about because of a can-do spirit on the part of the firefighters had unleashed the furies. Families were stunned by the charge that their loved ones, who could not speak for themselves, were being blamed for their own deaths, while some regional fire managers, who had neglected the fire for days, were given bonus pay increases and a congratulatory memo, signed by one of those same fire managers. The sense of betrayal extended to every level of the tightly knit wildland fire community. Many fire crews that summer flatly refused assignments they considered too dangerous. Senior fire executives publicly pledged a host of reforms, and many privately vowed never to blame victims for their deaths on their watch. One who made such a promise was Chief Bosworth, who as a regional forester in 1994 had been assigned to accompany home one of the South Canyon Fire victims. Bosworth then became chief in April 2001, just before the Thirtymile Fire.

Furnish, who was a few months from retirement, knew that heading a fatality investigation would make an unhappy ending for his career, no matter how it turned out. It wasn't really his turn to head an investigation. He had put his name at the top of the rotation list as a favor to a friend who had left town for a few weeks; even so, he accepted the assignment without complaint.

In describing the situation later, Furnish said that the previous chief, Mike Dombeck, had just scolded the senior leaders and told them that heading fatality investigations was a responsibility they could not duck. "The last time something bad happened," Furnish said, "they started calling people, and they went through a bunch of senior executives before finding one who would accept the responsibility. Dombeck said no more excuses; if you are on the top of the rotation list, you are expected to shoulder the responsibility."

Furnish told himself that his lack of fire experience could be a plus, helping him be objective. And the assignment was an opportunity to perform a meaningful, if thankless, service in his last days before retirement. "I felt literally and figuratively called to the responsibility," he said later. "Being a pretty deeply spiritual person, I thought, Well, there's a reason for this." The Thirtymile Fire investigation achieved far-reaching significance, to be sure, but not the kind Furnish anticipated.

He booked a morning flight to the West Coast, and before taking off he ran down Chief Bosworth, who was attending a meeting at a Washington hotel. They met for breakfast. Furnish appeared eager for the assignment, Bosworth said later. With only sketchy reports coming in from the field, the chief offered no special advice or counsel. The two men talked mostly about how to deal with Furnish's regular responsibilities while he was away. A rumor developed later that Bosworth, a Bush administration appointee, had deliberately stuck Furnish, a favorite during the previous Clinton administration, with the risky task. Both men, however, say that the rumor was groundless: Furnish headed the investigation only because his name came up on the rotation list.

THREE SEPARATE INVESTIGATIONS of the Thirtymile Fire were about to commence. The sheriff's department had the most immediate task, that of identifying and removing the bodies. Furnish's Forest Service team was to conduct a joint investigation with OSHA, or the Occupational Safety and Health Administration, which has responsibility for workplace safety for federal as well as private employees, to learn the lessons of the fire and gather facts for possible internal disciplinary action. And Forest Service arson investigators began a hunt for whoever had started the escaped campfire, with an eye to bringing criminal charges. While that may seem to be an imposing number of inquiries, the fire would prompt many more investigations and reinvestigations in the months and years ahead.

The canyon road was opened again at 9:30 the next morning, Wednesday, July 11. Detective Sloan was among the first to reach the entrapment site, and with time and daylight available, he began to examine the evidence on the roadway and sandbar. The equipment on the sandbar, unlike that on the road, had not been damaged by heat. There was a backpack, a two-way radio, and a 35mm camera that had spent time in the water. (The film was intact, but when developed produced images mostly taken at other locations before the fire.) Sloan took note of the many boot prints that headed from the sandbar into the water: they appeared to have been made by people walking, not running, a sign that there had been no panic, at least at this site. Sloan sent a sheriff's deputy up the road to look for more boot prints, perhaps of someone running away. The deputy walked most of a mile up the road without finding any more.

It was midafternoon before the necessary people, vehicles, and equipment were assembled for the sad chore of removing the victims. The bodies had not yet been identified by name, though there was no question of who had died. When investigators examined the body farthest in line down the canyon, they found hints of identity: a watch on the left wrist and, under the body, the charred remains of a cell phone.

The watch was small and feminine and had a silver wristband, slightly melted. The hands of the watch were stopped at 5:29, five minutes after the entrapment was first reported, which provided confirmation, if any was needed, of an approximate time of death. The watch and cell phone, it was later determined, had been gifts to Karen FitzPatrick from her family. It took a while to carry all the bodies to the road and place them aboard vehicles. When everything was ready for departure, Sloan, a man of precise habits, noted the exact time for his report. It was 5:29 PM, twenty-four hours to the minute after time had ceased to count for FitzPatrick and the others; when the link was pointed out to him, several years later, Sloan expressed surprise.

Sloan prepared the entrapment site for the incoming Forest Service team. He put rocks on the fire shelters to hold them in place and marked the pathway from the road to the shelters with yellow crime scene tape. At 6:27 PM, by his report, he left for the Twisp ranger station, where he was to meet with Furnish and his Forest Service team. The arrival of several key members of the team was delayed by travel problems and for other reasons, which added to the confusion of those first hours. Sloan met Furnish at the station about 7:45 PM and was invited to join a discussion with the team about to commence in the conference room. Sloan balked. Furnish should be out corralling witnesses while memories were fresh, Sloan thought, not wasting time talking.

"I'll give you what I've got here, and then I'm leaving," Sloan said abruptly. He made his report, handed Furnish a business card, and was headed for the door by 7:55 PM, ten minutes after he'd arrived. While Sloan's behavior might have seemed dismissive or even arrogant, Furnish later would conclude that indeed major mistakes were made in the early stage of the investigation because witness interviews were not properly handled.

Sloan spent the next several hours trying to run down the identities of the victims, though it proved frustrating because both survivors and gear were now scattered. The survivors had spent the early part of the day meeting with a team of grief counselors. "We were around this square table, and we talked about emotions and stuff," recalled Welch. "They didn't give you any information; it was just all this touchy-feely stuff. This is how you might react to tragedy: you might not eat, you might eat too much, you might drink. I thought it was kind of gay." After lunch, the survivors were moved to the Sun Mountain Lodge outside Winthrop. "We got to do whatever we wanted at this lodge, drink whatever we wanted at the bar any hour of the day," Welch said.

But they had to get out of their yellow shirts and green pants, to hide their identity as firefighters. "It turned out the media was staying at the lodge too," Kampen said later. "We were told to go right to our rooms and change, and if anybody tried to talk to us, we weren't supposed to talk." As they reassembled incognito on a patio, one crew member showed up wearing a T-shirt inside out, flip-flops, and three pairs of boxer shorts, with one pair turned backward. When asked about the strange getup, he answered, "I didn't have any shorts, so I put the boxers on backward to cover everything up," as if that explained everything.

Several news reporters caught on to the incognito almost immediately, but when asked to respect the crew's privacy, according to Kampen, they restrained themselves.

Sloan caught up with the survivors at the lodge about 9:00 PM. Daniels hunted up Johnson's backpack for him, but it contained no photo identification. Sloan rummaged through the green van but found no identity papers there either. He decided to call it a day, telephoned a report to the sheriff at 11:00 PM, and headed for home.

Furnish, in the meantime, had given his team a lecture at the Twisp ranger station. He had no intention, Furnish said, of letting his inquiry go the way of the South Canyon Fire investigation. "I said, 'I may have some things to learn, but you have some things to learn about me,'" Furnish recalled later. "I knew the South Canyon Fire investigation was not signed by all the team. I said, 'That's not going to happen here. I want everybody to feel comfortable with what our conclusions are. I don't want hidden stuff. I don't want stuff going on under the table. I don't want lingering innuendos that we dodged the truth.'"

The Forest Service investigation was everyone's best hope for a credible answer to calamity. Only the Forest Service could touch all the bases: gather facts, apportion responsibility, take internal disciplinary action, dig out and apply safety lessons, and offer expert analysis about why the fire had behaved in such an unexpected fashion. For this task, the Forest Service assembled what was probably the most highly qualified investigation team in its history. For the first time the agency hired—at a stiff rate of one thousand dollars a day—an outside investigator, Alan Chockie of Link Technologies, a company that had handled inquiries for other federal agencies. Another fresh but experienced eye was that of Tony Kern, who had been hired by the Forest Service after the South Canyon Fire; Kern had retired from the Air Force with decades of experience as an investigator and aviation safety expert. Kern was to deal with human factors, the role played by such matters as fatigue and state of mind.*

The team included several experts from the Missoula Technology and Development Center, or MTDC, who had much experience with investigations. The MTDC personnel brought voice recorders, purchased specifically to avoid repeating the mistake made during the South Canyon Fire investigation of inadequately documenting interviews with several key figures. Unfortunately, they had only enough recorders for themselves, and some of those were new, technologically sophisticated, and untried; Furnish's investigation, too, would suffer the plague of inadequately recorded interviews.

As the inquiry proceeded, an unprecedented level of cooperation developed between the Forest Service and OSHA, which had been at each other's throats over previous fatality investigations, most notably South Canyon. This time around, matters got off to a rocky start, which included a confrontation with raised voices in a public parking lot. That led to a settlement of differences, though, and from then on the OSHA

---

*Human factors became an issue for fatality investigations because of Ted Putnam, the investigator who never signed the South Canyon Fire Investigation Report. Putnam had complained during that investigation about a lack of consideration given to human factors such as fatigue and psychological state, which he thought vital to understanding the events of a fatal fire, the South Canyon Fire in particular. Putnam, an equipment specialist for the Forest Service's Missoula Technology and Development Center, organized the Human Factors Workshop a year after the fire, which resulted in the issue being added to the agenda of future fire fatality investigations—just in time for the Thirtymile Fire.

Then in 2005, a decade after his pioneering workshop, Putnam, who had retired by that time, was honored for his work at the Fire Safety Summit, a gathering of top fire safety professionals in Missoula. Dick Mangan, the other investigator who had refused to sign the South Canyon Fire report, had been Putnam's boss at the technology center, which is responsible for developing safety equipment such as fire shelters. Mangan, too, had retired from the Forest Service and in 2005 was serving as president of the International Association of Wildland Fire (IAWF), which sponsored the Fire Safety Summit. It was Mangan who handed Putnam two awards: the annual IAWF Safety Award, for making human factors an issue, and the Paul Gleason Lead by Example Award.

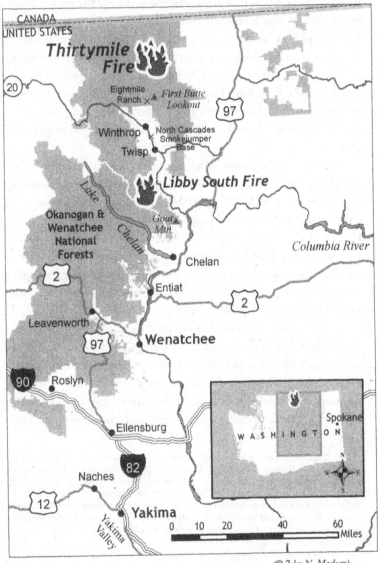

CANADA
UNITED STATES

Thirtymile Fire

20

Eightmile Ranch ×   First Butte Lookout

97

Winthrop
North Cascades Smokejumper Base

Twisp

Libby South Fire

Okanogan & Wenatchee National Forests

Lake Chelan

Goat Mtn.

Columbia River

2

Chelan

Entiat

2

Leavenworth

97

Wenatchee

90

Roslyn

Ellensburg

82

Naches

12

Yakima
Yakima Valley

WASHINGTON   Spokane

0   10   20   40   60
Miles

(© John N. Maclean)

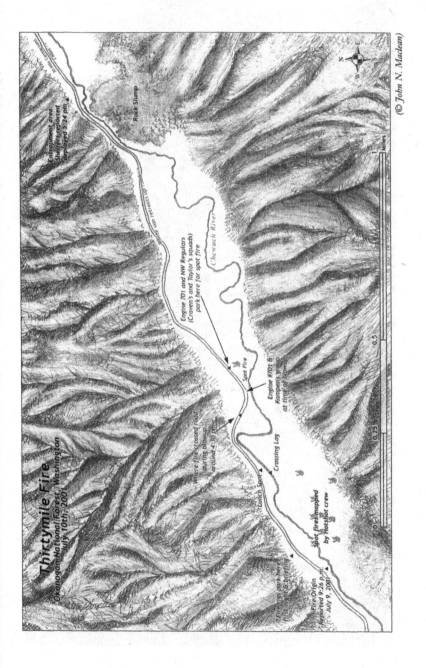

Thirtymile Fire
Okanogan National Forest, Washington
July 10th, 2001

Entrapment Creek
Shelters deployed
(explored 5:24 pm)

Rock Slump

Engine 701 and NW Regulars
(Craven's and Taylor's squads)
park here for spot fire

Chewuch River

Engine #701 &
Kampen's group
at time of blowup

Where fire crossed road
during blowup
around 1:50 pm

Spot Fire

Crossing Log

Lunch Spot

Spot fire mapped
by Hotshot crew

Fire rigs park here
11:31 lunch & briefing

Fire Origin
Reported 9:26 p.m.
July 9, 2001

N

Miles
0   0.25   0.5   1

(© John N. Maclean)

LEFT:
The view from the site of the neglected campfire showing the approximate path of the fire as it first developed. *(Photograph by author)*

BELOW:
The Northwest Regulars and Entiat Hotshots get a close-up look at flames across the Chewuch River from the Lunch Spot. *(Photograph by Matt Rutman, USFS)*

A fire engine barely escapes flames crossing the road at about the Lunch Spot, as seen through the window of a fire vehicle. *(Photograph by Kory Mattson, Entiat Hotshot, USFS)*

This photo of the Northwest Regulars, taken moments after they arrived at the entrapment site, became an icon of the fire. Thom Taylor is farthest to the left; next is Nick Dreis; then probably Devin Weaver, with his hands on his hips. Jason Emhoff walks toward the camera; to his left Karen FitzPatrick takes a self-portrait. Female figure at far right is unidentified. Smoke rises in the background from the arm of the fire that cut off and trapped the crew. *(Photograph by Matt Rutman, USFS)*

Thom Taylor, on a return visit to the entrapment site, motions to indicate how the fire approached him across the scree. *(Photograph by author)*

As the ember shower approached the entrapment site, firefighter Matt Rutman snapped the photo. *(Photograph by Matt Rutman, USFS)*

A double plume of smoke from the Thirtymile Fire, as seen from the Libby South Fire camp more than twenty miles away. *(USFS photograph)*

Firefighters who escaped the entrapment watch from below the fire as Pilot Paul Walters in helicopter 13N, in the upper left of the photo, bravely continues to make water drops. *(Photograph by Pete Kampen, USFS)*

Aerial view of the Chewuch River canyon taken after the fire. The Hagemeyers' pickup is in the foreground, at the entrapment site, with the sandbar to the left. *(USFS photograph)*

A series of maps showing the spread of the fire during the day, July 10, 2001. (© *John N. Maclean*)

Fire Progression Map

Spot Fires
X < Fire Ignition Point

Fire Area 10:00 a.m.

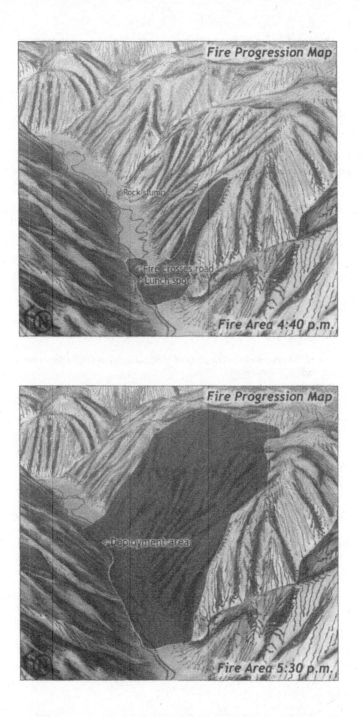

This photo of the fatality site was taken by Pete Kampen shortly after he arrived at the scene, in the immediate aftermath of the entrapment. Fire shelters are barely visible behind the tree in the center of the photo. *(Photograph by Pete Kampen, USFS)*

The melted camper on the Hagemeyers' pickup sent streams of aluminum onto the road. *(USFS photograph)*

Firefighter Nick Dreis sits in the spot where he survived inside a fire shelter, just off the road. *(Photograph by Matt Rutman, USFS)*

Pete Kampen at the scene of the Thirty-mile Fire in 2005—so much had changed from 2001 that it was a challenge to find some important locations. *(Photograph by author)*

Jason Emhoff puts a gloved hand on the boulder where he sat with Tom Craven's group as the fire approached. Photo was taken on a chilly day in November, the year of the fire. *(Photograph by author)*

Jessica Johnson
(Photograph courtesy of Jody Gray)

Karen L. FitzPatrick
(Photograph courtesy of Kathie FitzPatrick)

Devin Weaver
(Photograph courtesy of the Weaver family)

Tom Craven
(Photograph courtesy of the Craven family and Kay Evensen)

A stone memorial ledge, with images of the four firefighters who were killed—from left to right, Karen L. FitzPatrick, Devin Weaver, Jessica Johnson, and Tom Craven—stands alongside the road just below the fatality site. *(Photograph courtesy of Kathie FitzPatrick)*

and the Forest Service investigators worked side by side, to their mutual benefit, for the duration of the Thirtymile inquiry.

Despite these advantages—an all-star personnel roster, a cooperative spirit, and past example—the Forest Service investigation team produced what is arguably the agency's most troubled fatality report ever. The report blew up in their faces, repeatedly. Within a day of its release, survivors held a press conference to challenge one of the report's key findings. As a result, the chief of the Forest Service ordered a formal review of the report. When completed, the review backed up the contrary survivors and repudiated the key finding. When the Forest Service subsequently tried to fire three of the fire's managers based on facts in the report, plus a brief follow-up inquiry, none of the firings held up on appeal, which was conducted by yet another Forest Service team. The U.S. Congress became involved. Motivated by the upsets and by the outrage of the families of the victims, Congress passed legislation a year after the fire taking full control of fatality investigations out of the hands of the Forest Service, with far-reaching and unforeseen consequences.

How bright hopes and talented people produced such rocky results is, like the Thirtymile Fire itself, a story of how mistakes can link together, compound, and lead to disaster.

CHAPTER FOURTEEN

Make crystal clear in firefighting training that a "chimney,"
"narrow box canyon" or similar topographic feature is a
hazard area even if devoid of fuel.

—recommendation by Forest Service investigators
after California's Loop Fire of 1966, which
killed twelve firefighters

The Sun Mountain Lodge in the Methow Valley west of Winthrop has an expansive reception area that opens onto a flagstone veranda, which overlooks a well-tended lawn, beyond which lies a dry landscape of brown meadows and timbered foothills. The veranda surrounds a kidney-shaped pool. For athletic visitors there are ski, hiking, and horse trails, as well as spa services. The resort offers high-quality food and drink with a Northwest accent. The fire's survivors, transported to this haven of comfort the day after the fatalities, parked fire vehicles beside Mercedes Benzes, Porsches, and Aston Martins. They passed time at the bar, or mingled awkwardly with wealthy tourists, or retired to their rooms in confused boredom. Thom Taylor found a patch of grass outside where he sat and tried to regain a sense of place in the natural world. The stay was a freebie at government expense but quickly lost its novelty. The firefighters wanted to go home. Before this could happen, though, it would be necessary for each of them to relive the horrors of the fire in an interview with investigators.

One of the late-arriving investigators was Kern, the former Air Force investigator. By the time he made his way to the resort, on Thursday, July 12, two days after the entrapment, many key interviews already had taken place—with little regard for the qualifications of those doing the questioning. An OSHA investigator with scant experience in wildfire and a National Weather Service meteorologist, for example, had handled the most important interview, the one with Daniels. When Kern learned the details, he was startled to discover that the interrogators had not pressed Daniels for a thorough account of events at the entrapment site. They had asked only one question, "Then what happened?" They had not asked what, if anything, Daniels had said to Craven's group or if Craven's group had responded, and Daniels had said nothing about that himself.

"There was not a whole lot of organization at this point," Kern said later. "What I was struck by as I worked through some of the interviews was the lack of formal preparation for the interviews. There was no real discussion about sequence of events in command and control. It was clear to me there were two major players, Tom Craven and Ellreese Daniels. Everyone else around the periphery could provide yes, no, or maybe. But we needed to find out from the commander what was going on."

Kern determined to follow up himself; after all, as the man responsible for analyzing human factors, he needed to report on the psychological climate at the entrapment site. Someone pointed out Daniels in the lobby, and Kern introduced himself.

"I know you've been interviewed already," he told Daniels, "but I'd like to ask you some specific questions about the last few minutes there."

"Fine," said Daniels, and they found a table and chairs on the veranda.

Kern had no audio recorder—the team had to send out to purchase recorders—but he knew exactly what he wanted to find out:

"Was there something that broke down at the site? I asked Ellreese about that, and he said, 'I told them to come down out of the rocks; that's not the place to be.'" Kern wrote a summary of his half-hour talk with Daniels, which reads in its entirety:

Question: What communication took place between you and the group on the rock scree after you reached the site where you would eventually deploy?

I told them several times—at least three—I said "Come down out of the rocks, that's not the place to be. Come down out of the rocks, that's not the place to be. Come down out of the rocks" . . . over and over again.

Question: Are you certain they heard you?

Yes, they heard me. I'm sure.

Question: Do you have any idea why they did not do as you asked?

I don't. I wish I could have made them listen.

The text was appended without comment or explanation to the long, rambling transcript of Daniels's first interview. When both interviews were released to families and other interested parties weeks later, predictable suspicions were aroused. Daniels had said nothing in the long initial interview about calling people out of the rocks—and other survivors remembered him saying, "Stay near the road." Why was this crucial piece of information contained only in a second interview, the record of which appeared to be a brief summary, not a verbatim transcript? Was there a verbatim transcript to back it up? Had investigators slanted or even concocted the second interview to shift blame from supervisors to victims?

"I think the problem we had later is that we didn't capture hard data initially," Kern acknowledged, several years later. "There was a big rush. To the best of my knowledge there wasn't a single person there who was a trained interviewer. Without the benefit of taped interviews we were losing an opportunity that we would never regain. You've got to get people before they talk to each other. You don't have to talk to the survivors instantly as long as they don't talk to each other."

Furnish later acknowledged that initially he did not have control of the investigation process or even the makeup of his team. "I didn't have a good feel for how things would unfold for the first couple of days," Furnish said. "I felt in the first week I was losing control of the investigation team itself. Everybody wanted to put more people on the team, and they weren't talking to me about it. People were showing up, and I'm going, 'Who are you? What are you doing here? I'm the team leader, and nobody talked to me about this.'

"I just found that fascinating. I know how those things go. When there's excitement in the air, everybody wants to be there. I finally had some discussions with some people about this issue. I said, 'Hey look, some of these people have been good additions. But we need to have an understanding that when a team reaches a certain dimension it becomes unwieldy. We're at critical mass now. I cannot tolerate any more people showing up here without my knowing about it.'"

Other matters, too, spun out of control. Furnish held a press conference soon after his arrival, but the event left all parties unsatisfied. "The press is going gonzo," Furnish said later. "All we could tell them was, 'I'm the investigation team leader. I've got my team. We want to look into this.' They start asking me a lot of questions and get a lot of 'I don't knows.' There were eyeballs rolling."

With no facts to report, speculation and second-guessing made headlines. A huge wind had sprung up unexpectedly and caused the fatalities, just as had happened on the South Canyon Fire. The high proportion of rookies on the Northwest Regular crew was a significant cause of the deaths. The Endangered Species Act had dealt a crucial blow to firefighting efforts by delaying helicopter 13N and its water bucket for hours and hours. "So many lost their children for a fish!" lamented one firefighter—who was not on the fire—in an interview aired on national television. Political opponents of the act picked up the chant on conservative talk radio and in other media.* Forest Service officials were solicited for their response, to be sure, but for days no single, authoritative voice responded with facts.

"We were getting killed with rumor," Furnish said later. Six days after the fatalities, on July 16, he summoned the media to the Thirty-

---

*The effect of the Endangered Species Act on the Thirtymile Fire was briefly considered by a forest health subcommittee of the U.S. House Resources Committee at a hearing on other matters held July 31, 2001, less than a month after the fire. The subcommittee chairman, Representative Scott McInnis, a Colorado Republican who by chance represented the congressional district where the South Canyon Fire occurred, began the hearing by raising the issue of the role played by the Endangered Species Act, of which he was a longtime critic, in delaying the dispatch of helicopter 13N. "I have some very disturbing news that I want to discuss," McInnis told the Forest Service chief, Dale Bosworth, who appeared as the principal witness. Citing "confidential sources," McInnis said that helicopter water drops had been delayed for at least two hours because of the act, which may have contributed to the four deaths.

By then several media accounts and conservative commentators had put the delay many hours longer and had not hesitated to make the link to the deaths. An opinion piece in the *Washington Times*, quoting Fox News, said in early August that firefighters had "pleaded for more

mile Fire camp, by now set up at the Eightmile Ranch. The investigation was far from over, he acknowledged. But he wanted to share some preliminary findings. The big natural wind event that supposedly fanned the fire into a blowup simply had not occurred, Furnish said. High winds indeed had whipped through the canyon. But they had been generated when the fire "reached a critical mass and created its own strong wind."

The crew had many rookies, true again. But the proportion of rookies was not unreasonable on a Type II crew, and more important, the experience level of the supervisors should have provided an adequate balance. Investigators had found no link between the four deaths and the rookies' training level, he said.

It was also true that helicopter 13N had been delayed, Furnish acknowledged. But he pointed to the breakdown of the water pumps as the crucial failure. The pumps had the capacity to put many times more water on the fire than the helicopter could. If the pumps had been run properly, he said, the helicopter would hardly have been needed, though others maintain to this day that the helicopter would have helped a lot in early morning.

One issue that would not go away was whether the fire should have been fought in the first place. That question had been raised in the media on general grounds and because the fire lay within the boundaries of a Research Natural Area, or RNA, a place designated for the study of natural processes. To the contrary, Furnish argued, fighting the fire was consistent with national, Okanogan-Wenatchee Forest, and RNA guidelines for that specific area. The Chewuch River RNA was established to study the remarkable geologic features of the canyon—the rock slides,

---

than nine hours" for water, but by the time the first bucket drop was made, "four young firefighters, two women and two men, lay dead below." Neither assertion was factual: the overall delay for the helicopter was no more than five hours, only two hours of that were attributable to confusion over the act, and the first helicopter drop was made several hours before, not after, the fatalities.

Bosworth did not respond directly to McInnis's question about the delay. He said the matter was being looked into by the fire investigation team, which had not yet issued a report. But the ranking minority member of the subcommittee, Representative Jay Inslee, a Democrat from Washington, cautioned against turning the issue into a partisan battle over the Endangered Species Act. "Let us focus on the facts of this particular incident, rather than our ideological predispositions," said Inslee. The controversy faded, but did not disappear entirely, after Furnish publicly stressed the breakdown of the water pumps as the crucial failure, and not the delay over the Endangered Species Act.

valley cutting, and debris flows—and not the flora. The RNA guidelines called for "minimum impact suppression techniques," not a moratorium, when fighting fire. The Thirtymile Fire burned in a high-value recreation area in a time of extreme drought, Furnish said, and should have been fought for those reasons alone. But it also had been started by negligent humans, which virtually always requires that a fire be fought.

Despite those arguments, Okanogan-Wenatchee Forest managers subsequently sought authority to let more fires burn unmolested across the region. They quickly bumped into an environmental regulation, however, that required a detailed study of the effects of increased fire on any specially managed fauna or flora in the affected areas, which in this case amounted to tens of thousands of acres. Forest Service managers decided the enormous projected cost was prohibitive—budgets are tight, there are other priorities for spending. Though they continued to look for ways to make fire policy more flexible, the managers acknowledged that the Thirtymile Fire would be fought again today if it occurred under the same conditions.

Furnish's presentation brought a few weeks of public quiet. "We went to the mattresses," Furnish said, meaning he and his team hunkered down. Within team ranks, however, Furnish had to deal with seething resentments between Forest Service and OSHA investigators. One evening the combined team was meeting when someone on the Forest Service side made a snappy remark to someone from OSHA. "It was beyond, 'I disagree with you,'" Furnish said later. "It was like, 'I disagree with you, and you're an asshole. You've been barking up my tree ever since you got here, and I'm tired of it.'"

Furnish invited the OSHA team members outside for what he later dubbed the Parking Lot Talk. "I owned up to the long and painful history of OSHA and the Forest Service," Furnish said. For over a decade, OSHA had investigated Forest Service fatalities and issued safety reports, which sometimes denounced the Forest Service in stinging terms. The OSHA report on the South Canyon Fire, for example, had cited the Forest Service for "willful neglect" in the fourteen deaths.

The Forest Service, for its part, complained that OSHA investigators knew next to nothing about wildfire. In one past go-round the safety agency had asked for "all training materials related to wildfire," according to one forest agency participant. "Where do you want us to park the forty-foot vans?" was the response. In that case, Forest Service headquarters in Washington had to intervene and order its personnel to cooperate.

During the parking lot encounter, Furnish asked the OSHA personnel to let bygones be bygones. "I said, 'You guys have every reason to believe the Forest Service has not measured up to your standards historically. I am not going to have that happen here. I hope that after being with the team for a couple of weeks you have been reassured these are some of the best people we've got. The chief has given me every opportunity to conduct a thorough, complete, honest investigation.'"

The OSHA investigators, Furnish said, acknowledged the benefits of their being included in interviews and meetings and expressed appreciation for his remarks. The encounter eased the conflict, at least for the rest of this investigation.

The team, meanwhile, identified Thom Taylor as the witness who could best resolve several outstanding issues. Taylor was observant by nature. He had been present at important turning points. He had been skeptical enough of how things were going to break away and go up into the scree for a better look around. "You can almost always find somebody out there who saw things, someone who becomes your benchmark," Kern said. "Thom was the guy who would come close to capturing the truth for us."

The initial interview with Taylor, however, had been conducted by a National Weather Service meteorologist and an OSHA investigator, just as had happened with Daniels. Once again, no questions were asked about the key issue of what Daniels might have said to Craven and his group. As Kern read over the Taylor interview, it seemed to him the interrogators had avoided tough questions because they were overly sympathetic. "It was an innocent, honest mistake," Kern said later. "At that point we didn't know Taylor was the key guy."

Taylor had to be interviewed again, it was determined, and this time the most experienced investigators, Kern included, would handle the questioning. Taylor by then had left the Winthrop area, but he was quickly flown back. After a sit-down interview on July 17, Taylor led investigators on a walking tour of the fire site and retold the story in even greater detail, pointing out where things happened—a procedure that might well be a model for future investigation teams. "That interview was top-notch," Taylor said later. "They asked all the right questions. We went over things several times."

This time around, Taylor told investigators that Daniels in the first minutes at the entrapment site had told everyone to stay close to the road. Investigators took that as partial confirmation of Daniels's claim to have called people out of the rocks. But Taylor had lost touch with Daniels after he went up in the scree. From there, Taylor could hear Daniels over the radio, talking to Jasso. But the fire was getting louder, Taylor was far from the road, and his mind was on other things. "I was checking out the fire, that's where my attention was," he said later.

In short, Taylor could not back up Daniels's claim about calling directly to Craven and his group. Taylor, though, said that he didn't believe it had happened, because it had looked to him as though Craven's group was *already* on the road, a point that would be made by others as well. "I couldn't see any real separation between the people on the rocks and the people on the road," Taylor said later. "If someone had wanted them off the rocks, they could have pulled them down by their cuffs."

Two other witnesses had been better positioned than Taylor to hear Daniels during the crucial late minutes of the entrapment: Welch, who was with Craven and then moved down and was next to Daniels in those final minutes; and Emhoff, who was part of Craven's group until he threw off his shelter. These two did indeed have answers for the questions: Did Daniels call to Craven's group to come down? And did they hear him?

Welch was interviewed for the first time by the investigators two days after the entrapment. That interview was brief, only half of it was recorded, and she said nothing about Daniels calling to Craven's group. According to Welch, she was asked later informally if she had heard Daniels call and said she did not, but there is no available record of such an exchange.

Emhoff was in poor physical condition for many weeks after the fire. During a ten-week stay at Harborview Medical Center, he underwent seven surgeries and was heavily medicated for much of that time. His doctors said that a few decades earlier, he would have stood only a fifty-fifty chance of survival. Advances in burn treatments had upped his chances of living to 99 percent; his hands, though, were a different matter. Once before, doctors at the Harborview center had fought to save the hands of a firefighter who was terribly burned escaping a runaway blaze. The firefighter was Eric Hipke, a smoke jumper from the North Cascades base, and the event was the South Canyon Fire.

HIPKE HAD GONE over the crucial moment scores of times, but for him it always had a surreal quality, as though it had happened to someone else. Hipke, a legend among smoke jumpers for the power of his legs, had lunged for the safety of a ridgetop on Storm King Mountain as a blast of superheated air swept over him. Hipke raised gloveless hands to cover the back of his neck and let out a scream, which kept the fiery air from entering his nose and throat, but the heat blast shredded his hands. Flames engulfed a dozen firefighters behind him—and two others died higher up the mountain.

After his release from the Harborview center, Hipke, almost miraculously, returned to smoke jumping—that same fire season. Everyone expected him to be a changed man, to be sobered, to have a noticeably deeper appreciation of life. But he didn't feel a bit different, except for a nagging itch to go over those final moments on the ridge. Why had he left the others behind and raced alone for the ridge top? Had he deliberately lunged forward at the ridgetop, sensing the heat blast, and saved his own life? Or had he been shoved by the heat and his life saved by mere chance?

When the Forest Service offered him full-time employment in partial compensation for his injuries, Hipke opted to remain a seasonal smoke jumper, leaping out of airplanes and grubbing in the dirt. Hipke's turndown outraged the man who had made the job offer, Jack Ward Thomas, then chief of the Forest Service. "We offered him a *job!*" Thomas said later. "There aren't too many of those around."

Hipke returned to Storm King Mountain at every opportunity. He led tours of the fire site for other firefighters and hand-pruned undergrowth, as did others, to keep the fatal fireline open. He even re-created the final seconds of his race with fire, scream and all, for a History

Channel documentary based on the book *Fire on the Mountain*, which depicted his escape.

But now, seven years later, working a fire atop a Colorado mesa a few score miles from Storm King, Hipke still had a sense of unreality about that day in 1994. In a way, his big moment still did not belong to him. Hipke shouldered a hundred-pound pack and joined five other smoke jumpers as they prepared to hike down from the mesa top. It was Wednesday, July 11, the day after the Thirtymile Fire fatalities, and Hipke and the other jumpers had just put out yet another wildland fire—or in this case two fires. They had parachuted onto the mesa top toward dusk the evening before and had worked through the night to contain two small blazes, which had been started in juniper and brush by lightning. In a lighthearted moment, they had named the fires the Hawk Complex after one of their number, John Hawkins; the term *complex* is usually reserved for multiple fires covering thousands of acres. The jumpers thought that was pretty witty; the bigger of their two fires was less than a hundred feet wide.

The climb down the side of the mesa was short but rough, and the jumpers were glad to reach a road and flag a ride to the nearest town, Rangely. The smoke jumper base in Grand Junction, which had been the starting point for the smoke jumpers who fought the South Canyon Fire, was not far away, and the operations center there sent out a couple of vehicles to pick them up. One of the drivers brought grim news: four firefighters had been killed the night before on a fire in the North Cascades, and one survivor with badly burned hands had been airlifted to Harborview Medical Center.

The news was a shock on several levels. These were the first deaths by fire for the Forest Service since the South Canyon Fire. But for Hipke the connections ran even deeper. The North Cascades were home ground. He had grown up climbing the towering peaks and steep ridges around the summer cabin his family still kept on a lake near Leavenworth. He had been recruited into firefighting by George Marcott, the Naches Ranger District FMO who had helped carry the bad news to the FitzPatricks and Jody Gray. Hipke had been stationed for most of his fifteen-year career at the North Cascades Smokejumper Base in

Winthrop, where the survivors had been taken. One of Hipke's first thoughts upon hearing about Emhoff's injuries was to wonder whether Emhoff was on the same ward at the Harborview center, perhaps in the same bed, where Hipke had lain while his hands were being cared for.

"This wasn't supposed to happen," Hipke said later. "It was supposed to be another fifty years before people were dying again. It slapped me in the face with reality."

Hipke felt a need to contact Emhoff. Visiting a fellow firefighter in circumstances parallel to his own might help him come to final terms with his experience, he thought. Perhaps, too, he could make a difference for Emhoff. Getting in touch with Emhoff, though, proved a chore. It took ten days for Hipke to make the contact and arrange a leave from smoke jumping. "When I was in Harborview, people were calling and couldn't get through," Hipke said. "Now here I was on the other end of things, making the calls."

When he finally arrived at the medical center, he started for his old ward. Emhoff, however, had suffered burns over 25 percent of his body, compared with 10 percent for Hipke. Hipke was redirected to the intensive care unit. Emhoff was heavily medicated when Hipke finally found him, but not so woozy that he couldn't ask questions. He wanted to know all the details of Hipke's treatments. More than anything else, though, he wanted to know if Hipke was able to work hard again with his hands. "His hands looked fantastic, you couldn't tell they'd been burned at all," Emhoff said later. Hipke had expected the visit to last five minutes, but he stayed a half hour.

The discussion left both men feeling satisfied. The extent of Emhoff's injuries helped Hipke put his own wounds in perspective. "He was burned so much worse than I was, over such a larger area," Hipke said later. "My burns were minor by comparison." And Hipke was able to pass along his experience where it counted, with a firefighter who had burned his hands because, like Hipke, he liked to work without gloves.

Emhoff, for his part, took hope from Hipke's story of healing. If Hipke had made a complete comeback, perhaps he too could return to what he loved best: hard outdoor work with his hands. He had a much longer way to go. Not only were his hands in worse shape, but unlike

Hipke he had burns scattered over his body, though a heavy layer of body hair, along with his gear and clothing, had protected him somewhat. "I'm a pretty hairy guy, and that helped," Emhoff said. "I always thought hairy would be the enemy, but it actually added insulation." He'd had a goatee and hadn't shaved for a week, so the lower portion of his face was spared. He had raccoon eyes from wearing sunglasses. His calves had a sharp line, red above and white below, where his boot tops had reached. His wrists were scorched where he had rolled up his sleeves, against regulations. "That's another one we preach but don't do," he said, with wry humor.

Though Emhoff eventually lost his right pinkie finger, doctors saved both his hands. He kept an album of photos showing the various stages of treatment and proudly showed it to visitors, with a warning about the graphic images. In one operation, doctors had sewn his left hand into his belly, a procedure called a crane flap, to give the hand a chance to rebuild fatty tissue as a bed for skin grafts. It worked. Emhoff left the medical center on September 13, more than two months after the fire, though his physical therapy and other treatment continued long after that. The Forest Service paid his medical bills and the cost of putting up his parents near the medical center, and agreed to meet the agency's legal obligation to pay for follow-on treatment for the rest of his life.

The agency also offered him a full-time job, as a driver on an engine crew in California. He accepted. Handling the wheel of a truck was a major accomplishment, but Emhoff didn't stop there. After three years of ongoing treatments, he amazed everyone by qualifying as a rappeller, dropping down a rope from a helicopter to fight fires. He spent several seasons with the Wenatchee Valley Rappellers, a crew based near Yakima, and then went back to the Naches Ranger District, where he works to this day as a fuels management assistant.

Emhoff's contacts with Furnish's investigation team, by contrast, were a failure. A full-scale interview was put off for several weeks until Emhoff was strong enough to handle it. Then, three of the most experienced investigators arrived at the medical center with a new, technically advanced audio recorder, which they had little experience using. The recorder missed much of what was said: it apparently was placed too far from Emhoff; he mumbled; and when the recorder, which operates silently, ran out of audio space, no one noticed for a long time. The transcript of the interview has blank passages in almost every paragraph, similar to a heavily redacted national security document. Aware of the unfavorable impression this was going to make, the Forest Service attached a "Notice of Explanation" to the transcript that pleads, "The blank lines in Jason Emhoff's statement are due to inaudible portions of the audiotape used during the interview that could not be transcribed." The technical quality was so bad, and Emhoff was so drugged at the time, that he refused to sign the transcript.

When investigators asked the big question, whether Emhoff had heard Daniels give him and the others in Craven's group an order to come down to the road, Emhoff at first said he could not remember. The transcript of his response, given here as printed, is riddled with maddening blanks.

> Q: Do you remember hearing anybody, Ellreese or anybody else, saying that the road was the preferred deployment site or come out of the rocks or anything like that?
>
> No, I really don't. I don't remember any of that. I remember Tom being _____. We were hanging around, sitting on the rocks, kind of discouraged. As [we] were talking back and forth at the time we deployed, and it was _____. I know there was _____.
>
> I thought _____. I know I _____. _____ deploy up there _____.
>
> Q: Did he end up down in the creek though?
> A: Yeah.

The interview, taken in entirety, paints a confusing picture of events, because of Emhoff's drugged condition as well as the poor quality of the recording. Even so, the interview should have raised a warning flag for investigators. The one survivor who had been with Craven's group throughout their ordeal could not remember Daniels saying a word to them. But the many problems with the interview, and the long delay in obtaining it, apparently made Emhoff's recollections easy to discount.

Other survivors, most notably Rutman, who had stood near Daniels for most of the entrapment, appeared to support Daniels's version of events. Rutman's statement was taken down in notes, which he signed, but was not sound recorded. The notes contain this statement: "Ten minutes before deployment Ellreese had told those on the boulders to come down and got no response." The words *those on the boulders* had been jotted in to replace the word *them*, a change more likely done for the sake of clarity than for any dubious purpose. In any case, more serious difficulties for Rutman's statement lay ahead.

Furnish was determined to meet the forty-five-day deadline—the agency standard, though not a legal requirement—to issue a final report. The task was an emotional as well as intellectual challenge. On a series of trips to the site, Furnish, like many others who would follow him, was struck by the capricious way the fire had behaved, burning ferociously in one spot while sparing ground close by. Life and death had been a matter of inches and feet. All big fires jump around, but this one was an extreme case.

"The feeling was almost palpable—how could this have happened here?" Furnish said later, in a conversation with me. "It was so quiet, so benign. I am haunted by the images of the leaves on the trees that were still intact, still green. A lot of the pine needles around where the people died were twisted. They're flash-frozen from the heat.

"We would see a white mark where there had been a log. There was no ash, it was just gone. All you saw was white-hot memory in the rocks. Next to it, ten or fifteen feet over, you'd see a punky old log that was still there. I don't get that; I don't understand the mystery."

Furnish and his team struggled to fit eyewitness stories into a coherent narrative. "It was like a car accident," Furnish said later. "Everybody had a different recollection. You talk to eight people who saw it, and you get a different story from everyone, and everyone thinks they're right. It's only when you put eight stories together that things begin to converge."

A chain of little mistakes linked up and led to disaster, the investigation team found, but there were also two major failures of leadership. The first was the decision, taken without adequate thought or discussion, to reengage the fire. The second was when the trapped crew wasted "the luxury of time" and did nothing to improve their chances. "Instead of preparing for the worst, they hoped for the best," Furnish said later.

Those conclusions have all stood the test of time and inspired numerous fresh approaches to managing wildfires.

The investigation team also concluded that Daniels indeed had told Craven's group to get out of the rocks and had been ignored. "We did wind up putting a lot of weight on Ellreese's statement, particularly because we had a chance to go back and interview him a second time," Furnish said. That left Furnish with a daunting task. He had to tell families that their children had defied authority and bore heavy responsibility for their own deaths. In the countdown to the public release of the report, local Forest Service officials urged Furnish to brief the families beforehand, as a courtesy.

"I had bad vibes about doing this," Furnish said. "A lot of things could go wrong. There was no way we were going to please the families. But I ended up caving in."

CHAPTER FIFTEEN

We owe respect to the living.
To the dead we owe only the truth.

—Voltaire

Nothing brings out the best in rural folks like a shared tragedy. People rush to offer help, toss folding money into donation jars, pin on purple ribbons, and perform the unaccustomed task of expressing powerful emotion in public. Such acts of belonging testify to the unseen ties that bind isolated communities in ordinary times. It helps, too, if the nation joins in and offers its sympathy, as happened at first after the Thirtymile Fire. The story commanded national media attention. A network television crew arrived to compile footage for a documentary special. President George W. Bush, invited to a memorial service in Yakima in late July, declined only because he had to be in Italy for a trade conference that day, his aides said. Two of his cabinet secretaries did attend: Ann Veneman, Secretary of the Department of Agriculture, parent agency of the Forest Service; and Secretary of the Interior Gale Norton.

In a familiar ritual, fallen firefighters took their last journey home in a smoke jumper airplane. A prop-driven C-23 Sherpa carried the caskets of the three Naches Ranger District firefighters to McAllister Field in Yakima, just as smoke jumper aircraft had flown home victims of the South Canyon Fire. Families and friends gathered at the field in silence.

As each casket appeared, a Forest Service representative read out a name: Karen FitzPatrick, Jessica Johnson, Devin Weaver. The day before, Tom Craven had been taken by station wagon hearse to Ellensburg, though the town has a small airfield nearby; some friends sensed a slight. Four private funerals were held in as many days. At Craven's service, so many people showed up in yellow shirts, green pants, and purple ribbons that young T'shaun cried out, "Hey, Mom, they're wearing yellow shirts just like Dad!"

"Yes, Son, they're wearing yellow shirts just like Daddy," Evelyn replied.

"Hey, Mom, they have ribbons on their fire shirts. Daddy doesn't wear ribbons on his fire shirt."

"No, Son, Daddy doesn't wear ribbons," Evelyn said, and wept.

Karen FitzPatrick's funeral marked a turn for the good in the life of her sister, Jaina, who had been bedridden as a consequence of medication prescribed to control bipolar disorder. "I was not going drugged to my sister's funeral," she said later. She stopped taking the medication, rose from her bed, attended the funeral, and started down a long road to more normal living. For the next four years Jaina tried different doctors, therapies, and medication; she adopted strict eating habits, went to the gym regularly, and lost much of the eighty pounds she'd gained as a side effect of the drugs. "Today she is a size twelve, looking bright and feeling good," Kathie said of her daughter. "She is now the girl Karen would remember." Her struggle was so successful that her doctors nominated her for a paid position counseling others with bipolar disorder.

A memorial service for all four victims was held at the Yakima Valley SunDome, which is big enough to stage rodeos. More than three hundred fire vehicles from station houses across the nation paraded along a six-mile route to the SunDome. Thousands stood in tribute along the way. "Remember Our Heroes," read placards held up by teenagers. The SunDome filled with a checkerboard of fire units, each in uniforms ranging from the wildland badge of yellow shirts and green pants, to crew T-shirts in many colors, to crisp dress blues and ties. The service was strong on fanfare. A four-man military unit performed precision drill with rifles. The Forest Service provided an honor guard, which conducted a flag ceremony, and a chaplain-escort, Steve Seltzner, a fire veteran who had helped organize a standing memorial team to deal with line-of-duty deaths for wildland firefighters. "Outside people don't really understand what it's like," Seltzner said later; firefighter families, he had found, "need a shoulder, not a sermon."

Those who spoke included Washington governor Gary Locke and Chief Bosworth, both of whom had learned enough about each of the four to use their first names. Tom had been a standout athlete and devoted family man who mentored young firefighters. Karen, voted by classmates most likely to be the next Martha Stewart, had a devout faith and forgiving nature. Jessica had inspired friends with her high spirits and problem-solving skills. Devin, quiet and gentlemanly but with an edge to his humor, had found his best friend in his father.

"They were in the very best sense of the word Westerners," said Governor Locke. "Not the mythical Westerns of the cowboy and gun-slinging movies, but real Westerners, men and women who search and dream, plainspoken and honest, and independent and resourceful."

Chief Leitch of the West Valley Fire District, where Johnson had been a cadet, perhaps best caught their common spirit.

"We are an extended family, all with the last name 'firefighters,'" Leitch said. "All four were athletes, strong challengers, fierce competitors—all understanding the importance of a team. Firefighting is a team sport. They were there on that mountain as a team, there for each other. They died as a team. These young firefighters did not consider themselves heroes. They were well satisfied with a day's job done well.

"These four were high on the fresh Cascade Mountain air. They were high on life and all of its challenges. There were no drugs, gangs, or rap sheets. There was college, family, friends, God, and good times. They didn't wait until dark to see the world. They were future teachers of our children, future leaders of our battles. They represent the best of what America has to offer."

At the conclusion of the service, a fire bell was rung, and then the eerie electronic tones of the Last Alarm sounded: all units were home, the message said, and four firefighters had failed to answer roll call. The memorial service put a temporary cap on public events as the community stood back to await the release of the official fire report. Chief Leitch had remarked that investigators should not seek to lay blame, but rather to learn the lessons necessary to prevent another Thirtymile Fire. His generous sentiment was not universally shared; many people looked forward to a day of reckoning. With national and regional media on the alert, pressure built for a public accounting.

Then an event occurred that took the name of catastrophe; the date was September 11, 2001. The network television crew dropped the documentary project on the Thirtymile Fire and headed, as best they could with a national air traffic lockdown, for the East Coast. The terrorist attacks on the World Trade Center in New York City and at the Pentagon in the nation's capital did not simply dominate subsequent news coverage; for many months, the 9/11 disaster and its aftermath were virtually the only stories given prominence by national media. In the new age of terrorism, a fire report from the rural Northwest was off the radar screen. Interest remained high, however, in both the wildland fire community and the Northwest region, where there was much at stake: reputations, careers, lessons for the future, the need for justice to be done, and the desire to find healing in remembrance. When the fire report was unveiled at last, a month late on September 26, the impact on those directly involved was undiminished.

Furnish knew that he was the bearer of unwelcome news for the families. Yet he had not lived through the South Canyon Fire at the ground level of the wildland fire community, and neither had key members of his team: Kern, the human factors specialist, had been in the Air Force in 1994; Chockie, the professional investigator, in the private sector. That circumstance may help explain why Furnish and his team badly underestimated the uproar their findings would cause, not only among the families but also within the broader fire community.

The day before the report was to come out, a private briefing on its contents was held for the fire's survivors. The same courtesy ought to be extended to the families, regional Forest Service officials argued, even though the hour was late.

"The people on the Forest were adamant we have this meeting—they were being sensitive to the families," Furnish said. "I said, 'Something about this whole setup doesn't feel good to me.' But I got talked into it. The sense of hostility in that room was palpable. It was toxic. There was no way we were going to please the families."

An hour before the report was to be unveiled publicly, at the Yakima Civic Center, Furnish appeared before the families and a few of their close friends in a meeting room nearby. When he told them what was to come, the families were unbelieving.

"If my son was told to come down out of the rocks, he would have done it," Will Craven told Furnish. A Craven family friend, Kay Evensen, lashed out at Furnish: "And the next time you have a firefighter fatality, you have someone come to the door. No phone calls." Evensen had been with the Cravens the night of the notification.

After having his say, Will Craven became the least outspoken of the parents. He took out his grief by building an elaborate brick and stone memorial over his son's gravesite in the Roslyn cemetery, to which he kept making additions, working there day after day, year after year; Will and Virginia packed in paving stones for the job by hand. The cemetery isn't easy to find, but it's not unusual today to see a fire crew pull up in a rig to pay their respects, and have a word of greeting with Will Craven.

Others, too, spoke out at the meeting. "My daughter was not like that," said Jody Gray. "She was out to please. If Ellreese Daniels told my daughter to come out of the rocks, she'd have jumped." Tammie Blevins, Jessica Johnson's aunt, remarked on her way out the door, "We came here to get answers. I'm walking away from here just disgusted."

"Everyone just wanted to scream," Evelyn Craven said later. "When they briefed us alone, it sounded like Tom disregarded a direct order. It sounded like they were trying to put the blame on my husband. Tom disobeying an order? That's ridiculous."

"That's a lie, a bullshit lie," Ken Weaver later told the *Yakima Herald-Republic* newspaper. "None of those rookies would even propose to disobey an order from an incident commander."

Furnish cut the meeting off after an hour. "We have a press conference; we have to go," he said, curtly. He told the families they were not to make statements at the public meeting, but many did so afterward. Furnish tried to put the best possible face on matters years later. "The meeting with the families went as well as could be expected. It was respectful—no open hostility, shouting, or yelling," he said, though others who were there say there were many raised voices. "But it was very tense. There were tears. It was loaded with emotion—a lot of cynicism, suspicion."

The Thirtymile Fire Investigation Report was released to the media with a supportive word from Chief Bosworth, who attended the press conference. The report portrays a management fiasco that violated every basic safety rule in the book and a majority of the standing safety cautions. From the first moments, the report said, fire managers failed to appreciate the potential of a fire burning in a narrow canyon on a hot day in a time of extreme drought. Never mind the number of rookies; the veterans displayed an astonishing lack of situational awareness throughout the day. Too many people gave orders. Nobody was sure who was in charge. Orders were not enforced. The crew couldn't keep a set of relatively simple water pumps running.

The leadership stuck with unsuitable tactics as the fire grew in size and intensity, and failed even to properly communicate those tactics. Nobody bothered to ask for a weather update, and the dispatch office, which had an afternoon forecast, didn't bother to pass it along. There was no lookout posted after 3:00 PM, the most dangerous time of day for fire. The air observer who was supposed to keep watch couldn't see all of the fire because of smoke. When firefighters attacked the fire head-on in the afternoon, a mistake in itself, they fought it blind: they couldn't see the main fire, had no adequate escape routes or safety zones, and had "no viable strategy" to fight the fire, the report said. Once the entrapment occurred, preparation for a burnover was nonexistent. When a civilian couple unexpectedly showed up without protective clothing or gear, nobody paid them much attention, with the notable exception of Welch.

The report offered a detailed account of how every one of the venerable Ten Standard Firefighting Orders was violated, and how ten of eighteen Watch Out Situations were disregarded. The standard orders cover basics such as keeping up with weather conditions, knowing what the fire is doing, posting lookouts, identifying escape routes and safety zones, giving clear instructions, and maintaining effective control of the fire crew. The Watch Out Situations are safety issues that can be tolerated if cautionary steps are taken. If the basic safety rules had been followed,

Furnish told the news conference, no one need have died. "The fatalities were preventable," he said.

Furnish made a couple of positive points for balance. Daniels had acted wisely by not trying to run the white van and its passengers through flames once the fire crossed the road. Daniels had chosen the only survivable place in the upper canyon to ride out the fire. He had correctly identified the road as a good place to be. The rescue effort had been "quick and effective."

But the mistakes by Daniels and others were so numerous as to be overwhelming. Leadership was "ineffective" and "indecisive," the report said, adding a secondhand judgment about Daniels: "Crewmember testimony indicates that the IC was not a forceful leader and that may have impeded his ability to command the situation at the deployment site." Every member of the investigative team interviewed for this account, however, said without equivocation that Daniels should have acted more forcefully throughout the day, and most especially during the entrapment.

"I was around Ellreese, and he's pretty easygoing, pretty casual, not real directed, tough, or firm," Furnish said years later. "I think the crew sensed that. The order should have been conveyed convincingly, without question or equivocation. A leader would have gotten people to do as requested."

The report also contained a section devoted to the role played in the fatalities by human factors, mainly sleep deprivation, but which also offers a psychological insight. "At the deployment site, the crew's attention was 'turned inward,'" the report said. "The time and attention of experienced crewmembers was channelized almost exclusively on two non-fire issues. The first was keeping less experienced crewmembers calm and the second was the low key conflict between the IC/Crew Boss and the two squad bosses about coming down out of the rocks. This occupied the crew leadership and lowered the vigilance level as the fire approached and prevented any serious preparation from being accomplished at the site." While the remarks are illuminating in some ways, the criticism of the squad bosses, Taylor and Craven, for failing to make "serious preparation" seems to miss the mark. The "low key conflict" began when Taylor and Craven tried to talk Daniels into doing precisely that, and he turned them down, an episode that is only alluded to and not described in the report and its supporting documents. What contributed most to lowering the "vigilance level," it seems with hindsight, was the misjudgment repeated over and over as though it were a mantra—and especially between Daniels and Jasso—that the fire was going to pass by harmlessly.

The human factors section identified fatigue as a major underlying cause of the catastrophe. "The single overwhelming physiological factor that impacted upon this mishap was fatigue caused by sleep deprivation," the report claimed. "This may help explain a series of uncharacteristic lapses in judgment." Work hours and tours of duty for firefighters had been shortened after the South Canyon Fire, and were looked at again after the Thirtymile Fire. Some effective changes were made: for example, crews were to be called out after a full night's sleep and in daylight hours, when possible, rather than traveling overnight before starting work. But the accuracy of the data used in Kern's analysis was challenged by at least one of the fire's supervisors, who said he had a full night's more sleep than the report says, which undercuts the report's conclusion about the extent of the role played by fatigue.

The controversial finding that Craven's group had ignored a direct order from Daniels has a strong military flavor, as though it were a charge in a court-martial proceeding. It reads, "The firefighters on the rock scree were ordered to return to the road; however, these orders were disregarded."

The challenge to that finding was immediate and had a devastating effect on the report's credibility, and on Furnish. The day after the report was made public, three survivors—Dreis, Hurd, and Rutman—held their own press conference and said the charge wasn't fair or completely accurate.

"I didn't hear it [a direct order]," Dreis said. "I talked to other people there. They didn't hear it."*

"They weren't disobeying," said Hurd.

---

*Dreis was killed in January 2006, when he was ejected from and then pinned beneath his sport utility vehicle in an off-road accident in snowy conditions, in the Blue Grade area north of East Wenatchee.

"It's disrespectful to the people who passed away, to their families," said Rutman, in a milder dissent. He did not deny that he had heard Daniels call to the people in the rocks. But he flatly contradicted another claim in the report, namely that Daniels had given an order to deploy shelters when the flames arrived, though the report credits Daniels with saving lives by doing so. The only order Rutman says he heard Daniels give as the fire approached—and he was right beside him when it happened—was "Get your shelter out and cover your buddies."

What most offended the three survivors was the report's implication that the victims were to blame for their deaths. "They're not here to defend themselves," Dreis said. "Somebody's got to stand up for them."

Both the Thirtymile and South Canyon investigation reports have been tainted by the charge contained in each that firefighters were partly to blame for their own deaths. If such a charge is true, it should be pointed out and lessons learned. But even then the charge is sure to cause agonies for the living, and should be based on an unshakable foundation in fact. In the case of the Thirtymile Fire, there is no serious doubt that Daniels told people at the entrapment site several times to stay on or near the road. Numerous survivors heard him say those things early in the entrapment.

There is considerable—though less conclusive—evidence that Daniels indeed did tell Craven and his group to come down from the rock scree, but it's unclear when he made those remarks. Daniels thought he said it repeatedly. That's the story he told in the first hours after the fatalities, when he was emotionally distraught and unlikely to be concocting a fiction. According to Sheriff's Sergeant Dan Christensen's report on his interview with Daniels, conducted immediately after the fire, "Craven's group was up on some rocks and Daniels told them to get down on the road."

In Daniels's first interview with Furnish's fire investigators, he did not mention calling to Craven's group, though surely he would have done so if he was fabricating a story to save his own skin. When reinterviewed by Kern and asked direct questions, however, Daniels told the story the same way he had told it to Sergeant Christensen. Kern did not have an audio recorder, but there is no real reason to doubt the essential accuracy of his written summary, which has Daniels saying,

"I told them several times—at least three—I said 'Come down out of the rocks, that's not the place to be.'"

Daniels, then, almost certainly said something to Craven's group about coming down from the rocks. But was it an order? Was it heard? Was it deliberately ignored? The answer to those questions is essential to determining how much responsibility, if any, the four victims had for their deaths.

In fact, *Daniels never claimed that he issued an order.* He is quoted as saying only that he "told" Craven's group to move; nowhere in the official record does he say that he "ordered" them to retreat. Normally a directive from an IC is the same thing as an order, but in this case Daniels had not functioned as IC for most of the day, and at no time did he aggressively assert his authority. Daniels told Kern that he was certain he was heard and ignored, but he did not claim that anyone in Craven's group responded with so much as a word or a wave off. When Kern was questioned on this point years later, for this account, he said that Daniels based his assertion about being heard and ignored on eye contact with Craven's group. Eye contact is hardly irrefutable evidence for an accusation of this much consequence.

There is no independent, unchallenged testimony to back up Daniels's account in its entirety. Two survivors from Craven's group, Emhoff and Welch, maintain that they did not hear Daniels call to them. The official interview with Emhoff was botched, but Emhoff said years later for this account what he sketchily said then: if Daniels called to Craven's group, he didn't hear him. When Welch was interviewed for this account, she emphatically denied hearing Daniels call to her or anyone else in Craven's group. Granted, by then she was well aware of the denials by other survivors. But Welch is an unlikely liar. She proved her moral courage when she saved the lives of the Hagemeyers. The relevant exchange with Welch for this account, which was sound recorded, reads:

Question: Did you ever hear Ellreese Daniels say, "Come out of the rocks"?
Welch: No. He never said that. He never did. I don't think he talked to us the whole time. Like this stupid report says, he told me to come out of the rocks and it saved my life? He never did. I just think it was basic instinct or God telling me to come down.

The investigation team placed much weight, Furnish said later, on the testimony of one other witness, Rutman. But Rutman now says that his account to investigators, the one that he signed but that was not sound recorded, is wrong. In a series of interviews for this account, Rutman said that he, like many others, heard Daniels tell everyone to stay near the road. "The thing I remember hearing, Ellreese wanted us to stay together. That was early, when we first got there."

But when asked about Daniels's later communication with Craven's group, Rutman said, "If Ellreese told them to come down, I didn't hear it." This contradicts the signed notes of Rutman's interview with investigators, in which Rutman has Daniels calling to Craven's group ten minutes before the deployment. When Rutman was read that passage during one of the interviews for this account, he flexed his eyebrows Groucho Marx fashion and remarked, "They should have taped it, shouldn't they?"

Furnish and other members of the investigation team believe that Rutman and perhaps others changed their stories under peer pressure, and perhaps some did. "If there's ever a case study in how one witness influences another, it's this one," Kern said years later, bitterly. But the picture in the report of Daniels repeatedly issuing an order that was heard and then deliberately ignored by Craven's group is contradicted by every key witness—Emhoff, Welch, and Rutman—and even goes a step beyond what the soft-spoken Daniels, who never used the word *order*, claims happened. Further, in the judgment of Thom Taylor and others, Craven's group had good reason to think they were following Daniels's early instruction to stay on or close to the road. The place where they had gathered in the rocks is but ten steps up from the road; it was almost like being there.

"Where Tom was, that's on the road, well within the normal spread zone of a resting crew," said Tony Craven, one of Tom Craven's firefighting brothers. "I don't see how you consider it off the road. Tom knew Ellreese. We had worked with him since 1990. We knew and trusted him. If Ellreese had told Tom to come to the road, Tom would have come to the road."

About a year after the event, when he was mostly recovered from his physical injuries, Emhoff returned to the entrapment site where he offered this assessment of Daniels: "He never stood up and said, 'Hey, listen to me, we need to all get together and do this and this. We need to do something, even if it's picking your nose, as long as everyone's doing the same thing.' He never said that. He wasn't a verbally loud person. He was quiet and not really reserved, but shy about a lot of things. So if he ever asked us to get down off the rocks, we never heard it.

"And why would we disobey it?"

Emhoff's final question raises the issue of character. Was anyone in Craven's group *likely* to disobey orders? There is no scientific way to measure character, but the four victims had well-formed personalities that provide their own answers.

Craven embraced the fire world's rules and rewards, passing up his father's advice to use his education to pursue a safer career path. FitzPatrick chose a life of faith, discipline, and sacrifice, forswearing worldly temptations to follow the narrow way. Johnson had turned her life around only the weekend before, walking out on a damaging relationship and taking up a Spartan lifestyle in a fire barracks. Weaver was the forever faithful son, even in his dark period, always striving to fulfill parental expectations. Tom, Karen, Jessica, and Devin had bowed to authority in their lives. Though they could no longer speak for themselves, they had left traces of character in their final moments.

It never occurred to those trapped there at the bend in the river that conditions could change so fast and so catastrophically. One second the sky was blue, the sun was shining, and the wind was wafting the flames away from them. Then in the blink of an eye the sun disappeared, the sky turned black, and a thousand tiny particles of burning light raced toward them. The wave of superheated air that met Craven and the others as they started for the road was nonnegotiable. The road that had seemed a step away faded like a broken promise into a swirl of embers and darkness.

They turned around and clambered desperately up and away from the heat, sometimes on all fours, grabbing at rocks to help them upward and away from the firestorm. Their awareness of mortal danger ebbed and flowed. Several dropped their packs and other gear during the climb. Afterward, Detective Sloan found the debris and concluded that it was a sign of panic; in fact the opposite may be the case, though surely they were shocked and frightened. All four arrived at the deployment spot with the essential item: a fire shelter. They were trained to throw away their packs, with their fusees, and run with just their fire shelters in their hands. Managing this under calm conditions is a simple exercise, but a feat of considerable self-control with a flame wave hard on your heels.

Taylor, high above them, heard them call out in bewilderment, "Deploy? Deploy?" No place appeared safer than any other on that exposed, rocky slope. Taylor shouted down, "Deploy! Deploy!" and watched them shaking out their shelters.

What if they had started for the road seconds earlier? What if they had managed to struggle just a step or two higher, as Emhoff did, out of the heat wave's fatal footprint? The moment for such questions had passed away forever. Their world had shrunk down to a slight depression in the rock scree, the fire shelters, and the coming fire.

No one who lived heard another word from Craven after the shelter deployment began. His failure to anticipate the worst had been everyone's failure. But Craven had backed up Taylor's attempt to persuade Daniels to prepare for a burnover. He had kept his squad calm and together in the rocks. If he had lived, he likely would have gone on doing the same sort of things, bossing a fire crew, being head of a family, holding people together. Craven was the farthest one up the canyon and likely the first to be hit by the full fury of the heat wave. Perhaps because he led the way, he had not taken the time to jettison his pack and its deadly fusees; or perhaps he simply could not manage or forgot to throw off the pack—no one will ever know. Slag from the fusees, which burn at 1,500 degrees, was found under his body. The fire burned hard and long where he was, but his lungs were unmarked by soot, which indicates that for him death came within seconds.

The heat that struck Craven full-force overlapped Johnson as well, though it took perhaps a second longer. Johnson, who was right next to Craven, was able to exchange a word with Emhoff—"Hey, who kicked me?"—before she entered her shelter, fulfilling her presentiment about the level of danger. Next to Johnson was Weaver, who prepared for the flames in textbook fashion. He stretched out flat on his belly inside his shelter, gloves and hard hat in place. He was spared the most intense blast of heat, even though he was but a few feet from Johnson. When his body was found, he appeared as though asleep.

Afterward, Detective Sloan told Ken Weaver that his son had acted well in his final moments. "You could write the manual on shelter deployment by the way Devin deployed his shelter," Sloan said. "Your son did not lose his cool. I tell you that because I would have been proud of my son if he had acted the same way." Ken Weaver drew comfort from the words.

Last in line, FitzPatrick shook out her shelter and drew it over her back. She, however, did not lie down inside her shelter in the prescribed manner. The story spread afterward as a rural legend, but witness statements and photographs confirm it: FitzPatrick was found inside her shelter bowed on her knees, her hands on either side of her head, in an attitude of prayer.

In seconds, an unkind destiny forged the final link in the long chain of errors and betrayed the bright promise and changed lives of four young wildland firefighters.

CHAPTER SIXTEEN

*I woke up August 5 with the thought that the Mann Gulch
fire had started "thirty years ago today," and as I remembered
I could plainly see the Canyon Ferry Ranger Station as it used
to be, Bob leaving on a plane to scout his three fires....Did you
know that at the board of review (at Missoula), Bob was on the
stand giving testimony for six grueling hours? One secretary
told me, "He turned sort of green when they started asking
about the smoke jumper rescue, but he said, 'I will answer any
questions you want to ask about finding the bodies if I don't
have to look at you'—and he turned his chair to the wall."*

—Lois Jansson, wife of Ranger J. Robert Jansson,
who fought the 1949 Mann Gulch Fire,
from a letter to Norman Maclean, August 12, 1979

The survivors' challenge to the credibility of the Forest Service's Thirtymile Fire report found a receptive ear with the agency's chief, Dale Bosworth. "I'm sensitive to the fact, this feeling, that we're blaming the victims," Bosworth said several years later. "We could have a long-lasting hurt from that unless we're pretty doggone sure that's what happened." At the time of the South Canyon Fire, Bosworth had escorted the body of Smoke Jumper Jim Thrash home to McCall, Idaho—the chief in 1994, Jack Ward Thomas, had ordered Bosworth and other regional foresters to personally escort the caskets of South Canyon victims on their last flights home.

"I had been traumatized, and I wanted the regional foresters to be traumatized," Thomas said. In 1994 he got a late-night call at his home in Washington, D.C., and immediately booked a flight to Colorado. He was there the next day, not in uniform as chief, but wearing a yellow fire shirt, green pants, and battered White's boots. He joined the survivors, many of whom did not immediately recognize him, gathered in the bar of a motel. "I had never felt like that before," he said later, after the Thirtymile Fire. "I thought having the regional foresters accompany the bodies would make an impression, and that they would feel it too."

The experience had a lasting effect on Bosworth. "I saw a lot of the feelings of the people involved in Storm King," Bosworth said later, also in the wake of the Thirtymile Fire. "To say those persons caused their own . . . well, we need to be really, really careful about that."

One week after the survivors' contrary press conference, Bosworth ordered the fire investigation reopened. He directed the accident review board, already in place, to reevaluate the finding about Daniels's ignored order, and he passed along his concern about not blaming victims. "I'm sure we talked about it, though I don't recall specifically the discussion," Bosworth said later. "I don't want victims to be blamed, that's for sure."

Accident review boards for fire fatality investigations were another reform drawn from the South Canyon Fire. The one for the Thirty-mile Fire had already sent back an early draft of the report for more work, and that contributed to the monthlong delay in the report's release. "I would not accept the report as it was early on," said Tom L. Thompson, who headed the accident review board. Furnish's investigative team needed to nail down findings and explain matters such as the failure to find the Hagemeyers. The team had tried too hard to capture a mood and not hard enough to gather facts, Thompson said, citing the report's prologue, which begins: "The stillness of this place is eerie amidst the lingering smoke. The Chewuch River makes no sound as it glides by. Yet, there was violence here."

Thompson said he did not set out to exonerate the victims, but did appreciate the sensitivities involved. "Placing blame on someone who died isn't wrong," he said. "But it better be the truth." After reexamining testimony and documents for two weeks, the review board said the evidence did not sustain the finding that Daniels had issued an "order" to those in the rocks, but it did indicate that he had said something to them. The board offered two possible scenarios. In the first, Craven's group did not hear Daniels. "There is no verification or absolute knowledge that those sitting on the two rocks heard the directive," the board said.

In the second, Craven and his group did hear Daniels, but they thought he meant stay close to the road, not come down. Both scenarios raised the possibility that Craven and his group thought they were close enough to the road to move there when conditions worsened, and that they had planned to do so, the same possibility raised by Thom Taylor and Tony Craven.

"The bigger issue was the utter lack of leadership," Thompson said later. "Anybody could have stepped forward along the way and stopped it."

The review board recommended dropping the original finding about an ignored order and replacing it with this sentence: "The IC tried to get the firefighters sitting on the rocks to move to the road, but it is not known if they heard his directive." Other changes were recommended as well—four pages' worth—ranging from minor spelling corrections to dropping the assertion that Rebecca Welch left the rocks because Daniels ordered her to do so. Families and survivors expressed satisfaction when all the changes were adopted, though complaints persisted that the reversal did not go far enough.

"Much like the story that is told of the fourteen who died in Colorado in 1994, our daughter and the three others that also died were blamed for their own deaths," Jody Gray said later. "The Forest Service then retracted the statements, stating that the four who died may not have heard the order to come down off the rocks. The truth is known that the statement was never made for them to come down off the rocks. I personally have talked with some of the firefighters that survived the Thirtymile Fire, and their statements to me were that those orders never came to those who lost their lives. I do give the Forest Service some credit for changing the report and bringing it somewhat closer to the truth. They made a baby step to the truth without ever acknowledging exactly what happened."

Furnish, to the contrary, felt betrayed. He came to believe that Bosworth had bowed to outside pressures and "played a political game to appease the families." What particularly dismayed Furnish and others on his investigation team was the decision by Thompson's review board to disavow their finding about Daniels and the disregarded order.

"I think this is a time when Dale should have stood his ground," Furnish said later. "I thought it was a mistake for him to revisit that issue. And I didn't particularly appreciate the way Tom Thompson handled it. Tom basically cast out options, and one of the possible scenarios was not that Ellreese's repeated orders were disregarded by the crew. Now, personally, I chafe at that. I don't think that gave the investigation team enough credit. We worked that issue awful hard. Not even to list our conclusion as a possibility was, I thought . . . That bugged me."

The Forest Service, meanwhile, began disciplinary actions, unprecedented in the history of the agency, against its own personnel. To the surprise of many, the regional forester for the Pacific Northwest, Harv Forsgren, after a further administrative review, recommended firing three of the supervisors: Ellreese Daniels, Barry George, and Harry Dunn. He also recommended lesser penalties—ranging from removal from fire work to letters of reprimand—for eight others. Pete Kampen was to be suspended for a period and permanently removed from fire work. Gabe Jasso had to requalify for air attack. Pete Soderquist, Elton Thomas, Jack Ellinger, Dave Laughman, John Newcom, and Sonny O'Neal, the supervisor of the Okanogan-Wenatchee Forest, were subject to lesser disciplinary actions—some quite minor. None of the names, however, was publicly disclosed.

When the penalties were challenged on grounds they were "disproportionate" to past disciplinary actions, the Forest Service acknowledged that in the previous decade only one agency supervisor had been formally disciplined for negligence on a fire, in a case that did not involve either injuries or death. After the South Canyon Fire, which was actually the responsibility of the Bureau of Land Management, no one was publicly disciplined, though the Colorado state director for the BLM was quietly forced to retire.

"You could blow me over with a feather that they actually came out and handed down something substantive," said Ken Weaver, though he was not completely satisfied. The disciplinary measures "whitewashed" the severity of the misconduct, said Weaver, who wanted to see people charged with criminal offenses, and pursued the case in the courts for years afterward.

Every one of the eleven disciplinary cases was appealed. The appeals were handled by Regional Forester Linda Goodman, who had been deputy regional forester for Forsgren when they took the disciplinary actions—and signed off on them—and then was promoted to his post when he was transferred. Goodman assembled what amounted to a kitchen cabinet of managers and fire experts, each with long experience. She didn't hurry. She and her advisers reinterviewed survivors, invited them to talk at length, and asked questions based on the statements of others, cross-checking and stimulating memories. The advisers also spent a July day in 2002 walking through events at the site with Daniels, Kampen, Dunn, and Laughman. (Goodman did not accompany her advisers on that trip, to give them more freedom to hash things out among themselves.)

In an incident that later became famous on the Okanogan-Wenatchee, the administrative review team helping prepare the original disciplinary case for Forsgren had visited the site in January 2002, with several feet of snow lying on the ground. Driving snowmobiles into the remote area, they took a wrong turn and were lost for hours. They wound up spending forty-five minutes at the fire site—mostly staring at snowdrifts, according to the locals who accompanied them.

Goodman and her advisers also listened to the views of Tom Leuschen, the fire behavior analyst based at Twisp. Much had changed for Leuschen since 5:24 PM on the day of the fatalities, when he had heard the first radio report of a deployment on the Thirtymile Fire. Since then the fire had become his consuming passion. He had been a consultant to Furnish's investigation team, but the official fire report had left him unsatisfied. For him, a crucial element was missing, as though the fire was saying something and nobody was listening.

Barely three weeks after the fire, Leuschen's son, Jeff, came home from fighting a blaze not many miles from the site of the Thirtymile Fire. In a disturbing replay, Leuschen had listened to radio chatter during the day as his son's fire crew struggled against flames that should have been easy to extinguish, in normal times. Leuschen had contacted the fire's supervisors and warned them that the situation was anything but normal—conditions were hot, dry, and intense, just as they had been during the Thirtymile Fire. But Jeff's crew had stayed in the fight. By the end of the day, the blaze had burned beyond control.

"How'd it go?" Tom asked when his son came home that night.

"We were in and out of safety zones all day, Dad," Jeff replied.

Why are we doing this again? Leuschen thought. Why didn't everyone recognize the intense conditions and pull back?

Leuschen had a longtime interest, sparked by the South Canyon Fire, in the common denominators of fatal fires: the similarities of weather, degree of slope, kinds of fuels, and other factors that determine fire behavior. He discovered one element common to every fatal fire he studied: the presence of unburned fuel between the firefighters and the fire. If he could devise a formula for when to back off in that special case, when other conditions too were reaching the danger zone, it could be a guide for all firefighters and save lives.

"My disengagement guidelines were supposed to alert firefighters to change tactics during periods of high danger when working in unburned fuel, and tell them when the danger had subsided and it was all right to become more aggressive," Leuschen said later. His timing was good. The fire world was on the lookout for ways to be more selective about which fires to fight. But Leuschen's first guidelines proved unpopular because fire bosses saw them as a requirement to disengage every time a fire grew hot and fierce.

As Leuschen set about refining his system, he pored over witness accounts of the Thirtymile Fire and he reinterviewed survivors, many of them personal friends who spoke openly to him. "I need to know what you know," he told them. "Where was the fire? What did it look like? What were you doing?" He became the acknowledged local expert and even led tours of the fire site for families of the victims.

"If they had chosen any place else, we'd have lost them all," Leuschen told the family of Karen FitzPatrick a few weeks after the fire, while standing at the entrapment site. Kathie and Jaina, wearing yellow fire shirts and blue jeans, and using a portable video camera, made their way up to Karen's place in the rock scree. There, they gave each other a hug and placed a bouquet of flowers. "This is a kind of special time, an emotional time, a time to think about what happened here," Kathie said. "This will all probably grow back and be green and teeming with life this spring. But Karen, Jessica, Devin, and Tom won't come back, except in our hearts."

Despite his efforts, Leuschen could offer no solution to the biggest mystery of the fire's behavior. Why had the fatal arm of the fire taken that left hook into the rock scree, and why had the heat blast at the fatal site been so confined, so sustained in that one spot, and so intense?

"Without the blisteringly fast movement by the fire, the fatalities would never have happened," Leuschen said later. "I wanted to learn the answer of why that happened and carry the message forward."

The double plume of smoke that boiled violently up over the fire was one possible explanation. The chaos of counterrotating plumes could account for practically any effect, including that fatal left hook. Supporting this theory was a photograph of the double plume taken by a professional photographer, Sandor A. Feher, from the deck of his home near Winthrop. In his photo, both plumes are fully developed, their tops swept back like the horns of a massive ram. Joining the two tops are four horizontal bars of smoke, which might resemble a stairway or a furrowed brow, depending on the viewer's perspective. The camera automatically stamped the photo 5:30 PM, a moment when everyone was inside their fire shelters, and that's the way the photograph is identified in the official fire report. If the timing was correct, the double plume was a likely solution to the mystery.

Photos by a passing weather satellite, however, contradicted the photo's time stamp; those photos, too, are included in the official report. The more reliable time of the satellite photos shows that at 5:30 PM the fire was sending up a single plume of smoke. At this time, the first satellite photo made clear, the smoke from the smaller arm of the fire has not yet erected in a distinct second plume.

A second satellite photo, taken ten minutes later at 5:40 PM, shows the second plume erect and distinct, but by then the bulk of the fire has passed by the entrapment site. The contradiction between the timing of Feher's photo and the two satellite photos was later solved when Feher was asked by Leuschen and then again for this account if his time stamp could be wrong. Feher checked and reported that he had failed to put the timing mechanism on the camera an hour ahead in the spring to account for daylight saving time. The photograph was actually taken an hour later than the camera recorded, or at 6:30 PM. In other words, the satellite photos are correct, and the double plume did not develop in time to explain that fatal left hook.

Leuschen's main interest was the fire's behavior, but he found the disciplinary actions proposed by the Forest Service troubling. He could not believe that his friends and colleagues, Daniels, George, and Dunn, deserved to be fired. He accepted Daniels's claim about directing Craven's crew to withdraw from the rocks. George, Leuschen believed, had not taken over the fire from Daniels, which was later judged to be a serious mistake on George's part, because at the time George had good reason to believe that the crew had quit fighting the fire. He believed Dunn to be a conscientious engine captain, one who would not have attacked the fire without checking in first, and who would not lie about it afterward either.

On one occasion, Leuschen accompanied survivors and their union representatives to the site. As he listened to the survivors rehash and compare their stories, he realized that they were coming up with fresh insights, ones that never made the official report. "They started out passionate about their own personal accounts," Leuschen said. "But as they talked, they realized there were discrepancies and things they hadn't understood at the time, and they began to work out the differences." Why wasn't this process part of the Forest Service fire investigation? he wondered.

Of special interest to Leuschen was the fire's behavior when it cut off Kampen, Dunn, and the others, who then drove down the road to safety. As Dunn and Kampen described the event, it sounded to Leuschen like a wind shift, followed by a wave of embers and rapid ignition of numerous spot fires, and only then a crown fire. The official fire report said that flames racing through crowns of trees had cascaded over the road and trapped the firefighters. The difference is vital. Everyone had been expecting the main arm of the fire to keep flames heading up the south side of the canyon, away from the firefighters. An ember shower, Leuschen thought, could have instantaneously ignited hundreds of spot fires in a virtual "mass ignition" that happened so fast and unexpectedly no one reacted in time. If that's what had happened, it would weaken the charges against the fire's supervisors.*

"Fires do not always progress on the ground or in the crowns of trees; the fastest progress of flames is by ember shower," Leuschen said later, echoing a conclusion of Forest Service fire science studies in Canada's Northwest Territories in the late 1990s. "Seconds become deciding factors."

Leuschen acknowledged, however, that his virtual "mass ignition" idea does not apply to the fire's left hook higher up in the canyon, at the entrapment site. Survivors who were there described the fire's sudden advance as a column collapse—the smaller arm of the fire advancing horizontally—followed by a wave of heat and embers that somehow unexpectedly turned onto the roadway and scree, causing the fatalities. "Where did that convective heat blast come from?" Leuschen said. "We don't know."

Geography may have had something to do with the turning, though it's difficult to see the effect from the road. From higher up at the fatality site, though, an observer has a clear view down-canyon of the tunnel-like opening above the river and road, and that opening aims straight at the fatality site. "That's the mouth of the dragon," Leuschen said while standing with me at the fatality site, more than a year after the fire.

The bizarre left hook of the Thirtymile Fire attracted the attention of many fire scientists. These included some at the Forest Service's Fire Science Laboratory in Missoula, who thought that if the fire's explosive behavior could be explained, it would help fire supervisors select better safety zones in the future. Bret Butler, one of the scientists at the Missoula lab, obtained a complex software program from the energy industry to chart possible wind velocities and their results, and he applied it to the Chewuch River canyon. Initial computer runs were both instructive and frustrating. Though the computer program was the most advanced one available to Butler, it could not account for topographic features as significant as the massive rock slump in the canyon bottom.

---

*The term *mass ignition* can also apply to another kind of swift ignition on a wildfire, though it occurs only rarely: a gas-air explosion that erupts like napalm. But that's not what was meant here.

However, one computer run, of wind velocity unaffected by fire, showed airflow heading straight up the canyon with no side-to-side variation. A second simulation, with values inserted for mass and energy of the two centers of the fire just prior to the burnover, showed winds being drawn up the south side of the canyon and away from firefighters, as actually happened, but with no arm branching off toward the entrapment site, as also happened.

While that was an inconclusive finding, the second simulation also showed an area of high turbulence developing between the two centers of the fire. The simulation represented steady-state flow fields, whereas the air in the canyon would have been in a chaotic state during the fire, adding to the turbulence. The region of high turbulence identified by the second simulation might well have been a place where airflows oscillated back and forth, Butler said, resulting in "a region of high-velocity chaotic flow." That was as far as he would go. To take the argument a step further, an area of oscillating turbulence in the center of the canyon could have created, or helped to create, the conditions for a breakout—namely, that left hook.

Of more general importance, further simulation runs by Butler showed that even slight variations in the values for mass and energy at the origin of the fire resulted in great differences in the direction and spread of the fire at the entrapment site. What that means, in short, is that it's easy to predict that a fire will burn out a canyon, but it's a lot harder to say precisely how the fire will do it.

Leuschen had come to the same conclusion. "We are holding people accountable for things we don't have the criteria to assess," Leuschen told Goodman. The fire report says otherwise, Goodman responded, and Leuschen had been a contributor to that report.

"Why should I believe you now?" Goodman asked.

"Because we've learned more," Leuschen replied.

Leuschen convinced her, Goodman said later, that there had been "more of a fire storm" than originally thought, though his close ties to the accused made her skeptical of his conclusion about their accountability.

As Goodman's inquiry progressed, she kept Chief Bosworth informed of the changing picture of events. During this time, when asked for this account, "Shouldn't someone be fired for what happened on the

Thirtymile Fire?" Bosworth paused for a long moment before replying: "I cannot say that somebody ought to be fired. That's a wishy-washy answer. But I think you've got to look at all the parts of what happened." The consolidation of the Okanogan and Wenatchee forests had cut the number of fire supervisors, he noted. A major fire, the Libby South Fire, was being fought in the same region at the same time, which distracted attention. The Thirtymile Fire went from being a mop-up job to a raging conflagration with stunning speed, regardless of how you accounted for the transformation.

"I'm not convinced the public hanging of one person, which is going to make some people feel better, is the right solution," Bosworth said.

In the end, Goodman determined that no one should be fired, and she reduced most of the other disciplinary actions as well. In her judgment, Daniels had been qualified to handle the fire when it was a mop-up operation, but not later. His limits had been known for decades, and despite them the Forest Service had kept him in a supervisory position. "I didn't think someone we had put in that position should be fired, and I didn't fire him," she said later. Daniels was removed permanently from fire work and accepted a lesser position as a materials handler in the Forest Service's Wenatchee supply cache. When contacted for this account, he supplied a few biographical details, but he was under a threat of future legal action and nothing further was discussed.

The decision not to fire Daniels affected the firing case against George, who was not as responsible for the fire as Daniels. George was allowed to remain in his post as AFMO, but his fire qualifications were withdrawn, which meant he was able to plan for but not fight fire. He decided to retire.

The case for firing Dunn fell apart on factual grounds. The most serious charge against him was that he had failed "to provide truthful information" by claiming to have checked in with Daniels when he arrived at the fire. Lying is a firing offense. A letter notifying Dunn of the decision to dismiss him, dated May 24, 2002, said Dunn's conduct had "greatly contributed" to a dangerous situation that led to the deaths of four firefighters, and named each one; the same paragraph with the names and the accusation was in other disciplinary notices as well.

Dunn was devastated by the letter's charge that he personally was responsible for the four deaths. As far as he was concerned, he had been following orders, had checked in properly, and had told the truth about it afterward. By his account, he had been on patrol with his engine crew that afternoon in another part of the forest, and while listening to radio traffic had become concerned over the delay in launching helicopter 13N. He headed for the North Cascades Smokejumper Base, where the helicopter was waiting on the tarmac, to recommend some possible dip sites. On the way to the base, however, he was diverted by the dispatch office with an order to go to the Thirtymile Fire and check for spot fires along the road. Dunn thought he had a chance to put out the spot fires because he had seen it done in the canyon during the 1994 Thunder Mountain Fire.

If only that radio exchange had been recorded, Dunn said later, it would have proved he was acting under orders. But the dispatch operation had just been moved into new quarters, as part of the Okanogan-Wenatchee Forest reorganization, and a new system had been installed to record transmissions just like this one—except that someone apparently had either bumped or inadvertently knocked out the plug. The recorder at dispatch was somehow disconnected—or that's the explanation the Forest Service later offered. A dispatch log was kept the old-fashioned way, by hand. Unfortunately for Dunn, that handwritten log does not include any notes about orders to him for putting out spot fires.

According to the log, he did tell the dispatcher at 2:31 PM that he would reach the fire in about forty-five minutes. When interviewed for this account, Dunn maintained that he tried and failed to contact Daniels by radio on the way to the fire, but the log makes no mention of that, either. When Dunn drove up to the Lunch Spot, he said, he stopped his vehicle, stepped out on the running board, and made eye contact with Daniels. Dunn called over the hood of the engine, "I'm going up to check on spots." He remembered Daniels acknowledging that with a look and a gesture.

Initially, no one corroborated Dunn's story. When Dunn and Daniels returned to the Lunch Spot with Goodman's team, however, Dunn recounted his version of events, insisting that he saw Daniels sitting there with a sandwich in his hand. Daniels then changed his story, according to Goodman, and acknowledged Dunn had checked in. On top of that, another firefighter independently recovered a memory of the check-in, just the way Dunn described it.

"Dunn could say where Ellreese was sitting, what he was doing," Goodman said later, "though it wasn't a real 'check-in' as I would describe it." Dunn eventually gathered a stack of affidavits from fellow employees who said Dunn's check-in was standard procedure at the time; in the aftermath of the fire, requirements for check-ins were much stiffened.

Dunn hadn't lied, Goodman determined, and the firing charge against him was dropped, almost a year after it had been brought. Dunn was given a reprimand for failing to withdraw his engine in the face of extreme heat and with unburned fuel between him and the fire. Interviewed a year after that at the North Cascades base, where he was helping supervise a helicopter crew, Dunn could not speak of the episode without extreme agitation. The willingness of the Forest Service to revise its own findings, however, was remarkable for any governmental agency or other entity, and the methods employed during Goodman's appeals inquiry could be applied with profit to future investigations.

The issue of disciplinary action, however, did not end with the action by Goodman and her team. Under pressure from the families, Congress enacted legislation in 2002 that required oversight of Forest Service fatality investigations by the Inspector General's Office of the Department of Agriculture. No one was quite sure what the consequences would be of the Cantwell legislation, named for Maria Cantwell, the freshman Democratic senator from Washington who sponsored it. Would the legislation simply require one more layer of bureaucratic review? Or might it lead to criminal charges against fire managers? It would take another fatal fire, the Cramer Fire of 2003, before answers to those questions began to come in.

One investigative finding has stood the test of time with no qualification: the Thirtymile Fire was started by an abandoned campfire. Forest Service arson investigators began a search for those responsible, armed with the DNA sample from the half-eaten hot dog. Public appeals for information and the promise of a fifty-thousand-dollar reward brought many tips, but nothing panned out. Figuring the perpetrators might return to the scene, Ron Pugh, who headed the arson investigation for the Forest Service, hid a video camera in trees near the campfire site just before the first anniversary of the fire. Sure enough, the camera captured the images when a man and a woman stopped a pickup truck near the campfire ring, got out, and began to gesture in knowledgeable ways about what had happened. The camera caught their faces but was aimed just inches too high to record the truck's license plate number.

Pugh showed video stills of the couple to the families, survivors, law enforcement officials, and local businesspeople, warning everyone to keep mum. He described the couple as "potential witnesses," not as suspects, a caution that proved wise. When no one immediately recognized the faces, the photos were released to the news media, with much fanfare.

"They are people who may be able to tell us something about how the fire started, and that would help us in our ongoing investigation," Pugh remarked, again with restraint. "We have not forgotten the Thirtymile Fire or the employees who died or were injured."

The man and the woman soon came forward, identified themselves to Pugh, and convinced him that they were merely interested bystanders. With that, the investigation hit a dead end. But Pugh, who was later promoted and transferred to another region, vowed never to close the books on the inquiry.

The telltale hot dog DNA remains on file.

Not all the mysteries of the fire have clear answers even now, years after the event. The muddled fire investigation and its aftermath in a way have blocked the Thirtymile Fire from achieving the proper shape of tragedy by denying the event a cathartic ending, one that leaves the audience free to walk away. The rough edges of a real-life drama weather down with time, however, and so this yet may come to pass.

One big question that remains is this: how could the main lesson of the South Canyon Fire—to step back when conditions exceed capabilities—have been so grossly violated? In fact, that lesson was not entirely forgotten. The crew fully disengaged in midafternoon, and if matters had been left there everything would have turned out fine— except perhaps for the Hagemeyers. The reengagement came about bit by bit—until the fire's behavior and the firefighters' response to it gained momentum together, and the sum of the parts took on a life of its own . . . and the lesson of the South Canyon Fire faded away.

The solution to the mystery of why there was no effort to prepare for a burnover at the entrapment site is easier to grasp. Daniels lacked a command personality, and he and many others, notably Jasso, were lulled into complacency by their misperception that the fire would pass by harmlessly. If Daniels truly meant for people to come down from the scree and onto the road, he had the time and the opportunity to make the directive stick, but he didn't do it. If that message had been put across, everyone might have lived—as Thom Taylor generously remarked with hindsight, "Ellreese was right, the road was the place to be." Those two mistakes—to reengage the fire and then do almost nothing to prepare for the burnover—changed many practices in the fire world and contributed to the ongoing reassessment throughout society of how people get along with wildfire.

Traveling regularly up the Chewuch River canyon in the first years after the fire, an observer could mark changes that were also under way at other locations in fire-prone regions, from one coast to the other. Both fire crews and wildfire were clearing underbrush and small trees, giving the bigger trees a better chance to grow and making catastrophic wildfire less likely. Each year, the crews worked their way a few more miles up the canyon, thinning and burning. Above the thinned forest, and below the site of the Thirtymile Fire, the brush and timber were so dense that it was difficult to make out the trunks of even the biggest ponderosa pines. Brush piles, which would be burned in the fall or spring, marked the areas most recently treated. In the lower canyon, where work had been completed, the forest was open and healthy in appearance. The federal government plan, for burning 40 million acres of forest nationwide during the first years of the new century, includes treating half of that amount, or 20 million acres, and estimates that the other half will be cleared by wildfire. When the job is done, not only will those forests be healthier, but firefighters will be safer and people and property in and near those areas less threatened. Thus the Chewuch River canyon is an example, though an unfortunate one, of forest treatment by both prescribed and natural fires—the Thirtymile Fire is not the only fire to burn there in the past few years.

In 2003, three major fires in the surrounding area grew together into the Fawn Creek Complex, which eventually scorched more than eighty-one thousand acres and cost more than $37 million to contain. The fires were started by lightning on June 29 of that year and were not brought under control for well over a month. One of those three fires, the Farewell Fire, burned into the Chewuch River canyon. In a coincidence beating all odds, Joe Stutler, the incident commander on the Thirtymile Fire after the fatalities, two years later stood again at the old entrapment site, this time as a safety officer on the July 2003 Farewell Fire.

"I was standing twenty to thirty feet up from where they died," he said later, "and I saw a boiling vortex of flame up on the ridge. The fire had just blown up. I thought, This had to be what *they* saw—they were just a lot closer. It was an incredible experience. I watched the flames march around the old Thirtymile Fire perimeter for a couple of hours. It was history repeating itself."

The Farewell Fire backed down the canyon sides and moved slowly through the thinned areas. Very few trees in the canyon bottom were killed. Scorch marks on the big ponderosa pines aren't much higher up the tree trunks than the ones left by the prescribed fires, which indeed made the forest better able to handle fire.

The Farewell Fire, though, was fought with the Thirtymile Fire well in mind. At the outset, a "complexity analysis" was required to ensure that the fire managers assigned had adequate skills. Fire qualifications were more closely checked than before. The incident commander had to identify himself to all personnel. Anyone checking in on the fire was fully briefed on plans, hazards, and risks. If anyone tried to reengage the fire after backing off, they had to run through a long checklist similar to the one required for engaging a fire in the first place. Stricter attention was paid to work-rest guidelines for the more than 1,500 firefighters eventually assigned to the Fawn Creek Complex. The additional safety requirements, when added to the existing burden, brought the number of rules for decision making on a fire to more than 160, by one count—just too many rules, realistically, for anyone to follow. In a hopeful response, the fire world has begun to develop a more "experience and judgment"–based approach, turning away from the excessive reliance on rules.

"We are focused on defining those simple, clear principles that will encourage complex, intelligent behavior," Tom Harbour, national director of fire and aviation management for the Forest Service, said at a seminal training conference in 2005, named the Pulaski Conference for Ranger Edward Pulaski, the hero of the 1910 Big Blowup. New policies, training, and equipment are being developed to support this effort. A "foundational doctrine" has been developed to provide philosophic guidelines for fire suppression. Leadership courses have begun to emphasize real-life experience—tours of notable fire sites, sandbox exercises based on actual fires, small unit tactics adopted from the military—more than workbook exercises. A new fire shelter, with some added protection, was developed. Even more hopefully, the Forest Service, prodded by its own employees as well as by societal change, has begun to redefine its core mission as one of forest restoration after many years of drift and a legacy of serving as handmaiden for the timber industry. Such fundamental changes will take years to design and introduce; it will be a long time before they can be judged successful or not. The South Canyon Fire and its aftershock, The Thirtymile Fire, are strong motivators, though, for a new era of concern for firefighter safety, forest health, and the risks of living with fire. They are likely to provoke further beneficial changes for decades to come. Even constructive human responses, though, have their limits.

Fire on Earth is as old as oxygen, lightning, and life itself, and its basic nature remains unchanged: it's deadly dangerous and sometimes impossible to predict. The biggest remaining unsolved mystery of the Thirtymile Fire, for example, concerns the fire's erratic behavior. No one has yet answered why this fire, which was studied as few fires have ever been, took that fatal left hook and thus entered the history books. The experts grappled hard with this one, but the fire, it turns out, had a claim to the last word.

CHAPTER SEVENTEEN

*I feel this way. I see a certain beauty spring forth from the
ashes of the Thirtymile Fire that, in a way, gives me hope for
the future. The charred trees, the ghosts that still haunt from
the time of July 9th and 10th, 2001, stand amidst new life.*

—Kathie FitzPatrick, from an e-mail to the author
on the third anniversary of the fire, July 9, 2004

One day a few years after the fire, in early autumn when it was cool
in the shade and warm in the sun, the upper Chewuch River canyon was
a crazy quilt of black, gray, and green patches. Skeletons of burned trees,
honeycombed by woodpeckers, stood in bleak rows. Dead brush and
fallen trees lay in heaps and jumbles. Drifts of ash disguised burned-out
root pits, deep enough to break a leg. The old burn was a dirty, dangerous place to hike in on a calm day, and no place to be caught in a wind-
storm. Even so, there were many signs of returning life. Young aspens
had sprouted from the roots of burned ancestors. Grass had shot up in
the spring and turned brown during another dry summer. Wildflowers
had come out and were now a fading glory.

Standing at the entrapment site, where I had come for a last look
around, it was easy to make out the massive rock slump, which had
been mostly hidden by brush and trees at the time of the fire. The sight
of the exposed slump stirs the imagination. It's impossible to deny that
the huge pile of rock had acted as a barrier to the fire. The slump, a
series of ridges forty to sixty feet high with deep gulches in between,
stretches across the width of the canyon, minus the road and river, and

eight hundred to a thousand feet up and down the bottom of the canyon. It's a formidable obstacle.

But surely it had acted as a kind of ski jump as well, launching flames and gases into the air. This effect would help explain how the wave of heat lofted above the firefighters on the road, only to strike the four others with fatal intensity a hundred feet up in the scree, a mere twenty-five-foot difference in elevation. The ski-jump idea sounds promising, but it cannot explain the enduring mystery of why the heat blast veered toward the entrapment site in the first place.

Looking at the slump, I wondered what the events of that July day had been like from the fire's point of view. By now, I had walked the ground with survivors, had read witness accounts and reports, and had talked with families, investigators, and many others knowledgeable about the event. But the fire had left its own record, on the bleached rocks and blasted trees. Fire experts who tried to read that record had come away shaking their heads. Though much had been learned, no one had a convincing explanation for the fatal left hook. The best anyone could say was, "We don't know why it did that."

A mild wind was blowing up the canyon, just as it had on the day of the fire. I made my way across the river and up the face of the rock slump, which is almost naked of vegetation. The slump has a fresh look, as though it cracked off the canyon walls in recent times and not somewhere between ten thousand and fifteen thousand years ago, as the last glaciers withdrew. Along the looming canyon walls are outcroppings where giant clumps of rock sheared off. (The sound of rock walls crashing to the canyon floor must have played on a colossal scale.) The mightiest boulders came to rest in the canyon bottom, while smaller rocks and stones stopped short in long slides visible on the lower reaches of the canyon walls.

I climbed the face of the slump, in the lee of the wind. As I neared the top I could feel—and see—a strong wind, much stronger than the mild one in the bottom of the canyon, coming over the top of the slump. The wind whipped a stream of cottonlike fluff across the top of the slump at ten to fifteen miles an hour, giving away the wind's speed and direction. The fluff continued straight on up the canyon. If the fluff were the fire, it would have bypassed the entrapment site, as nearly everyone had expected. An exceptionally powerful force had been required to over-come the prevailing up-canyon trend, as well as the pull of flames surg-ing up the far side of the canyon, and turn a portion of the fire ninety degrees toward the entrapment site: the fatal left hook. The airborne fluff bore witness to the ski-jump effect, because it accelerated as it passed over the slump. But some additional power had to have caused the decisive turn.

As I looked down-canyon from the top of the slump, the series of rock ridges that make up the slump appeared like waves on a troubled ocean. The down-canyon ridges were at least as high as the one where I was standing. While I gazed down the canyon, I was thinking that those ridges must have turned the heat wave passing above the slump into a roller coaster, causing the heat to waffle up and down, making the atmosphere less stable and the fire easier to turn. Such an effect is well known in weather science: unstable air allows thermal layers to move up and down more easily. So why not from side to side, as long as there was some other force to give a push?

I decided to backtrack the fire. As I worked my way down the steep back slope of the ridge, I kept three points of contact with the rock, mountaineering style, to be on the safe side—two hands and a foot or two feet and a hand. The rock was gritty and sharp, and my apprecia-tion grew for what Emhoff and Taylor had gone through on their runs to the road. When I reached the top of the second ridge, I confronted another steep, narrow gully and beyond that another ridge. I had gone halfway into this gully when I noticed a curious phenomenon: the cot-tony fluff at midslope was no longer sailing up the canyon. Instead, it had made a turn of nearly ninety degrees and now followed the gully, at a sedate speed, on a path in the general direction of the entrapment site. At the same time I could see that the fluff at the top of the slump continued to blow straight up the canyon at high speed, so there had been no shift in the prevailing wind to account for the turn taken by the fluff. The fluff was showing that the gully between the ridges was able to turn a portion of the up-canyon wind into a side-canyon wind.

Was it possible that the many gullies in the slump had turned enough of the flames onto the entrapment site to account for the fatal left hook?

The trail of fluff poured out of the gully and into the tunnel-like opening above river and road—Leuschen's "mouth of the dragon" that aimed straight at the entrapment site. Following the fluff, I clambered out of the rock maze and made my way back to the place on the road where the survivors had ridden out flames. Behind me, a thin, continuous cloud of fluff emerged from the slump, danced across the river, and made a graceful turn toward the entrapment site.

Many influences had been at work when a portion of the fire had followed this same path. The dogleg turn of the canyon had given flames a nudge along the same course. The outcropping of rock directly below the entrapment site had created an eddy that drew a portion of the advancing fire in toward the entrapment site. The smaller arm of the fire had an effect, too, coming to the entrapment site by a more direct route—through the tunnel-like opening as well as over the outcropping of rock.

Everyone has a pet notion, well-considered idea, or deeply held belief about what caused the fatal left hook. Thom Taylor believes a gush of air down a narrow draw on the far side of the canyon pushed the fire onto the entrapment site. Kathie FitzPatrick and her family believe the fire represented a struggle between eternal forces of good and evil, and the deaths were part of a larger design. They call the photograph of the double smoke plume joined by four bands of smoke, one for each of the victims, the "Stairway to Heaven," and believe that Karen led the way for the others.

Fire has a life of its own beyond scientific absolutes. A decisive turning by fire can be traced to a thousand tiny forces, and to a few big ones, not unlike the course of human events. My hike had convinced me, however, that the rock slump had a lot to do with the mysterious left hook of the Thirtymile Fire.

I made my way down the canyon to the site of the campfire ring, where the fire had its beginning and the whole disastrous chain of events had been spawned. The flames had cleared a broad meadow from the opposite bank of the river to the far canyon wall. The meadow moved like a living thing, an undulating blanket in rose-to-lilac, green, and white, the colors of fireweed, the first volunteer to spring from ashes. Blazing fireweed covered the open spaces. After the fire, a bouquet of fireweed was found in the cab of Jessica Johnson's pickup; Jessica had loved the flower from childhood. "It was as though her life had come full circle," her mother, Jody, said.

In the fading warmth of the year, the rose-to-lilac blossoms with four flame-shaped petals each erupted into downy seed fluff. The fluff streamed upward, turning silver in the sunshine, and the light wind sent a great billowing cloud of it up the canyon, over the rock slump, and beyond, bearing the message of the past into the future.

The Ten Standard Firefighting Orders were created by a Forest Service task force in 1957 in the wake of a series of multiple fatality fires over several decades. Though criticized as being too numerous and difficult to remember, the ten orders have endured as the bedrock safety rules for fighting wildland fire. An abbreviated version, or checklist, also is in common use: LCES, for lookouts, communications, escape routes, and safety zones. The eighteen Watch Out Situations were added over time to address situations that are cause for concern, but which can be mitigated to allow firefighting operations to continue.

The Thirtymile Fire Investigation Report contains the following commentary, which has withstood the test of time, on how safety orders and guidelines were violated or stretched.

STANDARD FIRE ORDERS

All ten Standard Fire Orders were violated or disregarded at one time or another during the course of the incident. The following are some examples of these situations.

1. Fight fire aggressively but provide for safety first.

   The tactics implemented provided for aggressive suppression but lacked critical safety procedures, including mandatory escape routes.

2. Initiate all actions based on current and expected fire behavior.

   Aggressive attack with over-extended resources continued in spite of onsite indicators of an increased rate of spread, multiple spots, and crown fire.

3. Recognize current weather conditions and obtain forecasts.

   —Although received by Okanogan Dispatch, no afternoon fire weather forecast was transmitted to the Thirtymile Fire on the Methow Valley District.

   —No Spot Weather Forecast was requested by management or incident commanders.

4. Ensure that instructions are given and understood.

   —Instructions were given without any direct tie to strategy or tactics at the time of the entrapment.

   —At the deployment site instructions were given and not all were adhered to, but it is unknown whether they were heard or understood by all.

   —Instructions were coming from multiple sources adding to the confusion.

5. Obtain current information on fire status.

   —Air attack was utilized but due to smoke conditions could not always see the ground.

   —No assigned lookouts were used after 2 P.M.

6. Remain in communication with your crew members, supervisors and adjoining forces.

   Although the communication equipment was adequate, the lines of communications on the incident were poor due to lack of a plan and poorly established command structure. There was no viable strategy established during the afternoon of the incident.

7. Determine safety zones and escape routes.

   After the 3 P.M. lunch break, the crews were up the canyon during a frontal assault and had no alternative escape route or safety zone identified. They had nowhere to go when their only escape route was cut off.

8. Establish lookouts in potentially hazardous situations.

No lookouts were established during the burning period beyond what could be seen from the road and from air attack, who had limited visibility of the fire due to smoke.

9. Retain control at all times.

Leadership was fragmented and ineffective at all levels during the afternoon of July 10th. Resources were being ordered and directions given by others than the IC. While a suitable deployment site was found and orders were given there was no evidence of strong leadership on the deployment site to implement the orders as given.

10. Stay alert, keep calm, think clearly, act decisively.

—Supervisors, managers, and firefighters failed to stay alert and recognize changing conditions.

—Fatigue and collateral duties impeded the abilities of key leadership to think clearly and to act decisively to use available time on the shelter deployment site to prepare for the burnover.

WATCH OUT SITUATIONS

According to the Fire Investigation report, the following ten Watch Out Situations were present or disregarded at one time or another during the course of the incident as evidenced by the following non-inclusive set of examples.

Safety zones and escape routes not identified (Watch Out Situation #3)

- When they were working on the spots there was no clear instruction on safety zones or escape routes.
- The lunch site was not a safety zone and there were no safety zones up-canyon from the point of the fire origin once the fire behavior became severe.
- The shelter deployment site was not a safety zone.

*Unfamiliar with weather and local factors influencing fire behavior
(Watch Out Situation #4)*

- Fire fighters were unaware of the near record [weather] readings and how that affected fire behavior.

Uninformed about strategy, tactics, and hazards (Watch Out Situation #5)

- Chosen strategy and tactics were not achievable or viable due to fuel and environmental conditions.
- Hazards were never properly recognized, evaluated, and addressed.
- It was not recognized that the tactics needed to be changed when the fire began to leave the riparian area.

Instructions and assignments not clear! (Watch Out Situation #6)

- Instructions were given without any direct tie to strategy or tactics at the time of the entrapment.
- At the deployment site instructions were given and not all were adhered to, but it is unknown whether they were heard or understood by all.
- The incident commander did not make sure that all instructions were complied with.
- Many people throughout the incident gave instructions.

*Constructing fire line without a safety anchor point
(Watch Out Situation #8)*

- When action was taken on the spot fire at the head of the main fire there was no secure anchor point.

Attempting frontal assault on fire (Watch Out Situation #10)

- After the lunch break, two squads and two engines were actively suppressing spot fires ahead of the main fire.

Unburned fuel between you and the fire (Watch Out Situation #11)

- When engaged in suppression actions on the spots there was a large amount of unburned fuel between the main fire and the spots about 150 to 300 yards away.

Cannot see main fire, not in contact with anyone who can (Watch Out Situation #12)

- Air attack could not see the entire fire; no one could see the part of the fire that presented the greatest hazard.
- Terrain, smoke, and vegetation blocked firefighters' view of the main fire.
- A lookout who could continually view the main fire was not posted.

Spot fires frequently cross line (Watch Out Situation #16)

- The NWR #6 crew experienced spots across their control lines from when they began work at approximately 11 A.M. on July 10th.

Terrain and fuels make escape to safety zones difficult (Watch Out Situation #17)

- The identified safety zone did not satisfy the defined characteristics of a true safety zone.

Chapter Four

The legally mandated drive for equal employment, which has opened the Forest Service to women and ethnic minorities, has benefited many individuals. By the late 1970s, however, efforts to bring more women and minorities into the workforce were not producing sufficient results, and the pressure to do more was on—and still is—from both the national office and the courts.

A study by the Forest Service in 1990 called for "improved diversity" and for development of new leaders and managers, in part to make up for reductions in experienced staff caused by forced early retirements, which have come as a result of forest consolidations as well as normal attrition. More than a decade later, past the turn of the century, the Forest Service judged its own efforts a failure, though the agency acknowledged spending $600,000 a year in recruitment efforts for the fire service.

"This money has traditionally been used to fund individual regional diversity recruitment/outreach projects that have produced little result," the Forest Service reported in a briefing paper in 2003. "To date, diversity and retention issues among the fire workforce remain unimproved or worse."

The Forest Service's administrative arrangement of the Okanogan-Wenatchee National Forest, where the Thirtymile Fire occurred, is confusing to the outsider, as it proved to be for participants. The Forest Service combined the management staffs for the two forests in December 1999, but the forests retained their separate boundaries, which are set by Congress and not the Forest Service. Many national forests have undergone similar consolidation in recent years and are known informally as "hyphenated forests," which is no compliment.

At the time of the Thirtymile Fire, the combined forest had a single supervisor, Sonny O'Neal, and a single fire management officer, Elton Thomas, where formerly each forest had a supervisor and FMO of its own. Thomas was no stranger to fire; his father had been an FMO, and he had been in the fire post for two years at the time of the Thirtymile Fire. But he had spent the previous ten years of his career in natural resource work. During the 1980s, the Forest Service changed its management philosophy and began to emphasize administrative skills, not technical skills, as the primary qualification for advancement. Anyone who knew how to run an organization, it was thought, could run a fire program. After the Thirtymile Fire, this philosophy was called into question and remains a subject of debate today. In addition, forest consolidation and early retirements for fire supervisors meant that many people with little fire experience were placed in senior fire jobs.

The consolidated Okanogan-Wenatchee National Forest was divided into seven ranger districts, each with its own FMO and other staff. The Libby South and Thirtymile fires both were within the Methow Valley Ranger District, headquartered in Twisp. John Newcom was the ranger in charge of the Methow Valley district. The senior fire managers present at the Thirtymile Fire at different times, in addition to those who did the physical work of fighting the fire, were: Thomas, FMO for the Okanogan-Wenatchee Forest; Pete Soderquist, FMO for the Methow Valley district; and Barry George, Soderquist's assistant, or AFMO.

Chapter Six

Federal government policy statements unearthed after the Thirtymile Fire give clear directions about how to fight fire and respect the Endangered Species Act at the same time. But there was a general failure throughout government, caused in part by the extreme sensitivities within society about the act, to make the policies clear to those who had to do the fighting. The communications failure was generally acknowledged after the fire, and steps were taken to make the policies better known.

The overall policy calls for immediate action to suppress a fire, based on plans made up before fire season begins, and for later consultation on how to proceed if the fire grows into a major threat. "There is no need to consult on the wildfire itself," reads a 1995 policy memo from the Fish and Wildlife Service, which is responsible for implementing the act. The memo also states that consultation about a specific situation can wait until the emergency passes. "You do not need to delay response to a wildfire for this contact," the memo says. "If you have to wait until after the initial attack for the time to contact the Fish and Wildlife Service, by all means, then wait."

The 1995 memo says helicopters should try to avoid disturbing habitat for endangered species, a restriction which clearly did apply to the Chewuch River and its several endangered species. "When a known endangered species is in the area, attempts to avoid disturbance will be made," the memo says. But the memo is less than clear about how to go about doing this.

"Impacts to endangered species by helicopters during fire suppression activities have to be considered within the context of all other ground activities and the fire itself," the memo says.

A host of regulations, not just the Endangered Species Act, govern fire-fighting near streams—from where to site fire camps to the rules about how close to rivers a water drop can be made. The official Thirtymile Fire Investigation Report later acknowledged the difficulties in this instance. "There is no clear or consistent process on the Forest for helicopter bucket operations with respect to endangered species issues in relation to fire suppression operations," the report states.

Elton Thomas, the forest FMO, ultimately was given a mild reprimand for failing to fully communicate the forest policy on the Endangered Species Act to firefighters and others prior to the Thirtymile Fire. The disciplinary action did his career no harm. Thomas was celebrating his retirement day, April 1, 2005, when his lawyer telephoned and told him to retrieve his retirement papers immediately and return to active duty. It was no April Fool's joke. A series of unexpected twists in the legal proceedings in the aftermath of the fire had raised the possibility that Thomas might have to testify against the Forest Service. If he were to testify as a civilian, he would open himself to possible civil action. Thomas was reinstated by the end of that day. His old job as FMO had been filled by then, but a post was found for him: a promotion to deputy forest supervisor. He subsequently became acting forest supervisor when the regular forest supervisor took a medical leave. "I'm the only guy I know who went from retirement to a promotion," he said. Thomas retired for good in January 2006.

Chapter Fifteen

The official fire report states that fatigue was the single most important physiological element in causing the fatalities. But Pete Soderquist, the FMO for the Methow Valley Ranger District, said the data cited in the report for his sleep cycle is off by a good twenty-four hours, making him appear more exhausted than he was and raising questions about the reliability of the report's conclusion. "Tony

Kern interviewed me on the subject, and for some reason analyzed my cognitive effectiveness based on erroneous information derived from somewhere other than our interview," Soderquist said later. The fire report has Soderquist waking at 4:00 AM on Sunday, July 8, and not having a normal amount of sleep until after the fatalities on Tuesday, July 10. "At the key point where the DFMO [Soderquist, the district fire management officer] escorts and inbriefs NWR #6 at Action 103 . . . he has had less than thirty minutes sleep in the previous twenty-four hours (with little more than that the previous night)," the report declares.

On the contrary, said Soderquist. He indeed had been up for nearly twenty-four hours, as the report says, but had a normal night's sleep for the previous twenty-four-hour cycle, on Sunday night, and not "little more" than a half hour for that cycle as the report claims. Sunday was his day off, and he rose at a normal hour, about 6:00 AM, and went to bed at a normal hour that night. He rose at his regular time of 6:00 AM as well the next morning, Monday, July 9. He stayed up Monday night to plan for the Libby South and Thirtymile fires, and welcome the Northwest Regulars at Twisp. But, he said, "I had only been up since six that morning, not since four the night before."

Whatever failings there were in gathering the sleep-cycle data, they were carefully analyzed afterward. Kern submitted the data to the Air Force's Warfighter Fatigue Countermeasures team at Brooks Air Force Base, Texas. There, the data were compared to the effects of sleeplessness on soldiers during wartime. The work-sleep cycles of the firefighters were correlated to an effectiveness rating for a five-day period, from the weekend before the fire to the day after the fatalities. All the firefighters were given an effectiveness rating of 100 percent for the weekend preceding the fire. The rating for the managers of the Okanogan-Wenatchee and for the Entiat Hotshots began to drop on Monday, the day before the fatalities, because of their lack of sleep. By the end of the day Monday, these two groups had a rating of below 70 percent of normal effectiveness. Their rating went up and down throughout the day of the fire, from 75 percent to below 60 percent.

The Northwest Regulars, by contrast, had an effectiveness rating above 80 percent until directly after the fatalities when their rating dropped precipitously to below 50 percent. Citing scientific studies, Kern said that the loss of even a single night's sleep impairs decision making and vigilance similar to a blood alcohol content of .10, a level of intoxication generally considered unsafe for operation of a motor vehicle. Work-rest guidelines have been broadly adjusted several times since the South Canyon Fire; the Thirtymile Fire and Kern's study brought a new round of changes to the work-rest issue, but they did not solve all the problems and created some new ones, and adjustments continue to be made. The change most pertinent to the Thirtymile Fire is that today efforts are made to dispatch crews during daylight hours, not overnight as was done with the Northwest Regulars. In addition, fire crews now try to begin work as early as possible in the morning and not let those precious hours slip away, as happened on the Thirtymile Fire, though the effort is often not successful.

Chapter Sixteen

Less than a week before Christmas 2006, the U.S. Attorney's office in Spokane announced it would charge Ellreese Daniel with four counts of involuntary manslaughter and seven counts of lying. In a lengthy criminal complaint, the U.S. Attorney said that as incident commander Daniels had acted in a "grossly negligent" manner that was the "proximate cause" of the four fire deaths. An affidavit accompanying the complaint specifically cited Daniels for reengaging the fire in late afternoon without adequate thought or preparation and for failing to ready the crew for a possible burnover once the entrapment occurred.

The complaint alleged that Daniels lied, and knew he was lying, when he claimed that he had directed Craven and his group to come out of the rocks, and again when he claimed he didn't know why he wasn't obeyed. The complaint also alleged that he was lying when he claimed he told Rebecca Welch to allow the Hagemeyers into her fire shelter, and when he told investigators that the two engine bosses, Harry Dunn and Dave Laughman, had not checked in before they attacked spot fires along the road. A federal grand jury in Spokane indicted Daniels on all eleven counts in late January 2007. He faces up to six years' imprisonment for each manslaughter count and five years for the false statement charges. Each of the charges also carries a possible fine of $250,000.

Daniels pleaded not guilty to all charges stemming from the fire at a hearing before U.S. Magistrate Judge Cynthia Imbrogno in U.S. district court in Spokane. Daniels' trial was delayed when his public defender, after turning down a plea bargain, requested on several occasions more time to prepare the defense.

The criminal charges brought a strong and immediate negative reaction within the fire community. The families of the victims generally expressed a sense of vindication and a belief that the charges will lead to safer fire lines. The *Yakima Herald Republic* supported this view in an editorial titled "At Last, Justice May Prevail in the Thirtymile Fire." Many veteran firefighters, however, took an opposite tack. They said the unprecedented action will drive firefighters away from positions of responsibility and make serving fire managers less inclined to take on fires that should be fought. Another newspaper, the *Missoulian*, supported the latter view in an editorial titled "Charges Against Fire Boss Heap Travesty Atop Tragedy."

Kathie FitzPatrick said she was certain that fire supervisors now would think twice before committing crews in dangerous situations. "The Forest Service should have fired Daniels or put him in a warehouse long ago," FitzPatrick said. "They knew how bad he was. If they're going to pinch somebody, that's a good place to start."

"It's been a long time coming," said Jody Gray. "I mean, five and a half years, every day I've lived my life without my daughter." Ken Weaver said the level of negligence had been "criminal," but offered a word of sympathy for Daniels, who was the only person cited. "You have to feel bad for Ellreese as you would any human being that found himself in that pickle," Weaver told the *Yakima Herald-Republic*. Evelyn Craven refrained from early comment.

A surprising and contrary reaction came from Ken and Kathy Brinkley, whose son, Levi, was among the fourteen firefighters killed on Storm King Mountain in 1994. In the first years after the South Canyon Fire, the Brinkleys were among the most outspokenly angry of the victims' parents. "When Levi was killed I blamed many people," Kathy said, after the charges against Daniels were announced. "There were many mistakes made. Twelve years later I feel that the pendulum has swung too far the other way. The people in charge do not plan on having firefighters die. It will not help to charge someone for a firefighter's death; it will just cause good firefighters to not be squad bosses."

Meanwhile, efforts were put in motion within the fire community to raise money and provide expert witnesses for Daniels's defense. In Daniels's first court appearance in early January, Christina Hunt, his public defender, said it was unfair to "single out" Daniels and called the charges "a travesty of justice." A few hours after his first court appearance, however, Daniels was a passenger in an auto that was stopped by a State Patrol officer for a minor violation. The trooper found marijuana, pipes, and open beer cans in the vehicle. Daniels was cited for suspicion of marijuana and drug paraphernalia, which did nothing to strengthen his support in the fire community. "From the little bit that I have seen, it doesn't look like he was the one in possession of the drugs," his lawyer, Hunt, said directly following the incident. "From the looks of it, I'm not too concerned about it."

The criminal complaint against Daniels already has had a "chilling effect" on the willingness of firefighters to take on risk, according to the International Association of Wildland Fire (IAWF) and the Federal Wildland Fire Services Association (FWFSA), which together represent a broad spectrum of firefighters. "Firefighters have been coming forward stating their unwilling-

ness to accept the responsibilities of making the sometimes split-second decision, only then to find their decisions reviewed with 20-20 hindsight [after]
more than five years," the groups said in a joint statement.

The possibility of criminal indictments against fire managers has been a
mounting concern ever since the 1994 South Canyon Fire, which provoked
outrage because it resulted in little or no public accountability for individuals.
Wildland firefighters are not alone in being held to a rising and sometimes
unpredictable standard of accountability, though federal employees long have
operated under legal oversight in cases involving fatalities. This societal trend,
sometimes called "the criminalization of almost everything," has touched many
professions, from chief executive officer to Border Patrol officer to U.S. marine.

The charges against Daniels came as a consequence of the Cantwell legislation, which was passed by Congress at the express urging of the families of
the Thirtymile Fire victims. The legislation, which applies to the Forest Service and no other fire agency, requires oversight of its fatality investigations by
the Office of Inspector General of the Department of Agriculture, the service's parent agency. Many firefighters have called for repeal of the legislation.

For most of a century, since the founding of the Forest Service in 1905,
Congress had left responsibility for investigating line-of-duty deaths by wildfire
in the hands of the federal agencies that fight wildfire, mainly the Forest Service; the other principal fire agencies are the Bureau of Land Management, the
National Park Service, the Bureau of Indian Affairs, the U.S. Fish and Wildlife
Service, and the National Oceanic and Atmospheric Administration. By the
turn of the century, however, society was demanding more accountability for
everyone from chief executive officers of giant corporations to fire bosses in
backwoods canyons.

Following the release of the Thirtymile Fire Investigation Report, Senator
Maria Cantwell, a freshman Democrat from Washington, called for a Senate
hearing. Congress had an obligation to the families of the victims, she said, to
"ensure appropriate actions are taken to prevent future deaths." Why hadn't the
lessons of the 1994 South Canyon Fire prevented this tragedy? Senator
Cantwell asked, at a hearing held before the Senate Energy Committee's subcommittee on Forests and Public Land Management on November 14, 2001.
"Unfortunately, this situation sounds all too familiar," she remarked. The causes
of the Thirtymile Fire, she said, were "nearly identical" to the causes of the South
Canyon Fire. The same problems of leadership had been repeated seven years
later despite a host of interagency reviews, studies, and safety cautions. "Here
we are today, seven years and millions of dollars later, investigating yet another
horrible tragedy—one that the Forest Service says could have been prevented."

The Forest Service had to be made more accountable, said Cantwell, who was seconded by Representative Doc Hastings, a Republican who represented the district where the Thirtymile Fire occurred, and who appeared at the Senate hearing as a guest witness. "The responsible officials must be held accountable," said Hastings. "If there is a breakdown, there has to be accountability."

The Forest Service chief, Dale Bosworth, a witness at the hearing, defended the agency's safety record. The many reforms taken after the South Canyon Fire probably had saved lives, he said, though he acknowledged it was difficult to prove the point. "It is hard to know how successful we were after Storm King," Bosworth said. "We had two or three significantly difficult fire seasons where we do not know how many people our actions might have saved." It would be another three years before a Forest Service study justified Bosworth's remarks and reported a dramatic drop in the rate of deaths by fire among wildland firefighters in the decade after the South Canyon Fire, which includes the deaths on the Thirtymile Fire.

The agency's fatality study looked back to 1933, the time when the Depression-era Civilian Conservation Corps provided the manpower for the first organized wildfire crews and ushered in the modern era of firefighting. Over the next seven decades, as safety measures improved, entrapment fatalities for all wildland firefighters decreased from an annual rate of 6.39 in 1933 to 2.0 per year in 2003, the study showed. For the decade after the South Canyon Fire, from 1994 to 2003, the number of deaths in that category was cut by more than half, from 4.27 to 2.0.

The rate of deaths for Forest Service firefighters shows a similar decline. For the longer period, from 1933 to 2003, the rate of agency deaths fell from 3.65 per year to 0.67 per year. For the pertinent decade, from the 1994 South Canyon Fire until 2003, the annual rate decreased by more than half, from 1.6 deaths per year to 0.67. (The study did not include the deaths of five Forest Service firefighters on the Esperanza Fire in southern California in October 2006.)

"Even though the wildland fire environment continues to increase in complexity there is a steady, downward trend in the overall frequency of fire entrapment fatalities," said the study, which attributed the 1994–2003 drop to improvements in leadership, training, and safety practices initiated after both the South Canyon and Thirtymile fires.

The 0.67 annual rate is not rock bottom, but it is a low figure, and further dramatic reductions will be more difficult to achieve. Putting thousands of firefighters up against wildfire every year has inherent dangers, and accidents happen. But the incidence of multiple fatality fires, most of which can be traced to a long, unbroken chain of errors, can and hopefully will be reduced. There exists a remarkable willingness throughout the fire world, from top to bottom, to deal with safety issues in a forthcoming way.

The upshot of the Senate hearing on the Thirtymile Fire was a call by Senator Cantwell and Representative Hastings for legislation to require independent investigations of Forest Service fire deaths. The agency would continue to conduct its own inquiries, in order to learn safety lessons and support internal disciplinary actions. But someone else would look over their shoulder. "People are losing their lives, but no one is losing their jobs," said Cantwell.

A year to the month after the fire, on July 24, 2002, Congress passed a bill requiring the inspector general, or IG, of the Forest Service's parent agency, the Department of Agriculture, to conduct separate investigations into Forest Service wildland fire fatalities. The bill did not apply to other federal agencies engaged in firefighting: the Bureau of Land Management, the National Park Service, and others under the Department of Interior. It left open the question of what would be done with the results. Would the IG reports collect dust in a bureaucrat's drawer? Would they be used for criminal prosecutions? Or something in between? The legislation provided only that the IG submit reports to Congress and the Department of Agriculture.

The first major test of the Cantwell legislation came two years after the Thirtymile Fire when two firefighters, Shane Heath and Jeff Allen, who were members of a helicopter fire crew known as helitacks, were overrun by flames on Idaho's Cramer Fire on July 22, 2003. The Cramer Fire was started by lightning on July 19 in the Salmon-Challis National Forest, another "hyphenated forest" and some of the roughest country in the West, and by the time of the fatalities three days later had grown to two hundred acres.

Heath and Allen boarded a helicopter about 9:30 AM on the twenty-second, heading for a ridgetop above the fire where they were to clear a helicopter landing spot. At 11:00 AM and again at 12:30 PM they were asked how things were going and said they needed more time to finish the job. The fire flared up around noon, as it had done for the past several days. Allen asked an aerial observer to check billowing smoke, according to dispatch records. When the observer said there was a hot spot a half mile below the helitacks' position, Allen replied, "Okay, fine. We'll keep an eye on it."

At 1:26 PM, the incident commander, Alan Hackett, made a reconnaissance flight over the fire and asked Heath and Allen by radio if they were okay. They again said they needed more time. Hackett decided a little more than an hour later, about 2:30 PM, to pull Heath and Allen off the ridge. But tragically his order was never carried out.

At 3:05 PM, the two helitacks called for an immediate pickup. "Send them in a hurry," they said, according to a handwritten log. Four minutes later, they called again and said, "We need them right now." Two helicopters were in the area but were down for required maintenance and refueling. When the radio operator at the helicopter base told the two men at 3:13 PM that a helicopter was ready to launch, they responded, "Oh, God. We just got fire down below us. The smoke's coming right at us. Just make them hurry up."

The helicopter went aloft, and the pilot called in at 3:20 PM to report that heavy smoke made it impossible to land on the ridge. Heath and Allen reported winds of twenty to twenty-five knots at that time and said they were leaving the zone they had cleared. Four minutes later, one of them made a final call: "Could I get a helicopter up right now?" The fire, described as a "big flash front," swept over them at temperatures from 1,300 to 2,000 degrees, far beyond the protective capacity of a fire shelter. Two shelters were found near their bodies, which were discovered later not many yards from where the helitacks had landed, but neither shelter was deployed.

The subsequent Forest Service investigation cited the fire's supervisors for, among other things, failure to post lookouts, adequately monitor and oversee Allen and Heath, and follow routine safety procedures. The IG's investigation, required by the Cantwell legislation, went further and singled out Hackett, the incident commander. "Had existing Forest Service fire suppression policies and tactics been followed in a prudent manner, particularly by the IC, the fatalities of Heath and Allen may have been prevented," the IG report stated.

The results of the IG investigation, which focused on the crime of involuntary manslaughter, were passed along to the U.S. Attorney's Office in Boise, Idaho. Grand jury hearings were held in Boise, but no one was indicted. Then on November 30, 2004, federal prosecutors announced that Hackett, the incident commander, had accepted a deal. He would resign from the Forest Service and serve eighteen months of federal probation, with the promise that he would have no criminal record if his probation was successfully completed.

Hackett's case is not necessarily a precedent. He lacked the financial resources to hire defense lawyers, a cost estimated at about $100,000. And it is widely believed in the fire world that he could have won a court test.

The Thirtymile Fire also generated lawsuits by families of the victims and by Bruce and Paula Hagemeyer, the civilian couple trapped by the fire. The families of the victims were prevented from suing the Forest Service directly under the same legal protection afforded the federal government for military and law enforcement deaths.

In this case, however, the families adopted a novel legal maneuver. They sued private manufacturers of the Forest Service fire shelters in state court on grounds that the manufacturers failed to warn firefighters about the dangers of deploying fire shelters in rock scree, and that the shelters "failed due to improper and insufficient design." Because there was difficulty tracing the specific manufacturer of the shelters involved, the suit named five companies—Anchor

Industries, of Indiana; Weckworth Manufacturing, of Kansas; Weckworth-Langdon, of Kansas; International Cases and Manufacturing, of California; and Stilton Company, of California—and the National Association of State Foresters, a nonfederal agency with some responsibility for wildland fire training. The case was settled in March 2006; the amount of the award for the families and other details were not disclosed under a confidentiality agreement.

"This case was never about money," Mariano Morales, Jr., one of the lawyers for the families and himself a former firefighter, a hotshot, declared in a public statement. "It was about bringing attention to the unsafe instructions and making firefighting safer. We believe that by bringing this lawsuit, these objectives were met."

The Weavers subsequently filed an additional suit in federal district court alleging that two Forest Service officials destroyed or withheld evidence in the fire shelter case, and thus reduced the amount of the award, which was in the low seven figures. The suit alleged that Maureen Hanson, a Forest Service supervisor in Wenatchee, destroyed shelters used by the firefighter victims, and that George Jackson, a fire investigator and equipment specialist (who had retired by the time of the Weaver suit), withheld "crucial" information about the shortcomings of the shelters. The Weavers sought no less than $3 million in additional damages. "If I don't pursue the allegations, the next time they kill kids, it's going to partially be on my conscience, and that's not something I can live with," Ken Weaver told the *Yakima Herald-Republic*.

The Hagemeyers filed a separate suit claiming damages in the multimillion-dollar range that alleged the Forest Service had been negligent because the canyon road was not blocked when they went past the fire and because agency personnel had failed to discover them at the Thirtymile Campground. The Hagemeyers settled the suit in January 2007 for $400,000. The settlement included a promise by the Forest Service to consider several safety recommendations, including establishing a formal lookout post on fires, new standards for reasonable risk levels, and adding an employee representative to accident investigation teams. The settlement also included a statement declaring that the Forest Service did not concede liability.

Though the South Canyon Fire of 1994 set in motion a movement for greater accountability on the fireline, the process was evolutionary, not revolutionary. A new standard for accountability was set five years later, in 1999, following the Sadler Fire near Elko, Nevada, after six firefighters nearly lost their lives while conducting a burnout operation in front of an advancing fire. One of their supervisors was Tom Shepard, who had been in charge of the Prineville Hotshots when they lost nine crew members in the South Canyon

Fire. Though no one was fired on the Sadler Fire, the Type I team running the fire was formally disbanded, which was strong medicine at the time. Seven members of the team, including Shepard and a crew boss, were cited for negligence. After appeals the practical effect was that most of those cited, once again including Shepard, had to repeat training exercises to regain their fire qualifications, and most did. A disheartened Shepard retired from the Forest Service, bought a water tender vehicle, and continued to work as a firefighter.

One day right after the Thirtymile Fire fatalities, a film crew from the History Channel and I were driving up the Bitterroot Valley in Montana, to shoot scenes for a documentary film about the 1994 South Canyon Fire. We had arranged to meet with Bob and Nadine Mackey, whose ranch is in the valley and whose son, Don, had been a victim of the South Canyon Fire, which killed fourteen people on Storm King Mountain in west-central Colorado. We took along a copy of the *Missoulian* newspaper with a headline that read, "Wildfire Turns Fatal." When Nadine Mackey saw the headline, a repeat of the one seven years earlier for the South Canyon Fire, she said, "I know just what those families are going through."

Even in those first hours, connections were being made between the Thirtymile and South Canyon fires, and many more would become apparent over time. In fact there are so many links that this book amounts to what could be called a Storm King trilogy, though the books were not written with that intent: the trilogy started with my first book, *Fire on the Mountain*, about the South Canyon Fire, and continued through my second book, *Fire and Ashes*, which includes a story titled "The Ghost of Storm King" that follows the fortunes of Tom Shepard, supervisor of the ill-fated Prineville Hotshots, who lost nine crew members on Storm King. I have been drawn by flames and by the people who battle them.

A few months after the Thirtymile Fire, I received an e-mail from Jody Gray, who lost her daughter Jessica Johnson in the fire. The many similarities to the South Canyon Fire, she wrote, "brought an eerie chill to my soul." Once again, fire investigators were trying to blame victims for their own deaths, Gray said, just as happened after the South Canyon Fire. "The one thing about this story is that there were survivors of the blaze," she wrote, and the survivors were telling a different story from the official one. According to them, the Forest Service investigators had their facts wrong: the victims, according to survivors, were not to blame. Noting that *Fire on the Mountain* includes an account of a similar controversy, Gray asked if I would come to Washington and look into the Thirtymile Fire, and so I did.

Piecing together the story of the Thirtymile Fire has taken five years and involved the assistance of scores of people. I drove to Washington at least once a year during that time, covering nearly fifty thousand miles, and made numerous visits to the fire site—about the same mileage as when I researched the South Canyon Fire.

I am deeply grateful to the families of the fire victims and others close to them for speaking with me: Will, Virginia, and Tony Craven and the Craven family friend, Kay Evensen; Kathie, John, and Jaina FitzPatrick; Jody Gray and Nathan Craig (Craig went on to become a full-time firefighter, fulfilling his life's ambition, and was named training officer for the West Valley department; in 2005, he married Katie Fairbanks, a high school friend of Jessica Johnson); and Ken and Barbara Weaver. The support of Jody Gray and Kathie FitzPatrick was irreplaceable.

I thank all those survivors who shared their stories; Thom Taylor and Jason Emhoff did so repeatedly and deserve special thanks. I thank Pete Kampen for getting in touch and revisiting the scene with me. Tom Leuschen of the Forest Service (now retired but active as a speaker and trainer) was exceptionally open-handed with information and contacts, and always available.

Many of the sources of material are clear from the text, and I pointed out other sources where credibility was an issue—for example, in quotes from dispatch logs or official investigation interviews. The resulting narrative, however, blends personal interviews, official statements, news reports, and personal and official documents. The direct quotations are ones that participants remember themselves and others making. News coverage by the *Yakima Herald-Republic*, the *Seattle Times*, the *Seattle Post-Intelligencer*, the *Methow Valley News*, the *Wenatchee World*, and the Associated Press was most helpful. I filed numerous Freedom of Information Act requests and obtained many thousands of pages of background material. I thank Eileen Strauss, an attorney, for her assistance with document research.

The Forest Service chief, Dale Bosworth, Regional Forester Linda Goodman, and many other high-ranking Forest Service personnel, in the field and in the Washington headquarters, opened their doors to me, and I thank them.

I thank smoke jumpers at the Missoula and North Cascades bases who helped along the way. Eric Hipke, a smoke jumper and survivor of the South Canyon Fire, accompanied me on my initial visit to Washington, offered guidance, and opened many doors. Steve Dickenson, John Button, and Frank Clements, from the North Cascades base, gave assistance and hospitality.

Some people have provided counsel over more years than the span of this book. My thanks to Mike Apicello of the Forest Service, Lois Cunha of the Bureau of Land Management (BLM), Chris Cuoco of the National Oceanic and Atmospheric Administration, Justin Dombrowski, formerly of the Boulder Fire Department and now a Federal Coordinating Officer for the Federal Emergency Management Agency, Steve Dunsky of the Forest Service, Tim Eldridge of the smoke jumpers, John Hawkins of the California Department of Forestry and Fire Protection, Vi Hillman of the BLM, Jim Kitchen of the Forest Service, Dick Mangan (retired) of the Forest Service, and Kevin Milan of the Golden (Colorado) Fire Department. Steve Nemore, a retired smoke jumper but still an active fire supervisor, and Kelly Andersson have been longtime readers as well as counselors—that said, any errors are my responsibility alone.

I thank Jeff Lee and the Rocky Mountain Land Library, and Susan Tweit and Richard Cabe, for making possible a writer's residency at the Tweit-Cabe Railroad Cottage in Salida, Colorado, toward the end of the writing process.

My agent, Jennifer Lyons, and editor at Henry Holt, Jack Macrae, have been longtime sources of support and good counsel.

As always, my work would not be possible without the partnership with my wife, Frances.

INDEX

JOHN N. MACLEAN's *Fire on the Mountain* was the MPBA best nonfiction title of 1999. A newspaper reporter and longtime student of wildfire, he assisted in the posthumous publication of his father, Norman Maclean's *Young Men and Fire*. He divides his time between Washington, D.C., and Montana. *Fire and Ashes* was selected as a *Chicago Tribune* "best book" of 2003.